4th Financial Narrative Processing Workshop (FNP 2022)

Held at LREC 2022

Marseille, France
24 June 2022

Editors:

Mahmoud El-Haj
Paul Rayson
Nadhem Zmandar

ISBN: 978-1-7138-6120-1

Printed from e-media with permission by:

Curran Associates, Inc.
57 Morehouse Lane
Red Hook, NY 12571

Some format issues inherent in the e-media version may also appear in this print version.

Printed with permission by Curran Associates, Inc. (2023)

For permission requests, please contact the Association for Computational Linguistics at the address below.

Association for Computational Linguistics
209 N. Eighth Street
Stroudsburg, Pennsylvania 18360

Phone: 1-570-476-8006
Fax: 1-570-476-0860

acl@aclweb.org

Additional copies of this publication are available from:

Curran Associates, Inc.
57 Morehouse Lane
Red Hook, NY 12571 USA
Phone: 845-758-0400
Fax: 845-758-2633
Email: curran@proceedings.com
Web: www.proceedings.com

Proceedings of the 4th Financial Narrative Processing Workshop FNP 2022
Language Resources and Evaluation Conference
24 June 2022, Marseille, France.

Proceedings of the 4th Financial Narrative Processing Workshop (FNP 2022)

PROCEEDINGS

Editors:
Mahmoud El-Haj
Paul Rayson
Nadhem Zmandar

Proceedings of the LREC 2022 workshop on Proceedings of the 4th Financial Narrative Processing Workshop (FNP 2022)

Edited by: Mahmoud El-Haj, Paul Rayson and Nadhem Zmandar

For more information:
European Language Resources Association (ELRA)
9 rue des Cordelières
75013, Paris
France
http://www.elra.info
Email: lrec@elda.org

Message from the General Chair

Welcome to the 4th Financial Narrative Processing Workshop (FNP 2022). This year the workshop is held at the 13th Edition of the Language Resources and Evaluation Conference (LREC 2022) in Marseille, France on 24 June 2022 (a full-day event). This is an international gathering of researchers and speakers working on Financial Narratives from computing, accounting and finance. Following the success of the First FNP 2018 at LREC'18 in Japan, the Second FNP 2019 at NoDaLiDa 2019 in Finland, the Multiling 2019 Financial narrative Summarisation task at RANLP in Bulgaria, the 1st Joint Workshop on Financial Narrative Processing and MultiLing Financial Summarisation (FNP-FNS 2020) at COLING 2020 in Barcelona, Spain and the 3rd Financial Narrative Processing Workshop (FNP 2021) in Lancaster UK, we have received a great deal of positive feedback and interest in continuing the development of the financial narrative processing field, especially from our shared task participants. This has resulted in the organization of the 4th Financial Narrative Processing Workshop (FNP 2022). The FNP 2022 workshop achieved our aim of supporting the rapidly growing area of financial text mining. We ran three different shared tasks focusing on text summarization, structure detection and causal sentence detection, namely FNS, FinToc and FinCausal shared tasks respectively. The shared tasks attracted several teams from different universities and organisations from around the globe. The shared tasks resulted in the large scale experimental results and state of the art methods applied mainly to financial data. This shows the importance and growth of this field and we want to continue to be associated with top NLP venues. The workshop focused mainly on the use of Natural Language Processing (NLP), Machine Learning (ML), and Corpus Linguistics (CL) methods related to all aspects of financial text summarisation, text mining and financial narrative processing (FNP). There is a growing interest in the application of automatic and computer-aided approaches for extracting, summarising, and analysing both qualitative and quantitative financial data. In recent years, previous manual small-scale research in the Accounting and Finance literature has been scaled up with the aid of NLP and ML methods, for example, examining approaches to retrieving structured content from financial reports and studying the causes and consequences of corporate disclosure and financial reporting outcomes. We accepted 25 submissions. Each paper was reviewed by up to three reviewers. The submissions distribution is as follows: 6 main workshop papers and 19 shared task papers. The papers covered a diverse set of topics in financial narratives processing reporting work on financial reports from different stock markets around the globe presenting analysis of financial reports and using state of the art NLP methods such as the use of latest word embeddings. The quantity and quality of the contributions to the workshop are strong indicators that there is a continued need for this kind of dedicated Financial Narrative Processing workshop. We would like to acknowledge all the hard work of the submitting authors and thank the reviewers for the valuable feedback they provided. We hope these proceedings will serve as a valuable reference for researchers and practitioners in the field of financial narrative processing and NLP in general.

Organizers

Dr Mahmoud El-Haj, Lancaster University (General Chair)
Dr Paul Rayson, Lancaster University (FNP Program Chair)
Nadhem Zmandar, Lancaster University (Publication Chair and FNS Organiser)

FNS Organiser: Dr Marina Litvak, Shamoon Academic College of Engineering
FNS Organiser: Dr George Giannakopoulos, NCSR Demokritos
FNS Organiser: Dr Ahmed AbuRaed, University of British Columbia
FNS Organiser: Nikiforos Pittaras, NCSR Demokritos
FNS Organiser: Mahmoud El-Haj (Lancaster University)
FNS Organiser: Nadhem Zmandar (Lancaster University)
FNS Organiser: Paul Rayson (Lancaster University)
FNS Organiser: Nikiforos Pittaras (NCSR, Demokritos).
FNS Organiser: Marina Litvak (Sami Shamoon College of Engineering).
FNS Organiser: George Giannakopoulos (SKEL Lab – NCSR Demokritos)
FNS Organiser: Antonio Moreno Sandoval (UAM, Madrid).
FNS Organiser: Blanca Carbajo Coronado (UAM, Madrid)
FNS Organiser: Aris Kosmopoulos (NCSR, Demokritos),
FinToc Organiser: Dr Ismail El Maarouf, Fortia Financial Solution
FinToc Organiser: Abderrahim Aitazzi, Fortia
FinToc Organiser: Dr Juyeon Kang, Fortia Financial Solution
FinToc Organiser: Blanca Carbajo Coronado, Universidad Autónoma de Madrid
FinToc Organiser: Dr Ismail El Maarouf, Fortia Financial Solutions
FinToc Organiser: Dr Juyeon Kang, Fortia Financial Solutions
FinToc Organiser: Prof. Ana Gisbert, Universidad Autónoma de Madrid
FinToc Organiser: Prof. Antonio Moreno Sandoval, Universidad Autónoma de Madrid
FinCausal Organiser: Dominique Mariko, Yseop Lab
FinCausal Organiser: Hanna Abi-Akl, Yseop Lab
FinCausal Organiser: Hugues de Mazancourt, Yseop Lab
FinCausal Organiser: Estelle Labidurie, Yseop Lab

Program Committee:

Antonio Moreno Sandoval (UAM, Spain)
Vasiliki Athanasakou (SMU, Canada)
Martin Walker (University of Manchester, UK)
Marina Litvak (Sami Shamoon College of Engineering, Israel)
Mahmoud El-Haj (SCC, Lancaster University, UK)
John M. Conroy (IDA Center for Computing Sciences, USA)
Steven Young (LUMS, Lancaster University, UK)
Scott Piao (SCC, Lancaster University, UK)
Houda Bouamor (CMU, Qatar)
Paulo Alves (Accounting, Universidade Católica Portuguesa, Portugal)
Andrew Moore (Lancaster University, UK)
Nikiforos Pittaras (NCSR, Demokritos)
Paul Rayson (SCC, Lancaster University, UK)
Dominique Mariko (Yseop, France)

Table of Contents

FinRAD: Financial Readability Assessment Dataset - 13,000+ Definitions of Financial Terms for Measuring Readability
Sohom Ghosh, Shovon Sengupta, Sudip Naskar and Sunny Kumar Singh 1

Discovering Financial Hypernyms by Prompting Masked Language Models
Bo Peng, Emmanuele Chersoni, Yu-Yin Hsu and Chu-Ren Huang 10

Sentiment Classification by Incorporating Background Knowledge from Financial Ontologies
Timen Stepišnik-Perdih, Andraž Pelicon, Blaž Škrlj, Martin Žnidaršič, Igor Lončarski and Senja Pollak 17

Detecting Causes of Stock Price Rise and Decline by Machine Reading Comprehension with BERT
Gakuto Tsutsumi and Takehito Utsuro 27

XLNET-GRU Sentiment Regression Model for Cryptocurrency News in English and Malay
Nur Azmina Mohamad Zamani, Jasy Suet Yan Liew and Ahmad Muhyiddin Yusof 36

The Financial Narrative Summarisation Shared Task (FNS 2022)
Mahmoud El-Haj, Nadhem ZMANDAR, Paul Rayson, Ahmed AbuRa'ed, Marina Litvak, Nikiforos Pittaras, George Giannakopoulos, Aris Kosmopoulos, Blanca Carbajo-Coronado and Antonio Moreno-Sandoval 43

Multilingual Text Summarization on Financial Documents
Negar Foroutan, Angelika Romanou, Stéphane Massonnet, Rémi Lebret and Karl Aberer 53

Extractive and Abstractive Summarization Methods for Financial Narrative Summarization in English, Spanish and Greek
Alejandro Vaca, Alba Segurado, David Betancur and Álvaro Barbero Jiménez 59

DiMSum: Distributed and Multilingual Summarization of Financial Narratives
Neelesh Shukla, Amit Vaid, Raghu Katikeri, Sangeeth Keeriyadath and Msp Raja 65

Transformer-based Models for Long Document Summarisation in Financial Domain
Urvashi Khanna, Samira Ghodratnama, Diego Moll´a and Amin Beheshti 73

Financial Narrative Summarisation Using a Hybrid TF-IDF and Clustering Summariser: AO-Lancs System at FNS 2022
Mahmoud El-Haj and Andrew Ogden 79

The Financial Document Structure Extraction Shared Task (FinTOC 2022)
Juyeon Kang, Abderrahim Ait Azzi, Sandra Bellato, Blanca Carbajo Coronado, Mahmoud El-Haj, Ismail El Maarouf, Mei Gan, Ana Gisbert and Antonio Moreno Sandoval 83

ISPRAS@FinTOC-2022 Shared Task: Two-stage TOC Generation Model
Anastasiia Bogatenkova, Oksana Vladimirovna Belyaeva, Andrew Igorevich Perminov and Ilya Sergeevich Kozlov 89

swapUNIBA@FinTOC2022: Fine-tuning Pre-trained Document Image Analysis Model for Title Detection on the Financial Domain
Pierluigi Cassotti, Cataldo Musto, Marco DeGemmis, Georgios Lekkas and Giovanni Semeraro 95

GREYC@FinTOC-2022: Handling Document Layout and Structure in Native PDF Bundle of Documents
Emmanuel Giguet and Nadine Lucas 100

The Financial Causality Extraction Shared Task (FinCausal 2022)
Dominique Mariko, Hanna Abi-Akl, Kim Trottier and Mahmoud El-Haj 105

SPOCK at FinCausal 2022: Causal Information Extraction Using Span-Based and Sequence Tagging Models
Anik Saha, Jian Ni, Oktie Hassanzadeh, Alex Gittens, Kavitha Srinivas and Bulent Yener 108

Multilingual Financial Documentation Summarization by Team_Tredence for FNS2022
Manish Pant and Ankush Chopra 112

DCU-Lorcan at FinCausal 2022: Span-based Causality Extraction from Financial Documents using Pre-trained Language Models
Chenyang Lyu, Tianbo Ji, Quanwei Sun and Liting Zhou 116

LIPI at FinCausal 2022: Mining Causes and Effects from Financial Texts
Sohom Ghosh and Sudip Naskar 121

iLab at FinCausal 2022: Enhancing Causality Detection with an External Cause-Effect Knowledge Graph
Ziwei Xu, Rungsiman Nararatwong, Natthawut Kertkeidkachorn and Ryutaro Ichise 124

ExpertNeurons at FinCausal 2022 Task 2: Causality Extraction for Financial Documents
Joydeb Mondal, Nagaraj Bhat, Pramir Sarkar and Shahid Reza 128

ATL at FinCausal 2022: Transformer Based Architecture for Automatic Causal Sentence Detection and Cause-Effect Extraction
Abir Naskar, Tirthankar Dasgupta, Sudeshna Jana and Lipika Dey 131

MNLP at FinCausal2022: Nested NER with a Generative Model
Jooyeon Lee, Luan Huy Pham and Özlem Uzuner 135

Workshop Program

9:00–9:15 **Opening and Welcome**
Chair: Mahmoud El-Haj

9:15–10:00 *Keynote Speaker*
Dr Bayan Abu Shawar

10:00–13:30 **Session 1: Main Workshop Papers**
Chairs: Houda Bouamor, Paul Rayson

FinRAD: Financial Readability Assessment Dataset - 13,000+ Definitions of Financial Terms for Measuring Readability
Sohom Ghosh, Shovon Sengupta, Sudip Naskar and Sunny Kumar Singh

11:00–11:30 **Coffee Break**

Discovering Financial Hypernyms by Prompting Masked Language Models
Bo Peng, Emmanuele Chersoni, Yu-Yin Hsu and Chu-Ren Huang

Sentiment Classification by Incorporating Background Knowledge from Financial Ontologies
Timen Stepišnik-Perdih, Andraž Pelicon, Blaž Škrlj, Martin Žnidaršič, Igor Lončarski and Senja Pollak

Detecting Causes of Stock Price Rise and Decline by Machine Reading Comprehension with BERT
Gakuto Tsutsumi and Takehito Utsuro

XLNET-GRU Sentiment Regression Model for Cryptocurrency News in English and Malay
Nur Azmina Mohamad Zamani, Jasy Suet Yan Liew and Ahmad Muhyiddin Yusof

No Day Set (continued)

13:30–14:30 Lunch Break

14:30–15:30 Session 2: FNS Shared Task
Chair: Nadhem Zmandar

The Financial Narrative Summarisation Shared Task (FNS 2022)
Mahmoud El-Haj, Nadhem ZMANDAR, Paul Rayson, Ahmed AbuRa'ed, Marina Litvak, Nikiforos Pittaras, George Giannakopoulos, Aris Kosmopoulos, Blanca Carbajo-Coronado and Antonio Moreno-Sandoval

Multilingual Text Summarization on Financial Documents
Negar Foroutan, Angelika Romanou, Stéphane Massonnet, Rémi Lebret and Karl Aberer

Extractive and Abstractive Summarization Methods for Financial Narrative Summarization in English, Spanish and Greek
Alejandro Vaca, Alba Segurado, David Betancur and Álvaro Barbero Jiménez

DiMSum: Distributed and Multilingual Summarization of Financial Narratives
Neelesh Shukla, Amit Vaid, Raghu Katikeri, Sangeeth Keeriyadath and Msp Raja

Transformer-based Models for Long Document Summarisation in Financial Domain
Urvashi Khanna, Samira Ghodratnama, Diego Moll´a and Amin Beheshti

Financial Narrative Summarisation Using a Hybrid TF-IDF and Clustering Summariser: AO-Lancs System at FNS 2022
Mahmoud El-Haj and Andrew Ogden

No Day Set (continued)

16:10–16:40 **Session 3: FinTOC Shared Task**
Chair: Juyeon Kang

The Financial Document Structure Extraction Shared Task (FinTOC 2022)
Juyeon Kang, Abderrahim Ait Azzi, Sandra Bellato, Blanca Carbajo Coronado, Mahmoud El-Haj, Ismail El Maarouf, Mei Gan, Ana Gisbert and Antonio Moreno Sandoval

ISPRAS@FinTOC-2022 Shared Task: Two-stage TOC Generation Model
Anastasiia Bogatenkova, Oksana Vladimirovna Belyaeva, Andrew Igorevich Perminov and Ilya Sergeevich Kozlov

swapUNIBA@FinTOC2022: Fine-tuning Pre-trained Document Image Analysis Model for Title Detection on the Financial Domain
Pierluigi Cassotti, Cataldo Musto, Marco DeGemmis, Georgios Lekkas and Giovanni Semeraro

GREYC@FinTOC-2022: Handling Document Layout and Structure in Native PDF Bundle of Documents
Emmanuel Giguet and Nadine Lucas

16:45–17:55 **Session 4: FinCausal Shared Task**
Chair: Dominique Mariko

The Financial Causality Extraction Shared Task (FinCausal 2022)
Dominique Mariko, Hanna Abi-Akl, Kim Trottier and Mahmoud El-Haj

SPOCK at FinCausal 2022: Causal Information Extraction Using Span-Based and Sequence Tagging Models
Anik Saha, Jian Ni, Oktie Hassanzadeh, Alex Gittens, Kavitha Srinivas and Bulent Yener

Multilingual Financial Documentation Summarization by Team_Tredence for FNS2022
Manish Pant and Ankush Chopra

DCU-Lorcan at FinCausal 2022: Span-based Causality Extraction from Financial Documents using Pre-trained Language Models
Chenyang Lyu, Tianbo Ji, Quanwei Sun and Liting Zhou

LIPI at FinCausal 2022: Mining Causes and Effects from Financial Texts
Sohom Ghosh and Sudip Naskar

iLab at FinCausal 2022: Enhancing Causality Detection with an External Cause-Effect Knowledge Graph
Ziwei Xu, Rungsiman Nararatwong, Natthawut Kertkeidkachorn and Ryutaro Ichise

No Day Set (continued)

ExpertNeurons at FinCausal 2022 Task 2: Causality Extraction for Financial Documents
Joydeb Mondal, Nagaraj Bhat, Pramir Sarkar and Shahid Reza

ATL at FinCausal 2022: Transformer Based Architecture for Automatic Causal Sentence Detection and Cause-Effect Extraction
Abir Naskar, Tirthankar Dasgupta, Sudeshna Jana and Lipika Dey

MNLP at FinCausal2022: Nested NER with a Generative Model
Jooyeon Lee, Luan Huy Pham and Özlem Uzuner

Proceedings of the 4th Financial Narrative Processing Workshop @ LREC 2022, pages 1–9
Marseille, 24 June 2022

FinRAD: Financial Readability Assessment Dataset - 13,000+ Definitions of Financial Terms for Measuring Readability

Sohom Ghosh[†⋆], Shovon Sengupta[†], Sudip Kumar Naskar[⋆], Sunny Kumar Singh[‡]
[†]Fidelity Investments, [⋆]Jadavpur University, [‡]BITS, Pilani
[†]Bengaluru, India, [⋆]Kolkata, India, [‡]Hyderabad, India
{sohom1ghosh, ssg.plabon, sudip.naskar, sunnysingh.econ}@gmail.com

Abstract

In today's world, the advancement and spread of the Internet and digitalization have resulted in most information being openly accessible. This holds true for financial services as well. Investors make data driven decisions by analysing publicly available information like annual reports of listed companies, details regarding asset allocation of mutual funds, etc. Many a time these financial documents contain unknown **financial terms**. In such cases, it becomes important to look at their **definitions**. However, not all **definitions** are equally readable. Readability largely depends on the structure, complexity and constituent terms that make up a **definition**. This brings in the need for automatically evaluating the readability of **definitions** of **financial terms**. This paper presents a dataset, **FinRAD** (Sohom Ghosh, Shovon Sengupta, Sudip Kumar Naskar, Sunny Kumar Singh, 2022), consisting of **financial terms**, their **definitions** and embeddings. In addition to standard readability scores (like "Flesch Reading Index (FRI)", "Automated Readability Index (ARI)", "SMOG Index Score (SIS)","Dale-Chall formula (DCF)", etc.), it also contains the readability scores (**AR**) assigned based on **sources** from which the terms have been collected. We manually inspect a sample from it to ensure the quality of the assignment. Subsequently, we prove that the rule-based standard readability scores (like "Flesch Reading Index (FRI)", "Automated Readability Index (ARI)", "SMOG Index Score (SIS)","Dale-Chall formula (DCF)", etc.) do not correlate well with the manually assigned binary readability scores of **definitions** of **financial terms**. Finally, we present a few neural baselines using transformer based architecture to automatically classify these definitions as readable or not. Pre-trained FinBERT model fine-tuned on **FinRAD** corpus performs the best (AU-ROC = 0.9927, F1 = 0.9610). This corpus can be downloaded from https://github.com/sohomghosh/FinRAD_Financial_Readability_Assessment_Dataset.

Keywords: Readability, Financial Texts, Natural Language Processing, Financial Dataset

1. Introduction

Nowadays investors prefer to avail themselves of financial services online. This saves time as well as money. While making decisions relating to investments, they tend to read relevant content online. All financial content is not easy to comprehend due to the presence of unknown terms. In such cases, they have to look for definitions of these terms. Interestingly, not all definitions are easy to understand. Thus, it is extremely important to aid financial content writers to assess how readable are the definitions which are being written by them. Figure 1 depicts the same.

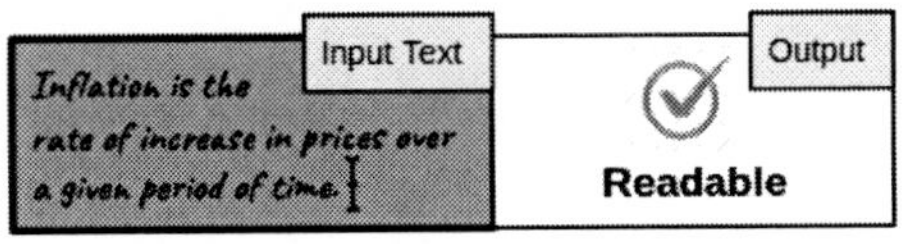

Figure 1: Readability of definition of "inflation"

We presented a basic tool, **FinRead** for demonstrating such a system in the 18th International Conference on Natural Language Processing (ICON-2021)[1] (Ghosh et al., 2021). It was trained using **definitions** of 8,401 **financial terms**. In this paper, in addition to extending this dataset to 13,112 **definitions** of **financial terms**, we release it publicly. Subsequently, we present several enhancements to the baseline architectures.

Our contributions

- We created a dataset comprising more than thirteen thousand **definitions** of **financial terms** along with their embeddings, standard formula based readability scores and assigned readability (**AR**) scores. We released it under the CC BY-NC-SA 4.0 license. To the best of our knowledge, we are the first to study readability in this context and provide the first dataset on financial terms and a proposed readability measure. A sample dataset can be downloaded from here[2]
- We showed that standard rule-based readability scores (like ARI, FRI, DCF, SMOG etc.) do not work well for financial texts.
- We proposed baseline architectures to automatically classify definitions of financial terms as readable or not.

[1] http://icon2021.nits.ac.in/coloc_events.html

[2] https://github.com/sohomghosh/FinRAD_Financial_Readability_Assessment_Dataset

The overall process flow is summarised in Figure 2. The rest of the paper is structured as follows. Section 2 states the prior works and their connection with this work. In section 3 we narrate the process we followed to collect, clean and label the data. Subsequently, we discuss various exploratory data analysis that we have performed. In section 4 we formally describe the task of assessing readability. We present various neural baseline architectures and their performances in section 5. Section 6 concludes the paper and provides some future directions of research.

2. Related Works

In this section, we discuss the prior works. Firstly, we narrate applications of readability in general and in the context of the financial domain. We then explore some of the related works and datasets.

2.1. Readability in general

For Natural Language Processing (NLP) practitioners, understanding readability of texts has always been an active area of research. Some of the standard readability scores include: "Flesch Reading Index (FRI)" (Flesch, 1948), "Automated Readability Index (ARI)" (Smith and Senter, 1967),"SMOG Index Score (SIS)" (Mc Laughlin, 1969) and "Dale-Chall formula (DCF)" (Chall and Dale, 1995). Flesh was one of the pioneers in this area. He proposed FRI which uses the ratio of total words to sentences and that of total syllables to total words as a measure of the readability. Smith et al. (Smith and Senter, 1967) defined ARI based on characters to words and words to sentences ratio. This score was used to assign the readability of a text to one of the fourteen predefined grade levels ranging from kindergarten to college student. Another new formula SIS for calculating readability was proposed by Mc Laughlin. It comprised of calculating the ratio between the number of polysyllables and sentences. However, it was only applicable for texts having at-least 30 sentences. In the paper, (Rush, 1985), Rush criticised these scores as they only dealt with the syntactic aspect of the texts and did not consider the aspect of the reading process which was interactive. Other papers which criticized these formulas include (Bruce et al., 1981) and (Anderson and Davison, 1986). Zamanian et al. (Zamanian and Heydari, 2012) presented a more detailed review of these formulas along with their advantages and disadvantages. Some of the papers which used language models to estimate readability include (Si and Callan, 2001), (Collins-Thompson and Callan, 2004), (Schwarm and Ostendorf, 2005) and (Heilman et al., 2007). In his recently published study of readability of "Policy Documents on the Digital Single Market of the European Union", Ruohonen(Ruohonen, 2021) argued that a PhD level eductaion would be required to study and understand the Digital Single Market (DSM) laws and policy documents. He further observed that there are critical differences in terms of the degree of agreement in various standard readability scores. The study also demonstrated, how the readability grades across time had evolved for the laws and policy documents in DSM as well. This in turn also indicates that the existing readability scores may fail to capture domain specific nuances for the different types of documents.

2.2. Readability in Financial Domain

Readability of financial texts has been widely explored. Most of these texts include Financial Disclosures (Loughran and McDonald, 2014), (Gosselin et al., 2021), Annual Reports and Management Discussions and Analysis (MD&A) (Arora and Chauhan, 2021), (Schroeder and Gibson, 1990), (Smith and Smith, 1971), (Lo et al., 2017). In addition to general features, Bonsall et al. (Bonsall IV et al., 2017) used the file size of 10-K documents to measure their readability. Bonsall et.al (Bonsall IV et al., 2017) proposed a new index "Bog Index" as a "plain English measure of financial reporting readability". It served as one of the standard approaches for the readability of financial reports. Loughran et al. (Loughran and McDonald, 2010) proposed a new method of measuring readability based on recommendations made by the U.S. Securities and Exchange Commission (SEC) in the year 1988. Readability scores were used for various downstream tasks like fraud detection (Othman et al., 2012), Stock Price Crash Risk prediction (Kim et al., 2019), etc. Readability of financial text books has been studied in (Chiang et al., 2008), (Plucinski and Seyedian, 2013) and (Plucinski et al., 2009). They also argued on the limitations of these popular scores as a measure of readability due to their inherent shortcomings to deal with domain specific language and jargon. Loughran et al. (Loughran and McDonald, 2014) also highlighted the need for alternative measures of readability for the financial documents like disclosures. Pitler (Pitler and Nenkova, 2008) proved that surface level standard readability scores do not correlate with the human assigned readability scores on the Wall Street Journal corpus. They further showed that a combination of entity coherence and discourse relations are the best features for assessing readability.

2.3. Related datasets

Related financial datasets on which readability has mostly been explored include 10-K SEC filing reports (Loughran and McDonald, 2009), disclosures (Ganguly et al., 2019), (Hoffmann and Kleimeier, 2021), and accounting textbooks (Chiang et al., 2008), (Plucinski et al., 2009).

2.4. Difference with prior works

To the best of our knowledge, we are the first ones to create a dataset consisting of definitions of financial terms along with their readability scores based on their complexity. We also propose transformer based neural baselines to automatically assess the readability of such definitions.

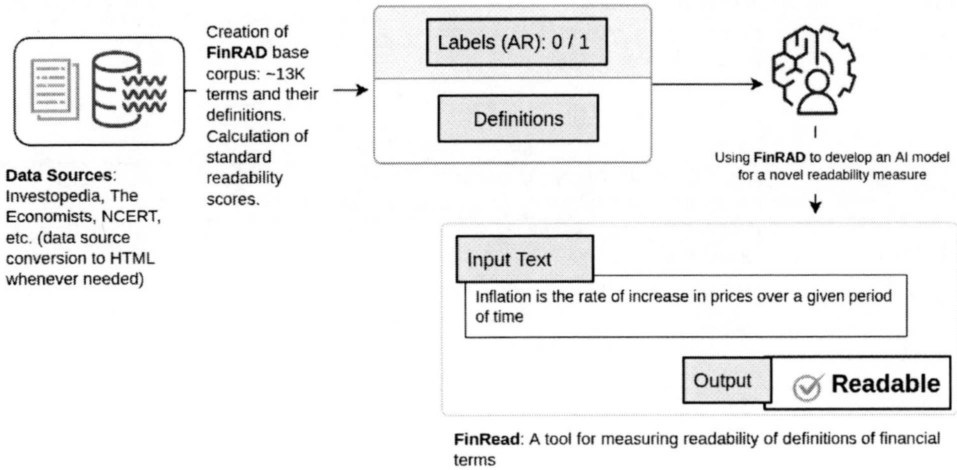

Figure 2: Overall process flow for **FinRAD**

3. Dataset

In this section, we narrate how we collected the data, cleaned and annotated it.

3.1. Data collection

Our dataset consists of 13,112 **financial terms** and their **definitions** written by experts across multiple sources. These sources include glossaries, dictionaries from financial websites, school and graduate-level textbooks relating to economics and finance. We collected the terms from 13 different sources and removed the duplicated terms during preprocessing. Source wise distribution of the dataset is presented in Table 1.

3.2. Data extraction and cleaning

Only three of the data sources considered were available as web-pages which we scraped directly. They include websites of The Economists, Federal Reserve Bank of St. Louis, and Investopedia. Other datasets were available in Portable Document Format (PDF). We tried extracting the terms and definitions directly from these PDFs first. However, we found that in most of the cases we were losing out on the structure. Thus, separating the terms from the definitions was challenging. Subsequently, we converted these PDF documents to the Hypertext Markup Language (HTML) format. For this, we used various freely available online services. We removed irrelevant texts like page numbers, the word "glossary", and texts which were mistakenly identified as terms. We removed the extra spaces and manually checked the final dataset to ensure that it is of high quality.

3.3. Data Annotations

Inspired by the method followed by Chakraborty et al. (Chakraborty et al., 2021), we consulted several professional financial experts. Subsequently, we decided to assign readability scores (**AR**) to the definitions of financial terms based on their sources. This was done since readability is subjective and manually annotating the entire dataset is expensive. Definitions from the following sources were assigned a readability score of 1.

- school-level textbooks (like NCERT textbooks, economics textbooks for begineers (Samuelson and Nordhouse, 2009))
- public websites suitable for masses (like Investopedia and The Economist).

The reason behind this is that the information from these sources is mostly consumed by beginners, school students, and by the masses. To understand the definitions which were obtained from other sources one needs to have at-least under graduate level knowledge specific to the financial domain. Thus, they were assigned a readability score of 0. This gave us 7,604 and 5,508 instances with readability scores of 1 and 0 respectively. An **AR** score of 1 represents the terms' definitions that are easily readable and 0 represents the definitions that are comparatively complex in nature or less readable. To validate this assumption we identified 112 additional terms and extracted their definitions from both kinds of sources (i.e. with **AR** = 0 and 1). We manually inspected each of the definitions and assigned them a readability score (0 or 1). In 79.91 % of the cases the manual assignment was in agreement with the assumption.

3.4. Exploratory Data Analysis

In this section, we present an overview of the **FinRAD** dataset and its contents. The dataset consists of 4 key fields:

Tag	Source Description	AR	# Terms/Definitions
prin	*Principles of Corporate Finance* by Richard A. Brealey, Stewart C. Myers, Franklin Allen (Brealey et al., 2019)	0	177
zvi	*Investments* by Zvi Bodie Alex Kane Alan J. Marcus (Bodie and Kane, 2020)	0	492
palgrave	*The Palgrave Macmillan Dictionary of Finance,* Investment and Banking by Erik Banks (Banks, 2010)	0	3925
opod	*Options, Futures, and Other Derivatives,* Global Edition by John C. Hull (Hull, 2003)	0	527
fmi	*Financial Markets and Institutions* by Frederic S. Mishkin Stanley Eakins (Mishkin and Eakins, 2006)	0	387
ncert_keec111	*NCERT Indian Economic Development Economics Class 11*[3]	1	95
ncert_kest	*NCERT Statistics for Economics Class 12*	1	53
ncert	*NCERT Introduction to MacroEconomics Class 12*	1	115
ncert_class12_econ	*NCERT Introduction to MicroEconomics Class 12*	1	41
investopedia	*Investopedia* Data Dictionary[4]	1	5946
economist	*The Economist* terms dictionary[5]	1	457
6_8_louis	*Glossary of Economics and Personal Finance Terms* from Federal Reserve Bank of St. Louis[6]	1	342
9_12_louis	*Glossary of Economics and Personal Finance Terms* from Federal Reserve Bank of St. Louis	1	188
pre_louis	*Glossary of Economics and Personal Finance Terms* from Federal Reserve Bank of St. Louis	1	36
sam	*Economics Textbook* by Paul Samuelson and William Nordhaus (Samuelson and Nordhouse, 2009)	1	331

Table 1: Source wise distribution. AR: Assigned Readability, #: Count

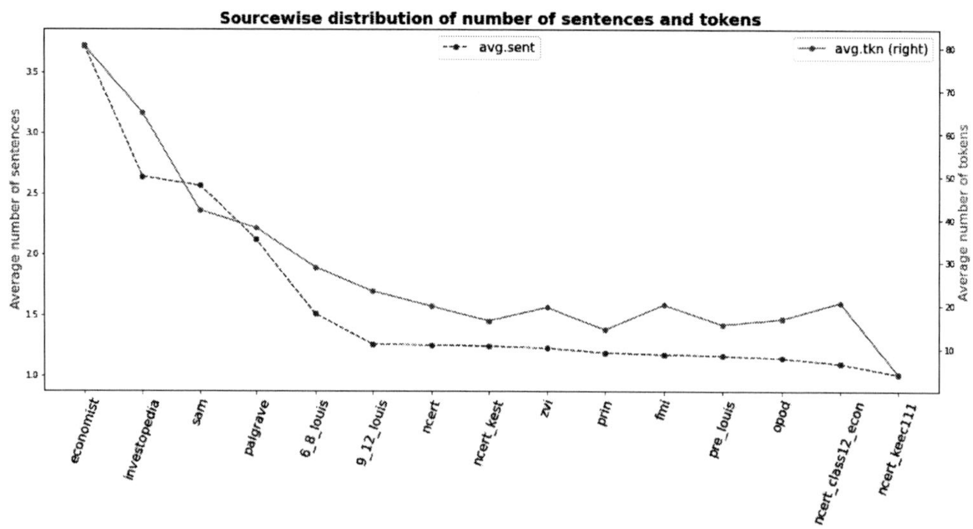

Figure 3: Source-wise distribution of the average number of sentences and tokens per definition

- **`financial terms`** (i.e. the terms that have been collected from different sources)
- **`definitions`** (i.e. the descriptions or definitions of these terms)
- **`source`** (i.e. the sources from which these terms have been collected)
- assigned readability (**`AR`** i.e. the annotated readability)

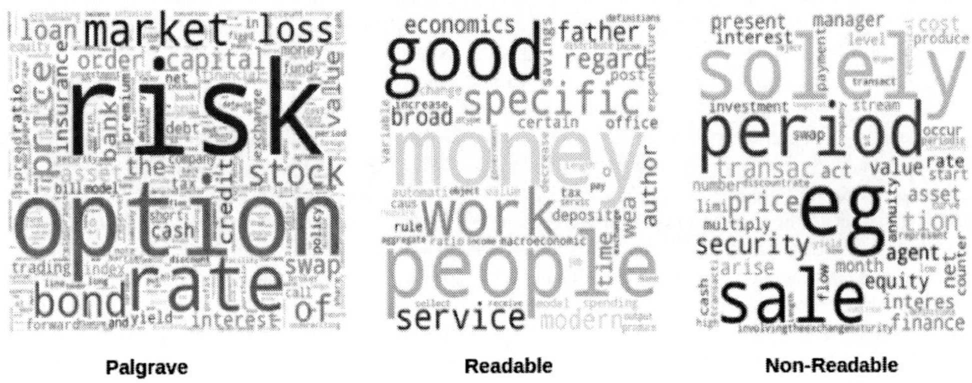

Figure 4: Word clouds of definitions from "Palgrave", readable and non-readable sources

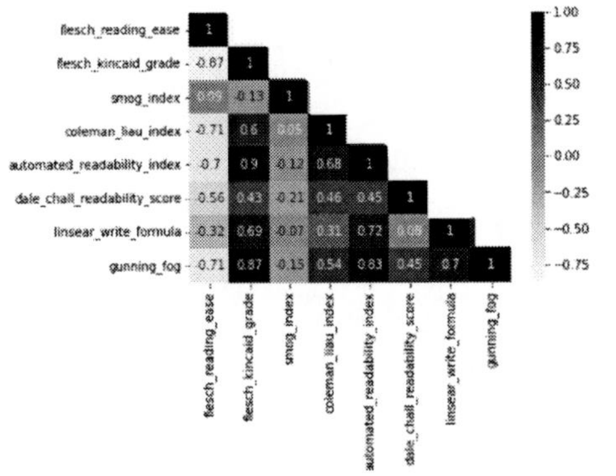

Figure 5: Correlation between standard readability scores

Apart from these 4 fields, the dataset also includes readability scores extracted using traditional methods. So far, 8 different scores have been provided for the definitions of the financial terms: Flesch Reading Ease (FRE) Score(Flesch, 1948), Flesch-Kincaid Grade Level (FKGL) Score(Kincaid et al., 1975), SMOG Index(SI) Score(Mc Laughlin, 1969), Coleman – Liau Index(CLI) Score(Coleman and Liau, 1975), Automated Readability Index(ARI) Score(Smith and Senter, 1967), Dale – Chall Readability (DCR) Score(Chall and Dale, 1995), Linsear write Formula and Gunning's Fog Index (FOG) Readability Formula. For all the definitions, these scores have been calculated using the textstat[7] library.

We started by studying the distribution of the number of sentences in the definitions across different sources. Figure 3 summarizes the distribution of the average number of sentences per definition used to define the terms across various sources. As evident from this

[7]https://pypi.org/project/textstat/

Readability type	Avg. sentences	Avg. tokens
Non-readable (0)	1.8529	32.2912
Readable (1)	2.5494	59.7701

Table 2: Average number of sentences and tokens per definition

plot, "The Economist" have definitions with the highest average number of sentences (approximately 4 sentences). We further compared the average number of sentences per definition across assigned readability segments in Table 2. It is quite interesting to note that the average number of sentences per definition in the readable set is higher than that of the non-readable set. Moreover, the average sentence length (i.e. number of tokens per sentence) for the readable set is 24.03 and that for the non-readable set is 17.22. This is because authors tend to use more words and shorter sentences to simplify concepts.

Subsequently, we studied the distribution of the average number of tokens present in the **`definitions`** across different sources. Figure 3 illustrates this. The average number of tokens per definition are approximately 80 and 64 for the definitions obtained from the readable sources "The Economist" and "Investopedia" respectively. This reconfirms our previous findings that authors tend to explain more to simplify concepts. In addition to this, we compared the average number of tokens across different readability segments. We observe that readable definitions have around 27 tokens more than that of non-readable ones. We provide more details and exact numbers in Table 2.

Word clouds are quite helpful to generate meaningful insights about text data. They offer an interesting option to visually represent the frequency of different words present in a corpus.

For ease of exposition, we have presented the word clouds of terms for one of the key sources ("Palgrave") in Figure 4. It accounts for almost 30% of the entire dataset of terms. Furthermore, for effective comparison we also present word clouds of non-readable and readable definitions of financial terms in the same figure. Quite evidently, the frequent terms present in the non-readable definitions (**AR**=0) are more complex than those of the readable ones (**AR**=1).

Lastly, we study the correlation between the standard readability scores and present them in Figure 5. Now, it is apparent that all the scores can not be directly compared as they are generated using different mathematical principles. However, for a few scores which are comparable like Flesch Reading Ease formula (Flesch, 1948) and The Flesch-Kincaid Grade Level (Kincaid et al., 1975), the positive correlation is high. Similar conclusions can be drawn for other scores as well.

4. Task

Given a set $\mathfrak{D} = \{d_1, d_2, d_3, \ldots, d_n\}$ of **`definitions`** of **`financial terms`** and a set $\mathcal{R} = \{r_1, r_2, r_3, \ldots..., r_n\}$ of readability scores where r_i is the assigned readability (**AR**) corresponding to the definitions of financial term d_i and $r_i \in \{0, 1\}$. **AR**=0 denotes non-readable and **AR**=1 denotes readable. The task is to develop a system capable of classifying a definition as readable or not. Furthermore, it shoud be able to automatically compute readability score r_t for **`definition`** of any unknown **`financial term`** d_t. Note: $0 \leq r_t \leq 1$. We use Area Under the Receiver Operating Characteristic curve (AU-ROC) score as the evaluation parameter.

5. Models and Results

We divided the dataset into two parts keeping the event rate same - the training set (67%) and the validation set (33%). Firstly, we studied how standard readability scores (like FRI, ARI, SIS, DCF, etc.) performed in a domain-specific setting like this. Most of these scores provided grade levels as outputs. We calculated the AU-ROC, F1 and Accuracy considering readability of grade level higher than 12 as 0 and rest as 1. This was done following our assumption stated in section 3.3. The performance of these standard scores in measuring readability on the validation set are presented in Table 3. The performance on the validation set which was calculated using these scores was not up to the mark. The best AU-ROC was only 0.4986 using the Flesch Reading Index. Thus, we trained machine learning based classifiers to assess the readability of the **`definitions`**.

We represented **`definitions`** of the terms numerically using a Term Frequency - Inverse Document Frequency (TF-IDF) matrix. We trained various machine learning based classifiers over it such as Logistic Regression, Random Forest (Ho, 1995) and Gradient Boosting Machine (Friedman, 2001) and the results of these models are presented in Table 4. Furthermore, we experimented by replacing TF-IDF with sentence embeddings (Reimers and Gurevych, 2019) created using BERT (Devlin et al., 2019) and FinBERT (Araci, 2019). In addition to this, we tried using other machine learning based classifiers like LightGBM (Ke et al., 2017) and XG-Boost (Chen and Guestrin, 2016). This improved the AU-ROC on the validation set to 0.969. Finally, we fine-tuned the financial domain-specific language model FinBERT (768 dimensions) (Araci, 2019) for the downstream task of classifying definitions. It was trained for 20 epochs with a batch size of 256, maximum sequence length of 64 and a learning rate of 0.00002. This model out-performed all the other algorithms (**AU-ROC** = 0.9927, **Matthews Correlation Coefficient** = 0.9063, **Accuracy** = 0.9540 and **F1 Score** = 0.9610) on the validation set. The corresponding ROC curves are presented in Figure 6.

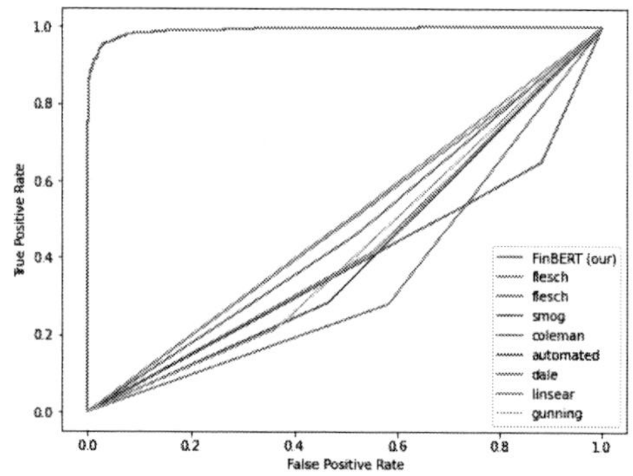

Figure 6: ROC curves

6. Conclusion

In this paper, we presented a new dataset **`FinRAD`** for the task of evaluating the readability of **`definitions`** of **`financial terms`**. We explored the limitations of various standard formula based readability scores which were developed to assess the readability of English texts in general. Finally, we proposed a neural architecture that outperformed all such scores in terms of AU-ROC.

There are several directions in which this research can be extended in future. We present some of the research questions (RQ) here.

- **RQ1:** *Do the predicted readability scores correlate with human judgements?*
  To understand this, we need to perform a qualitative analysis of the predicted readability scores generated automatically using machine learning algorithms. This may need additional manual tagging which is subjective and expensive. If the correlation is less, it would be essential to manually tag more definitions before developing any machine learning based classifier.

Readability Score (RS)	RS Description	AU-ROC	F1	Accuracy
flesch_reading_ease	The Flesch Reading Ease formula (Flesch, 1948)	0.4986	0.5516	0.5034
flesch_kincaid_grade	The Flesch-Kincaid Grade Level (Kincaid et al., 1975)	0.4320	0.4573	0.4296
smog_index	The SMOG Index (Mc Laughlin, 1969)	0.3841	0.5661	0.4250
coleman_liau_index	The Coleman-Liau Index (Coleman and Liau, 1975)	0.4710	0.4995	0.4691
automated_readability_index	Automated Readability Index(Smith and Senter, 1967)	0.4100	0.3494	0.3906
dale_chall_readability_score	Dale-Chall Readability Score (Chall and Dale, 1995)	0.4922	0.6793	0.545
linsear_write_formula	Linsear Write Formula[8]	0.3492	0.3295	0.3388
gunning_fog	The Fog Scale (Gunning FOG Formula)[9]	0.4259	0.2908	0.3936

Table 3: Performance of standard readability scores

Algorithms	Validation AU-ROC
TF-IDF vectors + Logistic Regression	0.9038
TF-IDF vectors + Random Forest	0.8866
TF-IDF vectors + Gradient Boosting Classifier	0.9116
BERT ST embeddings + Logistic Regression	0.9544
BERT ST embeddings + Random Forest	0.8801
BERT ST embeddings + Gradient Boosting Classifier	0.9063
FinBERT ST embeddings + Logistic Regression	0.9691
FinBERT ST embeddings + Random Forest	0.9434
FinBERT ST embeddings + Gradient Boosting Classifier	0.9523
FinBERT ST embeddings + Light GBM Classifier	0.9640
FinBERT ST embeddings + XGBoost Classifier	0.9626
FinBERT (fine-tuning [CLS] token)	**0.9927**

Table 4: Performance of models trained using Machine Learning

- **RQ2:** *Can we have better metrics to measure the performances of the models?*
  Presently, we use the Area Under the Receiver Operating Characteristic curve (AU-ROC) to measure the performance of the models. An interesting direction would be to develop a new metric that correlates more with human judgements.

- **RQ3**: *Can we develop unsupervised formulae based readability scores specific to the financial domain?*
  Machine learning based supervised models are computationally expensive and needs lots of data. Thus, it would be nice to explore if we can generate unsupervised formulae based readability scores specifically for the financial domain.

- **RQ4**: *Can we use Natural Language Generation methods to simplify definitions?*
  We removed duplicate terms while creating the **`FinRAD`**. A dataset consisting of readable as well as non-readable definitions for a given term would complement this. Simplification of complex definitions using Natural Language Generation techniques could be a new dimension to this research.

7. Bibliographical References

Anderson, R. C. and Davison, A. (1986). Conceptual and empirical bases of readability formulas.

Araci, D. (2019). Finbert: Financial sentiment analysis with pre-trained language models.

Arora, S. and Chauhan, Y. (2021). Do earnings management practices define the readability of the financial reports in india? *Journal of Public Affairs*, n/a(n/a):e2692, 05.

Banks, E. (2010). *The Palgrave Macmillan Dictionary of Finance, Investment and Banking*. Palgrave Macmillan, London, UK.

Bodie, Z. and Kane, A. (2020). Investments.

Bonsall IV, S. B., Leone, A. J., Miller, B. P., and Rennekamp, K. (2017). A plain english measure of financial reporting readability. *Journal of Accounting and Economics*, 63(2-3):329–357.

Brealey, R., Myers, S., and Allen, F. (2019). *Principles of Corporate Finance*. Economia e discipline aziendali. McGraw-Hill Education, USA.

Bruce, B., Rubin, A., and Starr, K. (1981). Why readability formulas fail. *IEEE Transactions on Professional Communication*, PC-24(1):50–52.

Chakraborty, S., Nayeem, M. T., and Ahmad, W. U. (2021). Simple or complex? learning to predict readability of bengali texts. *Proceedings of the AAAI Conference on Artificial Intelligence*, 35(14):12621–12629, May.

Chall, J. and Dale, E. (1995). *Readability Revisited: The New Dale-Chall Readability Formula*. Brookline Books, USA.

Chen, T. and Guestrin, C. (2016). XGBoost: A scalable tree boosting system. In *Proceedings of the 22nd ACM SIGKDD International Conference on*

Knowledge Discovery and Data Mining, KDD '16, pages 785–794, New York, NY, USA. ACM.

Chiang, W.-C., Englebrecht, T. D., Phillips Jr, T. J., and Wang, Y. (2008). Readability of financial accounting principles textbooks. *The Accounting Educators' Journal*, 18:47–80.

Coleman, M. and Liau, T. L. (1975). A computer readability formula designed for machine scoring. *Journal of Applied Psychology*, 60(2):283.

Collins-Thompson, K. and Callan, J. P. (2004). A language modeling approach to predicting reading difficulty. In *Proceedings of the Human Language Technology Conference of the North American Chapter of the Association for Computational Linguistics: HLT-NAACL 2004*, pages 193–200, Boston, Massachusetts, USA, May 2 - May 7. Association for Computational Linguistics.

Devlin, J., Chang, M.-W., Lee, K., and Toutanova, K. (2019). BERT: Pre-training of deep bidirectional transformers for language understanding. In *Proceedings of the 2019 Conference of the North American Chapter of the Association for Computational Linguistics: Human Language Technologies, Volume 1 (Long and Short Papers)*, pages 4171–4186, Minneapolis, Minnesota, June. Association for Computational Linguistics.

Flesch, R. (1948). A new readability yardstick. *Journal of applied psychology*, 32(3):221.

Friedman, J. H. (2001). Greedy function approximation: A gradient boosting machine. *The Annals of Statistics*, 29(5):1189–1232.

Ganguly, A., Ganguly, A., Ge, L., and Zutter, C. (2019). Shareholder litigation and readability in financial disclosures: Evidence from a natural experiment.

Ghosh, S., Sengupta, S., Naskar, S. K., and Singh, S. (2021). Finread: A transfer learning based tool to assess readability of definitions of financial terms. In *Proceedings of the 18th International Conference on Natural Language Processing (ICON): System Demonstrations*, Silchar, India, December. NLP Association of India (NLPAI).

Gosselin, A.-M., Le Maux, J., and Smaili, N. (2021). Readability of accounting disclosures: A comprehensive review and research agenda*. *Accounting Perspectives*, 20(4):543–581.

Heilman, M., Collins-Thompson, K., Callan, J., and Eskenazi, M. (2007). Combining lexical and grammatical features to improve readability measures for first and second language texts. In *Human Language Technologies 2007: The Conference of the North American Chapter of the Association for Computational Linguistics; Proceedings of the Main Conference*, pages 460–467, Rochester, New York, April. Association for Computational Linguistics.

Ho, T. K. (1995). Random decision forests. *Proceedings of 3rd International Conference on Document Analysis and Recognition*, 1:278–282 vol.1.

Hoffmann, A. O. and Kleimeier, S. (2021). Financial disclosure readability and innovative firms' cost of debt. *International Review of Finance*, 21(2):699–713.

Hull, J. C. (2003). *Options futures and other derivatives*. PearsonPrentice Hall, Boston, USA.

Ke, G., Meng, Q., Finley, T., Wang, T., Chen, W., Ma, W., Ye, Q., and Liu, T.-Y. (2017). Lightgbm: A highly efficient gradient boosting decision tree. *Advances in neural information processing systems*, 30:3146–3154.

Kim, C., Wang, K., and Zhang, L. (2019). Readability of 10-k reports and stock price crash risk. *Contemporary accounting research*, 36(2):1184–1216.

Kincaid, J. P., Fishburne Jr, R. P., Rogers, R. L., and Chissom, B. S. (1975). Derivation of new readability formulas (automated readability index, fog count and flesch reading ease formula) for navy enlisted personnel. Technical report, Naval Technical Training Command Millington TN Research Branch.

Lo, K., Ramos, F., and Rogo, R. (2017). Earnings management and annual report readability. *Journal of Accounting and Economics*, 63(1):1–25.

Loughran, T. and McDonald, B. (2009). Plain english, readability, and 10-k filings.

Loughran, T. and McDonald, B. (2010). Measuring readability in financial text.

Loughran, T. and McDonald, B. (2014). Measuring readability in financial disclosures. *the Journal of Finance*, 69(4):1643–1671.

Mc Laughlin, G. H. (1969). Smog grading-a new readability formula. *Journal of reading*, 12(8):639–646.

Mishkin, F. S. and Eakins, S. G. (2006). *Financial markets and institutions*. Pearson Prentice Hall, Boston, USA.

Othman, I. W., Hasan, H. H., Tapsir, R., Rahman, N. A., Tarmuji, I., Majdi, S., Masuri, S. A., and Omar, N. (2012). Text readability and fraud detection.

Pitler, E. and Nenkova, A. (2008). Revisiting readability: A unified framework for predicting text quality. In *Proceedings of the 2008 Conference on Empirical Methods in Natural Language Processing*, pages 186–195, Honolulu, Hawaii, October. Association for Computational Linguistics.

Plucinski, K. J. and Seyedian, M. (2013). Readability of introductory finance textbooks. *Journal of Financial Education*, 39(1/2):43–52.

Plucinski, K. J., Olsavsky, J., and Hall, L. (2009). Readability of introductory financial and managerial accounting textbooks. *Academy of Educational Leadership Journal*, 13(4):119.

Reimers, N. and Gurevych, I. (2019). Sentence-BERT: Sentence embeddings using Siamese BERT-networks. In *Proceedings of the 2019 Conference on Empirical Methods in Natural Language Processing and the 9th International Joint Conference on Natural Language Processing (EMNLP-IJCNLP)*, pages

3982–3992, Hong Kong, China, November. Association for Computational Linguistics.

Ruohonen, J. (2021). Assessing the readability of policy documents on the digital single market of the european union.

Rush, R. T. (1985). Assessing readability: Formulas and alternatives. *The Reading Teacher*, 39(3):274–283.

Samuelson, P. and Nordhouse, V. (2009). Economics: a textbook.

Schroeder, N. and Gibson, C. (1990). Readability of management's discussion and analysis. *Accounting Horizons*, 4(4):78–87.

Schwarm, S. E. and Ostendorf, M. (2005). Reading level assessment using support vector machines and statistical language models. In *Proceedings of the 43rd Annual Meeting on Association for Computational Linguistics*, ACL '05, page 523–530, USA. Association for Computational Linguistics.

Si, L. and Callan, J. (2001). A statistical model for scientific readability. In *Proceedings of the Tenth International Conference on Information and Knowledge Management*, CIKM '01, page 574–576, New York, NY, USA. Association for Computing Machinery.

Smith, E. A. and Senter, R. (1967). Automated readability index.

Smith, J. E. and Smith, N. P. (1971). Readability: A measure of the performance of the communication function of financial reporting. *The Accounting Review*, 46(3):552–561.

Zamanian, M. and Heydari, P. (2012). Readability of texts: State of the art. *Theory & Practice in Language Studies*, 2(1):43–53.

8. Language Resource References

Sohom Ghosh, Shovon Sengupta, Sudip Kumar Naskar, Sunny Kumar Singh. (2022). *FinRAD: Financial Readability Assessment Dataset - 16,000+ Definitions of Financial Terms for Measuring Readability*. distributed via GitHub: `https://github.com/sohomghosh/FinRAD_Financial_Readability_Assessment_Dataset`.

Proceedings of the 4th Financial Narrative Processing Workshop @ LREC 2022, pages 10–16
Marseille, 24 June 2022

Discovering Financial Hypernyms by Prompting Masked Language Models

Bo Peng, Emmanuele Chersoni, Yu-Yin Hsu, Chu-Ren Huang
Department of Chinese and Bilingual Studies, The Hong Kong Polytechnic University
The Hong Kong Polytechnic University, Yuk Choi Road 11, Hung Hom, Kowloon, Hong Kong
{peng-bo.peng,emmanuele.chersoni,yu-yin.hsu,churen.huang}@polyu.edu.hk

Abstract

With the rising popularity of Transformer-based language models, several studies have tried to exploit their masked language modeling capabilities to automatically extract relational linguistic knowledge, although this kind of research has rarely investigated semantic relations in specialized domains. The present study aims at testing a general-domain and a domain-adapted Transformer model on two datasets of financial term-hypernym pairs using the prompt methodology. Our results show that the differences of prompts impact critically on models' performance, and that domain adaptation to financial texts generally improves the capacity of the models to associate the target terms with the right hypernyms, although the more successful models are those which retain a general-domain vocabulary.

Keywords: Transformers, Semantic Relations, Language Modeling, Financial Natural Language Processing

1. Introduction

Since their introduction, Transformer architectures (Vaswani et al., 2017; Devlin et al., 2019) have quickly become the dominant paradigm in modern Natural Language Processing (NLP). On the one hand, their capacity for generating contextualized representations of words in context has led to performance improvements in several supervised tasks. On the other hand, the *masked language modeling* abilities of models like BERT attracted the attention of linguists and NLP scientists to propose experiments with *natural language prompts* to probe the semantic and pragmatic knowledge in the internal representations of the networks (Ettinger, 2020; Ravichander et al., 2020; Pandia et al., 2021; Hanna and Mareček, 2021). Roughly speaking, a prompt is a natural language sentence in which a token has been masked, such that a language model has to predict the hidden token and reconstruct the original sentence. The assumption of the literature on probing language models is that, given a prompt, "filling the gap" requires some specific linguistic knowledge. For example, with a prompt like *A robin is a type of* `[MASK]`, a language model will be able to assign the highest probability to *bird* for that given prompt only if it possesses some knowledge of lexical-semantic relations (and more specifically, the hyponymy-hypernymy relation existing between *robin* and *bird*).

As NLP technologies are frequently used in accounting and finance, detecting hypernymy and other semantic relations can substantially improve results in financial tasks, such as numeral understanding and records management. Hypernyms correspond to higher-level categories for target concepts, and thus they play an important role in the organization of the terminology of specialized domains (Espinosa-Anke et al., 2016).

Despite the popularity of prompt-based methods in NLP (Liu et al., 2021), there are still open questions about their usage in specialized domains: *Can they retrieve lexical-semantic relations in a specialized domain? What is the impact of domain adaptation on relation discovery? And how does the choice of different linguistic prompts affect the models' performance?*

To answer these questions, in our paper, we focus on the specific problem of *hypernymy discovery in the financial domain*. We use the data from two benchmarks in recent FinSim shared tasks (El Maarouf et al., 2021; Mansar et al., 2021). We treat the problem as an unsupervised task and test three different Transformer models (a general domain model and two domain-adapted ones) by using 5 types of prompts, and we report their results in identifying the right hypernym for the financial terms in the datasets. We found that domain adaptation tends to improve the retrieval of the right hypernym. Surprisingly, however, we found that a general-domain vocabulary leads to better retrieval performance than a finance-specific one.

2. Related Work

Lexical-semantic relations such as hypernymy have been investigated in computational linguistics for a long time, especially in the Distributional Semantics community (Weeds and Weir, 2003; Lenci and Benotto, 2012; Weeds et al., 2014; Roller et al., 2014; Santus et al., 2014a; Santus et al., 2014b; Santus et al., 2015; Santus et al., 2016; Chersoni et al., 2016; Roller and Erk, 2016; Shwartz et al., 2017; Liu et al., 2019; Xiang et al., 2020). Hypernymys have received special attention in the literature, since they correspond to higher-level categories of concepts and represent the backbone of ontologies and lexical networks (Chersoni and Huang, 2021). A research trend based on pattern-based methods use external corpora to exploit the co-occurrence of a hyponym and its hypernyms in specific linguistic patterns (e.g., *is a type of*) (Boella and

Di Caro, 2013; Flati et al., 2016; Camacho-Collados and Navigli, 2017). Machine learning models relying on distributional representations as input features have also been trained for prediction and detection of hypernymy relations (Shwartz et al., 2016; Sanchez and Riedel, 2017; Nguyen et al., 2017).

After the introduction of Transformers in NLP, several researchers tried to take advantage of their abilities of *masked language modeling* to analyze to what extent they are able to associate nouns with their hypernyms. A simple methodology consists of feeding the masked language model with a sentence of the form "The TERM is a HYPERNYM." then masking the hypernym token and letting the model fill the blank spot. Although the results were not always consistent, previous work showed that the Transformers can perform the hypernymy discovery task well, especially when the right hypernymy has to be picked from a close set of candidates (Ettinger, 2020; Ravichander et al., 2020). Moreover, Chersoni and Huang (2021) recently reported a positive effect of Transformer-based features in supervised hypernymy detection for the financial domain. The target term was masked in a manually constructed probe sentence, and a pre-trained Transformer-based language model was asked to assign probability scores to the candidate hypernyms of the target terms.

In the last few years many domain-adapted versions of BERT and other Transformer architectures have been made available by NLP researchers (Araci, 2019; Yang et al., 2020; Liu et al., 2020). However, to the best of our knowledge, the impact of domain adaptation on the systems' capacity for retrieving lexical-semantic relations has not yet been explored. In theory, a Transformer that has been adapted to a specific domain should have access to a more specific lexical-semantic knowledge for the words of that domain, and therefore one would expect it to perform better in term categorization tasks.

In the present work, we compared a general domain BERT (Devlin et al., 2019) and two domain-adapted FinBERT models (Yang et al., 2020) on two datasets for financial hypernymy detection that have been used for the recent FinSim shared tasks (Keswani et al., 2020; El Maarouf et al., 2021; Mansar et al., 2021). We adopted the masked language modeling approach, feeding the model with 5 types of natural language prompts (Hanna and Mareček, 2021), and we analyzed the capacity of the systems to associate the terms in the datasets with the correct hypernym labels.

3. Experimental Settings

3.1. Datasets

For our study, we used the datasets from the FinSim (El Maarouf et al., 2021) and the FinSim-2 shared task (Mansar et al., 2021). The FinSim dataset is composed of a training set and a test set of, respectively, 100 and 99 financial terms and their corresponding hypernyms, which a system has to identify out of 8 possible alternatives (**Bonds, Forward, Funds, Future, MMIs, Option, Stocks, Swap**). The FinSim-2 has a training set of 614 terms and a test set of 212 terms, and 10 possible hypernym labels (the same as FinSim, with the addition of **Credit Index**, and **Equity Index**). Examples of instances from FinSim-2 are shown in Table 1. In both datasets, the hypernyms correspond to the high-level classes of the Financial Business Ontology (FIBO) [1]. Since the gold labels of the FinSim-2 test set are not publicly accessible, we were able to conduct experiments only on the items of the training set. On the other hand, most of the one-word hypernym pairs are the same in both the FinSim-1 and the FinSim-2 datasets. Thus, we merged the two datasets and to delete the duplicates. After this step, we obtained 202 one-word and 405 two-word term-hypernym pairs (607 pairs in total). The number of unique word-types in the dataset vocabulary is 546, among which 185 and 134 words are not included in the general-domain and in the finance-specific vocabularies of the models, respectively.

Term	Label
S&P 100 Index	Equity Index
Green Bond	Bonds
Index Forward	Forward
Preference Share	Stocks

Table 1: Examples of term-hypernym pairs from the FinSim-2 dataset.

3.2. Systems and Settings

We used **BERT Base** (Devlin et al., 2019) as a general-domain Transformer model. BERT consists of a series of stacked Transformer encoders, and was trained using a masked language modeling and a next sentence prediction objective on a concatenation of the Books Corpus (Zhu et al., 2015) and of the English Wikipedia. For the domain-specific models, we used two versions of the FinBERT model introduced by Yang et al. (2020), namely **FinBERT BaseVocab** (FV w/ BV) and **FinBERT FinVocab** (FB w/ FV). The main difference is that the former was initialized from the original BERT Base (i.e., it also uses the same general-domain vocabulary) and further pretrained on three financial corpora (the Corporate Reports 10-K & 10-Q from the Securities Exchange Commission [2], the Earnings Call Transcripts from the Seeking Alpha website [3] and the Analyst Reports from the Investext database), while the latter was trained afresh on financial corpora for 1M iterations and uses a domain-specific financial vocabulary. As in Peng et al.(2021), we specifically chose the model by Yang and colleagues because of the availability of two versions obtained with different methods for domain adaptation. This allows us to measure the impact of the vocabulary on task performance.

[1]https://spec.edmcouncil.org/fibo/

[2]https://www.sec.gov/edgar.shtml

[3]https://seekingalpha.com/

Type	Prompt	Example
A	a(n) TERM is a(n) [MASK].	A Share is a [MASK].
B	TERMs are [MASK].	Shares are [MASK].
C	a(n) TERM is a type of [MASK].	A Share is a type of [MASK].
D	a(n) [MASK], such as a(n) TERM.	A [MASK], such as a Share.
E	a(n) TERM is a(n) [MASK], so is a(n) CO-TERM.	A Share is a [MASK], so is a quota.

Table 2: List of the prompt templates.

For each target term in the dataset, we fed a prompt including the term, and asked the masked language models to assign a probability score to each candidate hypernym. The hypernyms were then ranked, for each term, by decreasing probability value. Following Schick and Schütze (2021), we only modeled the probability of the hypernym labels, i.e., the probabilities of the rest of the vocabulary were not taken into account.

We conducted experiments with 5 types of prompts, including using a linking verb to form two basic types of prompts, and using *type-of*, *such-as*, and multiple hyponym. The details of the prompts are shown in Table 2 (Notice that all the prompts have been built with the appropriate determiner *a* or *an* for both the term and the masked hypernym). Type **A**, the classic **is-a** pattern, is the most basic form of hypernym prompting. Specifically, the terms and labels are pluralized in type **B** for checking the consistency of the prediction: if the systems have some actual knowledge about hypernymy-hyponymy relations, we would expect the attribution of a hypernym to a term to be the same, regardless of whether the term is singular or plural. For instance, if the system knows that the hypernym of *apple* is *fruit*, then the system should also be able to recognize the correct hypernym *fruits* for *apples*. However, previous studies showed that, in Transformers' predictions, this is often not the case (Ravichander et al., 2020). For all the other prompts, instead, both the hyponym term and the hypernym label are singular. Type **C** is the **type-of** pattern, a variation of the basic Type A prompt. Type **D** is the **such-as** pattern: although it is a sentence fragment rather than a full sentence, it represents a more natural pattern of co-occurrence of lexemes in a hyponym-hypernym relation (it is quite rare to see the lexemes co-occurring specifically in patterns A-C, except in text like encyclopaediae and wikis). Type D, in particular, has been reported to be one of the most effective ways of prompting the hypernym relation (Hanna and Mareček, 2021).

Type **E** is the **multiple hyponyms** prompt. A co-hyponym, the CO-TERM, is automatically found by using pretrained FastText embeddings (Bojanowski et al., 2017). At first, we looked for the nearest neighbor of each word to find co-hyponym examples. However, after inspecting the results, we chose to use the second nearest neighbor as the hyponym instead of the closest one, because the nearest neighbor always turned out to be the capitalized version of the word itself. As shown by Hanna and Marecek (2021), inserting a co-hyponym in the prompt is likely to query the desired hypernym more precisely. Using off-the-shelf FastText vectors allow us to automatize and speed up the procedure of finding the co-hyponym word. Intuitively, adding a co-hyponym in the sentence makes the prompt more informative, because it gives the language model more semantic information about the general category that needs to be predicted.

The hypernym *MMIs*, which is present in both datasets, is not included in BaseVocab, nor in FinVocab (neither in the singular, nor in the plural form). Meanwhile, after pluralization (pattern of type **B**), the hypernym label *Swaps* is not included in BaseVocab, but it is included in FinVocab. During the encoding procedure, the words not included in the vocabulary will be split into subwords, e.g., *Swaps* $\rightarrow$ *Swap##* and *##s*. The language model will be unable to guess these hypernyms with one single [MASK] token. Therefore, as the prompt-based learning requires that we convert the hypernym to a corresponding identification number in the vocabulary, the missing hypernym labels are added to the vocabulary of the pretrained language models, so that they can be identified with unique numbers. However, the word representations of these added words are randomly initialized without optimization.

Finally, prompt-based learning requires mapping each hypernym label to a word from the vocabulary of the language model. For two-word hypernyms, e.g., *Equity Index* and *Credit Index*, we first merge them into a single category *Index* and jointly evaluate with other one-word hypernym labels. Then, we perform an extra disambiguation step to discriminate between these two-word hypernyms, by creating an additional prompt. See examples below for the prompts of Type **A** and **C**.

1. *A S&P 100 Index is a/an* [MASK] *Index.*

2. *A S&P 100 Index is a type of* [MASK] *Index.*

In this case, the language model is asked to assign the probabilities of words *Equity* and *Credit* only.

3.3. Metrics

The predictions were evaluated in terms of *Accuracy* and *Mean Rank*. The systems are not expected just to output a prediction for each instance; they have to output a rank of the candidate labels, from the most to the least likely one. The Accuracy and Mean Rank metrics are defined as follows:

Type	BERT Base		FB w/ BV		FB w/ FV		Average	
	ACC	Mean Rank	ACC	Mean Rank	ACC	Mean Rank	ACC	Mean Rank
A	64.42	1.49	69.19	1.41	57.50	1.82	63.70	1.57
B	38.72	2.23	13.84	3.19	43.49	2.39	32.02	2.60
C	72.32	1.65	71.17	1.69	49.75	2.15	64.42	1.83
D	75.12	1.39	**82.21**	**1.28**	39.87	2.27	65.73	1.65
E	74.79	1.38	78.42	1.32	50.74	2.15	**67.98**	**1.62**
Average	**64.78**	**1.63**	62.97	1.78	48.27	2.15		

Table 3: Accuracy(%) and mean rank of hypernym detection on the merged dataset. The best scores are in **bold**.

$$Accuracy = \frac{1}{n} * \sum_{i=1}^{n} I(y_i = y_i^l[0]) \quad (1)$$

$$MeanRank = \frac{1}{n} * \sum_{i=1}^{n} rank_i \quad (2)$$

Notice that, in Equation (2), $rank_i$ corresponds to the rank of the correct label if the latter is among the top 3 predictions and 4 otherwise, as in the Semeval 2018 evaluation of the hypernymy discovery task (Camacho-Collados et al., 2018).

4. Results and Discussion

Table 3 illustrates the accuracy and mean rank scores of the three language models and prompt templates on the merged dataset. We observe that the prompt can heavily affect the detection results. For example, without any fine-tuning, the accuracy score of the FinBERT w/ BV model can be changed from 13.84 to 82.21 by changing the prompt from the basic plural type **B** to type **D** (**such-as**). If we exclude the prompt of type **B**, which was included to check the prediction consistency, the average scores tend to improve by using more complex prompts, with the models generally doing better with prompt-types **D** and **E**. The result is in line with the findings of Hanna and Mareček (2021).

The accuracy and mean rank scores for the basic types are lower than the others in both BERT Base and FinBERT w/ BV. It is striking that, after changing the prompt sentence from singular to plural, all the models have a sharp performance drop. FinBERT w/ BV models is, apart from Type **B**, the model achieving the best scores (82.21 in accuracy and 1.28 in mean rank), but on the other hand, it is also the model having the largest drop after the pluralization of the prompt. This finding is consistent with previous studies on hypernymy detection with masked language models (Ravichander et al., 2020; Hanna and Mareček, 2021), and it suggests that the models might only be exploiting some surface lexical cues to predict the hypernyms, rather than learning actual semantic relations between word representations (Rambelli et al., 2020; Pedinotti et al., 2021).

From the language models' perspective, BERT Base and FinBERT w/ BV outperform the FinBERT w/ FV model, confirming previous findings in financial text sentiment analysis and numeral understanding tasks (Peng et al., 2021). Curiously, the only model with finance-specific vocabulary is the only one that achieves its best score with the basic prompt **A** among the 5 prompt types, and it is outperformed by the competitor models with prompts **B**, **C**, and **E**, suggesting that domain-specific vocabulary does not necessarily represent an advantage for this kind of tasks. This contrasts with findings in other domains such as the biomedical domain, where models with a domain-specific vocabulary have been shown to be more efficient (Gu et al., 2021; Portelli et al., 2021). Between the two models with general domain vocabulary, FinBERT w/ BV is generally better at guessing the right hypernyms, with the exceptions of prompt-types **B** and **C**. Excluding the value of the plural prompt, which gives particularly low scores for FinBERT w/ BV, the accuracy and mean rank scores of this model would be 75.16 and 1.43, against 71.66 and 1.48 of BERT Base. Since FinBERT w/ FV was only trained on financial corpora and was missing the training on general-domain text (Yang et al., 2020), the model may not have acquired a good knowledge of the semantic relations. It is also possible that hypernymy patterns such as "is a" or "is a type of" are not very frequent in financial texts, because these patterns are likely to appear in definition-like statements, while financial texts are generally read by specialists that do not need definitions for the meaning of the domain-specific terms.

Figures 1a and 1b show the confusion matrices of the two best prompts, **D** and **E**, in the FinBERT w/ BV model, respectively. The two prompts are both good at associating terms to hypernyms. For example, the detection accuracies of *Bond* and *Option* are almost 100%. Moreover, despite the unbalanced distribution of the labels (e.g., Forward), we did not observe accuracy drops for rare labels. Both prompts failed to recognize *MMI*, as expected, as it is not included in the vocabulary of the language model. The merged label *Index* is the primary source of errors for both models, with many instances of *Option* being erroneously associated with *Index*, particularly with type **E** prompts.

We show some term-hypernym pairs that are misclassified by FinBERT models with type **D** and **E** prompts in Table 4. Only the terms CDS and To Be Announced are included in both base and financial vocabularies, while the others are split into subwords. This might have misled the language models, making them unable to guess the right hypernym. On the other hand, some

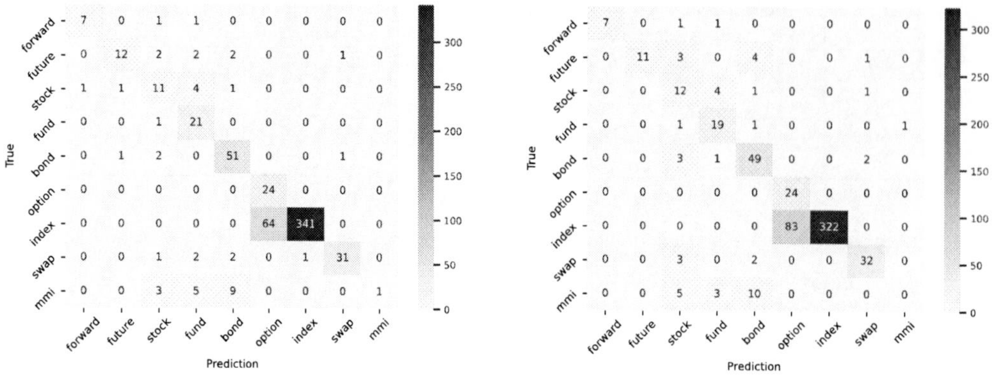

(a) Type **D** (b) Type **E**

Figure 1: Confusion matrices of FinBERT w/ BV model with type **D** and **E** prompts, respectively.

Term	Label	FinBERT w/ BV				FinBERT w/ FV			
		Rank		Prediction		Rank		Prediction	
		Type **D**	Type **E**	Type **D**	Type **E**	Type **D**	Type **E**	Type **D**	Type **E**
Sukuk	Bond	2	3	Stock	Stock	2	2	Future	Stock
To Be Announced	Bond	5	7	Future	Future	8	4	Future	Future
CDS	Swap	4	4	Bond	Bond	4	8	Index	Index
Wisdomtree Europe Hedged	Index (Equity Index)	2	2	Option	Option	3	9	Future	Future
CDX Swaption	Index (Credit Index)	2	2	Option	Option	4	2	Future	Option

Table 4: Misclassified terms of FinBERT models with type **D** and **E** prompts, respectively. The rank of probability of the correct label and the prediction result are reported as well.

in-vocabulary terms may have special meanings in the financial domain, e.g. CDS (Credit Default Swap), and they are also misclassified by FinBERT models. This may due to a failure of the language models in extracting the domain-specific meanings of the terms (e.g., the models may interpret CDS as Compact Discs). FinBERT w/ FV model generally got a worse probability rank for the hypernyms, which once again suggests that domain-specific vocabulary does not necessarily represent an advantage for this kind of task.

Finally, for the original two-word hypernyms (*Equity Index* and *Credit Index*) we further analyzed the detection accuracy by creating an additional disambiguation prompt, using the word *Index/Indices*. The language models are asked to fill the [MASK] with only *Equity* or *Credit* as illustrated in Section 3.2. Table 5 shows the accuracy score of two-word hypernyms detection. We still observe large drops for the plural prompts, while the basic type **A**, and the types **D** and **E** are the most effective patterns. Considering all models, type **A** achieves the more stable performance. Patterns D and E also obtained perfect scores, but the average is pulled down by the low performance of FinBERT w/ FV. Among the language models, FinBERT w/ BV is the top-scoring model as it manages to guess all the hypernyms correctly in three cases out of five.

Overall, the results prove that training Transformer language models on specialized corpora can improve hypernymy detection. Apart from the consistency issue with plural prompts, FinBERT w/ BV is the model achieving most often the highest scores, and it tends to perform better than BERT Base for the more informative prompts (types **D** and **E**). BERT Base is still competitive with the domain-adapted model, and shows more consistency with the basic prompts. Finally, FinBERT w/ FV performs the worst of the three, suggesting that knowing financial-specific vocabulary *per se* does not help hypernym detection. Almost all the hypernymy labels and the majority of the terms to be classified were included in both vocabularies, with a slightly better coverage using FV (only 134 missing terms against 185 for BV). The fact that this small advantage did not help the FinBERT w/ FV model suggests that the internal representations of the Transformers are able to efficiently exploit lexical cues from the

Type	Bert Base	FB w/ BV	FB w/ FV	Average
A	**100.00**	**100.00**	94.57	**98.19**
B	69.14	78.27	71.85	73.09
C	72.10	74.07	67.90	71.36
D	**100.00**	**100.00**	76.54	92.18
E	99.51	**100.00**	89.63	96.38
Average	88.15	**90.47**	80.10	

Table 5: The accuracy(%) scores of two-word hypernym label detection. The best scores are in **bold**.

context to make their predictions, even when the target words are not included in their vocabulary. However, it should also be noticed that FinBERT w/ FV achieved a higher accuracy than the competitors with the plural prompt of type **B** (see Table 3). This might be due to the fact that this model is the only one that includes the pluralized forms of all the hypernym labels (except for MMI) in its vocabulary.

5. Conclusion

In this paper, we proposed a comparison between general and domain-adapted pretrained language models' performance of the task of financial hypernym detection via masked language modeling. We also tested different types of prompts used to search for hypernym. The results indicate that the domain adaptation can improve the language model's capacity to retrieve the right hypernym, although the models are more efficient when they also retain a general-domain vocabulary. In addition, we observed that different prompts have an important impact on hypernym detection; that is, more natural and informative prompts generally lead to better scores. Future work will experiment with new methods to refine the Transformers' internal representations to identify hypernyms and other lexical-semantic relations. For example, one could explore fine-tuning the model on triples from knowledge graphs (Bosselut et al., 2019), or extracting relation embeddings from the language model output (Ushio et al., 2021).

Acknowledgements

The authors acknowledge the support from the projects "Analyzing the semantics of Transformers representations for financial natural language processing" (ZVYU) and "Conversational Brains: A Multidisciplinary Approach" (ZG9X), funded by the Hong Kong Polytechnic University.

6. Bibliographical References

Araci, D. (2019). FinBERT: Financial Sentiment Analysis with Pre-trained Language Models. *arXiv preprint arXiv:1908.10063*.

Boella, G. and Di Caro, L. (2013). Supervised Learning of Syntactic Contexts for Uncovering Definitions and Extracting Hypernym Relations in Text Databases. In *Machine Learning and Knowledge Discovery in Databases*.

Bojanowski, P., Grave, E., Joulin, A., and Mikolov, T. (2017). Enriching Word Vectors with Subword Information. *Transactions of the Association for Computational Linguistics*, 5:135–146.

Bosselut, A., Rashkin, H., Sap, M., Malaviya, C., Celikyilmaz, A., and Choi, Y. (2019). COMET: Commonsense Transformers for Automatic Knowledge Graph Construction. In *Proceedings of ACL*.

Camacho-Collados, J. and Navigli, R. (2017). Babel Domains: Large-Scale Domain Labeling of Lexical Resources. In *Proceedings of EACL*.

Camacho-Collados, J., Delli Bovi, C., Espinosa-Anke, L., Oramas, S., Pasini, T., Santus, E., Shwartz, V., Navigli, R., and Saggion, H. (2018). SemEval-2018 Task 9: Hypernym Discovery. In *Proceedings of SemEval*.

Chersoni, E. and Huang, C.-R. (2021). PolyU-CBS at the FinSim-2 Task: Combining Distributional, String-Based and Transformers-Based Features for Hypernymy Detection in the Financial Domain. In *Companion Proceedings of the Web Conference*.

Chersoni, E., Rambelli, G., and Santus, E. (2016). CogALex-V Shared Task: ROOT18. In *Proceedings of the COLING Workshop on Cognitive Aspects of the Lexicon*.

Devlin, J., Chang, M.-W., Lee, K., and Toutanova, K. (2019). BERT: Pre-training of Deep Bidirectional Transformers for Language Understanding. In *Proceedings of NAACL*.

El Maarouf, I., Mansar, Y., Mouilleron, V., and Valsamou-Stanislawski, D. (2021). The FinSim 2020 Shared Task: Learning Semantic Representations for the Financial Domain. In *Proceedings of the IJCAI Workshop on Financial Technology and Natural Language Processing*.

Espinosa-Anke, L., Camacho-Collados, J., Delli Bovi, C., and Saggion, H. (2016). Supervised Distributional Hypernym Discovery via Domain Adaptation. In *Proceedings of EMNLP*.

Ettinger, A. (2020). What BERT Is Not: Lessons from a New Suite of Psycholinguistic Diagnostics for Language Models. *Transactions of the Association for Computational Linguistics*, 8:34–48.

Flati, T., Vannella, D., Pasini, T., and Navigli, R. (2016). MultiWiBi: The Multilingual Wikipedia Bitaxonomy Project. *Artificial Intelligence*, 241:66–102.

Gu, Y., Tinn, R., Cheng, H., Lucas, M., Usuyama, N., Liu, X., Naumann, T., Gao, J., and Poon, H. (2021). Domain-specific Language Model Pretraining for Biomedical Natural Language Processing. *ACM Transactions on Computing for Healthcare (HEALTH)*, 3(1):1–23.

Hanna, M. and Mareček, D. (2021). Analyzing BERT's Knowledge of Hypernymy via Prompting. In *Proceedings of the EMNLP Workshop on Analyzing and Interpreting Neural Networks for NLP (BlackBoxNLP)*.

Keswani, V., Singh, S., and Modi, A. (2020). IITK at the FinSim Task: Hypernym Detection in Financial Domain via Context-free and Contextualized Word Embeddings. In *Proceedings of the IJCAI Workshop on Financial Technology and Natural Language Processing*.

Lenci, A. and Benotto, G. (2012). Identifying Hypernyms in Distributional Semantic Spaces. In *Proceedings of * SEM*.

Liu, H., Chersoni, E., Klyueva, N., Santus, E., and Huang, C.-R. (2019). Semantic Relata for the Evaluation of Distributional Models in Mandarin Chinese. *IEEE Access*, 7:145705–145713.

Liu, Z., Huang, D., Huang, K., Li, Z., and Zhao, J. (2020). FinBERT: A Pre-trained Financial Language Representation Model for Financial Text Mining. In *Proceedings of IJCAI.*

Liu, P., Yuan, W., Fu, J., Jiang, Z., Hayashi, H., and Neubig, G. (2021). Pre-train, Prompt, and Predict: A Systematic Survey of Prompting Methods in Natural Language Processing. *arXiv preprint arXiv:2107.13586.*

Mansar, Y., Kang, J., and Maarouf, I. E. (2021). The FinSim-2 2021 Shared Task: Learning Semantic Similarities for the Financial Domain. In *Companion Proceedings of the Web Conference*, pages 288–292.

Nguyen, K. A., Köper, M., Schulte im Walde, S., and Vu, N. T. (2017). Hierarchical Embeddings for Hypernymy Detection and Directionality. In *Proceedings of EMNLP.*

Pandia, L., Cong, Y., and Ettinger, A. (2021). Pragmatic Competence of Pre-trained Language Models through the Lens of Discourse Connectives. In *Proceedings of CONLL.*

Pedinotti, P., Rambelli, G., Chersoni, E., Santus, E., Lenci, A., and Blache, P. (2021). Did the Cat Drink the Coffee? Challenging Transformers with Generalized Event Knowledge. In *Proceedings of *SEM.*

Peng, B., Chersoni, E., Hsu, Y.-Y., and Huang, C.-R. (2021). Is Domain Adaptation Worth Your Investment? Comparing BERT and FinBERT on Financial Tasks. In *Proceedings of the EMNLP Workshop on Economics and Natural Language Processing.*

Portelli, B., Lenzi, E., Chersoni, E., Serra, G., and Santus, E. (2021). BERT Prescriptions to Avoid Unwanted Headaches: A Comparison of Transformer Architectures for Adverse Drug Event Detection. In *Proceedings of EACL.*

Rambelli, G., Chersoni, E., Lenci, A., Blache, P., and Huang, C.-R. (2020). Comparing Probabilistic, Distributional and Transformer-Based Models on Logical Metonymy Interpretation. In *Proceedings of AACL-IJCNLP.*

Ravichander, A., Hovy, E., Suleman, K., Trischler, A., and Cheung, J. C. K. (2020). On the Systematicity of Probing Contextualized Word Representations: The Case of Hypernymy in BERT. In *Proceedings of *SEM.*

Roller, S. and Erk, K. (2016). Relations such as Hypernymy: Identifying and Exploiting Hearst Patterns in Distributional Vectors for Lexical Entailment. In *Proceedings of EMNLP.*

Roller, S., Erk, K., and Boleda, G. (2014). Inclusive Yet Selective: Supervised Distributional Hypernymy Detection. In *Proceedings of COLING.*

Sanchez, I. and Riedel, S. (2017). How Well Can We Predict Hypernyms from Word Embeddings? A Dataset-centric Analysis. In *Proceedings of EACL.*

Santus, E., Lenci, A., Lu, Q., and Im Walde, S. S. (2014a). Chasing Hypernyms in Vector Spaces with Entropy. In *Proceedings of EACL.*

Santus, E., Lu, Q., Lenci, A., and Huang, C.-R. (2014b). Taking Antonymy Mask Off in Vector Space. In *Proceedings of PACLIC.*

Santus, E., Yung, F., Lenci, A., and Huang, C.-R. (2015). Evalution 1.0: an Evolving Semantic Dataset for Training and Evaluation of Distributional Semantic Models. In *Proceedings of the ACL Workshop on Linked Data in Linguistics: Resources and Applications.*

Santus, E., Lenci, A., Chiu, T.-S., Lu, Q., and Huang, C.-R. (2016). Nine Features in a Random Forest to Learn Taxonomical Semantic Relations. In *Proceedings of LREC.*

Schick, T. and Schütze, H. (2021). Exploiting Cloze-Questions for Few-Shot Text Classification and Natural Language Inference. In *Proceedings of EACL*, pages 255–269.

Shwartz, V., Goldberg, Y., and Dagan, I. (2016). Improving Hypernymy Detection with an Integrated Path-based and Distributional Method. In *Proceedings of ACL.*

Shwartz, V., Santus, E., and Schlechtweg, D. (2017). Hypernyms under Siege: Linguistically-motivated Artillery for Hypernymy Detection. In *Proceedings of EACL.*

Ushio, A., Camacho-Collados, J., and Schockaert, S. (2021). Distilling Relation Embeddings from Pre-trained Language Models. In *Proceedings of EMNLP.*

Vaswani, A., Shazeer, N., Parmar, N., Uszkoreit, J., Jones, L., Gomez, A. N., Kaiser, Ł., and Polosukhin, I. (2017). Attention Is All You Need. In *Advances in Neural Information Processing Systems*, pages 5998–6008.

Weeds, J. and Weir, D. (2003). A General Framework for Distributional Similarity. In *Proceedings of EMNLP.*

Weeds, J., Clarke, D., Reffin, J., Weir, D., and Keller, B. (2014). Learning to Distinguish Hypernyms and Co-hyponyms. In *Proceedings of COLING.*

Xiang, R., Chersoni, E., Iacoponi, L., and Santus, E. (2020). The CogALex Shared Task on Monolingual and Multilingual Identification of Semantic Relations. In *Proceedings of the COLING Workshop on Cognitive Aspects of the Lexicon.*

Yang, Y., Uy, M. C. S., and Huang, A. (2020). FinBERT: A Pretrained Language Model for Financial Communications. *arXiv preprint arXiv:2006.08097.*

Zhu, Y., Kiros, R., Zemel, R., Salakhutdinov, R., Urtasun, R., Torralba, A., and Fidler, S. (2015). Aligning Books and Movies: Towards Story-like Visual Explanations by Watching Movies and Reading Books. In *Proceedings of the IEEE International Conference on Computer Vision*, pages 19–27.

Proceedings of the 4th Financial Narrative Processing Workshop @ LREC 2022, pages 17–26
Marseille, 24 June 2022

Sentiment Classification by Incorporating Background Knowledge from Financial Ontologies

Timen Stepišnik-Perdih[1,3], Andraž Pelicon[1,2], Blaž Škrlj[1,2], Martin Žnidaršič[1], Igor Lončarski[4], Senja Pollak[1]
[1]Jožef Stefan Institute, Ljubljana, Slovenia
[2]Jožef Stefan International Postgraduate School, Ljubljana, Slovenia
[3]Faculty of Computer and Information Science, Ljubljana, Slovenia
[4]School of Economics and Business, University of Ljubljana, Slovenia

tstepisnikp@gmail.com
igor.loncarski@ef.uni-lj.si
{andraz.pelicon, blaz.skrlj, martin.znidarsic, senja.pollak}@ijs.si

Abstract

Ontologies are increasingly used for machine reasoning over the last few years. They can provide explanations of concepts or be used for concept classification if there exists a mapping from the desired labels to the relevant ontology. This paper presents a practical use of an ontology for the purpose of data set generalization in an oversampling setting, with the aim of improving classification models. We demonstrate our solution on a novel financial sentiment data set using the Financial Industry Business Ontology (FIBO). The results show that generalization-based data enrichment benefits simpler models in a general setting and more complex models such as BERT in low-data setting.

Keywords: Sentiment classification, Financial ontology, Generalization

1. Introduction

From the perspective of financial economics, capturing and understanding the impact of non-financial information, such as sentiment or subjectivity conveyed in textual (language) form, has become increasingly more important. Identification and estimation of the sentiment are important in order to better understand and be able to predict investor behavior and the impact on supply and demand for financial assets and, in turn, the effect on asset prices, mainly from the perspective of disentangling fundamental drivers of asset prices from those based on perceptions/sentiment.

There has been a range of natural language processing approaches to automatically assess financial sentiment from texts (Man et al., 2019; Xing et al., 2020), which can be categorized into unsupervised, semi-supervised and supervised approaches. Financial text sentiment analysis is most frequently used for predictive analytics on financial markets (e.g., (Jin et al., 2019; Xing et al., 2018; Day and Lee, 2016; Smailović et al., 2014)), while on the other hand, a growing body of literature (e.g. (Smailović et al., 2017b)) is dedicated to the analysis of relations between financial and non-financial information in financial reports, which is motivated by the fact that the issue of the quality of financial reporting has become one of the central issues during the recent financial crisis and has received considerable attention from the society at large ever since.

Domain ontologies are becoming increasingly available. Containing background knowledge in a computer-readable form inspires the creation of new systems that try to solve problems in a way, more similar to domain experts. Provision of semantic information allows the learner to use features on a higher semantic level, possibly enabling better data generalizations. The methods, leveraging background knowledge (from domain or general resources), have been proposed in various fields (e.g. biology (Kim et al., 2018; Chang et al., 2015), sociology (Freeman, 2017)), short text classification (e.g. (Škrlj et al., 2020), fake news detection (Koloski et al., 2021)). Developing and using domain ontologies in financial economics could thus facilitate more accurate identification and classification of sentiment.

This paper discusses the use of background knowledge in the form of financial ontologies, more specifically the FIBO ontology, for improving classification models by text generalizations. While FIBO ontology has been previously used in automated approaches to classify the financial concepts (Stepišnik Perdih et al., 2021b), the potential of domain ontologies has not yet been sufficiently exploited for financial sentiment analysis. We use FIBO for text generalization, and more specifically assess it as a method for oversampling, where one transforms the original data set so that the new one is potentially more suitable for learning with the aim of improving a model's performance. The main contributions of this paper are as follows:

- we propose new text generalization methods using FIBO financial ontology;

- we assess their potential to be used in financial sentiment classification tasks using simple symbolic as well as neural transformer models in high- and low-data settings;
- we evaluate the method on a novel sentiment-annotated data set of random sentences from a selection of annual reports of companies listed on US or UK stock exchanges.

Our paper is structured as follows. In Section 2 we discuss work related to this paper: approaches modeling sentiment in financial texts and data upsampling approaches. Section 3 presents the financial sentiment data we use in our study and the Financial Industry Business Ontology (FIBO) which we use as background knowledge. In Section 4 we discuss the methodology of term generalization and our approaches of enriching data sets with generalized terms. In Section 5 we lay out the experimental evaluation of our methods and present the results. We draw conclusions and discuss further work in Section 6 and in Section 7 we discuss the reproducibility of our experiments.

2. Related work

There has been a range of natural language processing approaches developed to automatically assess financial sentiment from texts (Man et al., 2019; Xing et al., 2020). Financial sentiment analysis can be performed on various data sources including microblog posts (Cortis et al., 2017a), news (Cortis et al., 2017a) or corporate disclosures. El-Haj et al. (2016) gathered a dataset, similar to the one presented in this work, and annotated it for tone expressed in the text. In contrast to our dataset, which was gathered from financial reports, their dataset was gathered from earning announcements of UK comapnies.

In terms of annual reports, which are also the source of our data, several approaches have been proposed for prediction of financial phenomena such as: next year performance through indicators such as return on equity (Qiu et al., 2006; Butler and Kešelj, 2009; Li, 2010; Balakrishnan et al., 2010), contemporaneous returns around filing dates (Feldman et al., 2008; Amel-Zadeh and Faasse, 2016), stock return volatility (Kogan et al., 2009; Loughran and McDonald, 2011a), earnings forecast dispersion (Kothari et al., 2009; Loughran and McDonald, 2011a), costs of capital (Kothari et al., 2009), financial distress (Hájek and Olej, 2013; Hajek et al., 2014) and bank failure (Gupta et al., 2016). Another line of research (e.g. (Smailovic et al., 2017a), is dedicated to the analysis of relations between financial and non-financial information in financial reports, which is motivated by the fact that the issue of the quality of financial reporting has become one of the central issues during the recent financial crisis and has received considerable attention from the society at large ever since.

In terms of methods, we can distinguish between dictionary-based, supervised and hybrid methods. In the first category, the collection of dictionaries by (Loughran and McDonald, 2011b) is the most widely-used resource. In addition, general lexica like Opinion Lexicon (Hu and Liu, 2004) and MPQA Subjectivity Lexicon (Wilson et al., 2009) are being used by various researchers (e.g. (Chen et al., 2013; Goel and Uzuner, 2016) including by high-ranked teams in SemEval 2017 competition(Cortis et al., 2017a).

On the other side, supervised approaches are being developed. In older research, a lot of attention has been put on feature engineering, and several algorithms have been used. In the context of analyses of the financial reports it has been employed to categorize tone and content of forward-looking statements in 10-K fillings (Li, 2010) and to detect financial constraints based on word stem frequencies (Buehlmaier and Whited, 2015). Decision trees are not common in financial sentiment analysis, but were used among several other approaches in the study by (Hajek et al., 2014) on relations of report text sentiments and financial performance indicators, Random Forest approach has been used to predict short-term stock price changes on the basis of sentiment in 8-K reports (Lee et al., 2014), other non-neural approaches use logistic regression (e.g. (Hajek et al., 2014)), while the most frequently used algorithm is Support Vector Machine (SVM), e.g. in fraud detection models (Goel and Uzuner, 2016), classification of companies as out-performing or under-performing on the basis of narrative of disclosures (Balakrishnan et al., 2010), discriminating between failed and non-failed banks based on the sentiment of their reports (Gupta et al., 2016), picking out financially distressed companies on the basis of sentiment in reports (Hájek and Olej, 2013; Hajek et al., 2014), predicting financial risk from text features of reports (Kogan et al., 2009), predicting risk through stock return volatility on the basis of sentiment (Wang et al., 2013) or ranking companies as to their risk level on the basis of textual information on their reports (Tsai and Wang, 2012).

Several recent works tackled the problem of modeling sentiment in financial texts using deep learning methods. (Zhang et al., 2018) developed a neural architecture based on gated recurrent units which embedded textual and user information into a shared embedding space for mining financial opinions (e.g., bullish or bearish) from Twitter data. (Dong and Liu, 2021) note that quality annotated data for financial sentiment classification is scarce. They try to mitigate this limitation by training their convolutional neural network model on cross-domain data with the addition of an adversarial domain-adaptation module. (Araci, 2019) performed additional pretraining of the original BERT language model on texts from the financial domain. The updated finBERT model has shown improvement on two financial sentiment analysis data sets over the baselines. (Lee, 2021) use the adapted finBERT model in their work to train a financial sentiment classifier on social media posts and include its predictions as features for predicting stock returns. Additionally, through investigation of feature importance, they are able to quantify the impact these features have on stock return predictions.

The branch of research of high relevance to the presented publication considers *data upsampling*. This process, given the input data set, outputs a *transformed* data set which is potentially more suitable for learning. Upsampling regimes can be based solely on the input data (Halterman and Radford, 2021), however, upsampling based on external knowledge has also been of increasing interest in the last decades (Schneider et al., 2016; Lu et al., 2006). Incorporation of taxonomy-like background knowledge, however, was recently also shown to have performance-beneficial effects when considering texts(Škrlj et al., 2020). Semantic enrichment has shown promising results also when annotating scientific literature (Bertin and Atanassova, 2012). Another line of research related to data upsampling is *data augmentation*. With this process, given the original dataset, we obtain an upsampled dataset by adding slightly modified instances of the original instances or newly created synthetic instances. Several data augmentation approaches were developed explicitly for textual data: using WordNet as a dictionary to randomly replace words/phrases with their synonyms in an instance (Zhang et al., 2015), replacing words using the nearest neighbour of the word from a given word embedding (Wang and Yang, 2015), or replacing random words in a sentence based on the predictions of those words from a BERT model conditioned on the label for a particular instance. (Wu et al., 2019)

3. Data

In this section, we introduce the corpus of annotated sentences that we have used (Section 3.1), as well as the financial ontology used in our generalization method (Section 3.2).

3.1. Corpus

For our experiments, we have created a new data set of sentences from annual reports of companies that are listed on US or UK stock exchanges and cover the period between the years 2017 and 2019. Reports in PDF format were transformed into raw texts with the pdfminer[1] library, as well as some post-processing editing steps. Annual reports were first split into sentences and for each annotator, we created a data set containing 480 randomly sampled sentences. In order to include proper and relevant sentences from the reports, we have included only sentences from the first part of the report that begins with a capital letter and end with a full stop, contain at least 20 words or numbers and where at most 15% of characters are numeric. We additionally randomly sampled 20 sentences from the reports for annotation by all the annotators, for a total of 500 sentences per annotator. For annotating the data set, we engaged thirteen annotators. Annotators were the second-year graduate students of MSc in Quantitative Finance and Actuarial Sciences at the School of Economics and Business, University of Ljubljana. Given their field and length of studies, we believe they were very much suitable for the task of annotating financial texts from the perspective of domain experts in the area of financial sentiment. Annotators were then asked to annotate each of the sentences according to several criteria. First, whether the sentence is relevant from the perspective of corporate business. Second, whether the sentence conveys positive/negative/neutral financial sentiment. Third, whether the sentence expresses an opinion (subjectivity) or states the facts (objectivity). Four, whether it is forward-looking or not. Finally, whether it relates to sustainability issues or not.

In this work, we are using the labels with regards to the sentiment of the sentences to train a financial sentiment text classifier. The financial sentiment classification is posed as a three-class classification problem where each sentence can be classified as either positive, negative or neutral.

Given that our data set was annotated by several annotators, we estimate the agreement in annotations using labels for the 20 common sentences which were labeled by all the annotators. The inter-annotator agreement was estimated using Krippendorff's Alpha-reliability (Krippendorff, 2018), an established measure for estimating agreement between human annotators. While the measured alpha reliability was relatively low (α=0.3937) we note that it is comparable to other studies in the domain of sentiment analysis, especially when it comes to annotating sentiment in short texts (Pelicon et al., 2020; Bobicev and Sokolova, 2017; Santos et al., 2021). The low scores can be attributed to the fact that sentiment classification is a hard and rather subjective task.

This final financial sentiment data set was additionally preprocessed before conducting the experiments. We included the 20 common sentences, originally used to calculate the inter-annotator agreement, in the data only once and averaged the labels from several annotators into the final gold standard label. Next, we removed all the instances that were not labeled by the annotators. The final data set used for experiments contained 5994 labeled instances. The class distribution of this data set is presented in Table 1.

positive	neutral	negative	total
2194	3033	767	5994

Table 1: Class distribution of the financial sentiment classification data set.

We opted for the development of this specific new data set as most of the available financial texts with sentiment annotations originate from social media or news

[1] `https://github.com/euske/pdfminer`

(e.g., (Cortis et al., 2017b)) and we are not aware of any suitable sentiment annotations of texts from annual reports.

3.2. The Financial Industry Business Ontology

Ontologies are studies of all that exists in a given domain. In information science, an ontology is a model representing knowledge as a set of concepts connected with different relations. They are often represented by a directed graph where nodes represent concepts of the domain and edges represent relations connecting concepts.
The Financial Industry Business Ontology (FIBO), that we use in our generalization approach presented in Section 4, defines the sets of things that are of interest in financial business applications and the ways that those things can relate to one another. In this way, FIBO can give meaning to any data (e.g., spreadsheets, relational databases, XML documents) that describe the business of finance (fib, 2021a). Visualization of a part of FIBO is presented in Figure 1.
In this work we considered the following FIBO relations: "subClassOf", "isProvidedBy", "type", "isUsedBy", "isMemberOf", "hasJurisdiction" and "isPartOf", which connect 36,344 FIBO concepts. These represent the subset of FIBO that we use.

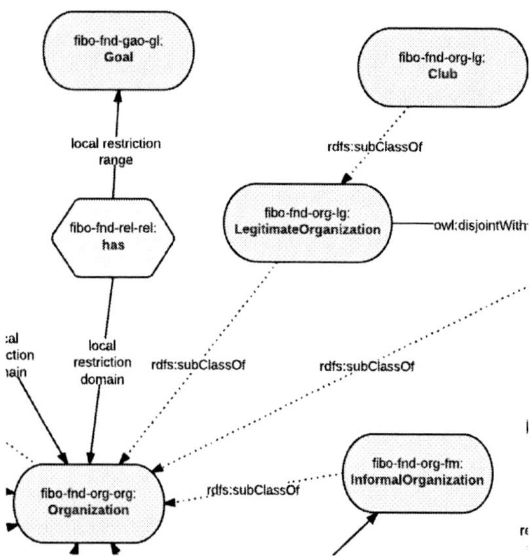

Figure 1: Visualization of a part of FIBO (fib, 2021b). The graph shows domain entities like "Organization", "LegitimateOrganization" and "Club" connected with relations like "subClassOf".

4. Methodology of term generalization for data set enrichment

In this section, we discuss generalizing terms using a domain ontology. In section 4.1, we first explain how we generalize financial terms using the Financial Industry Business Ontology (which was introduced in Section 3.2), and next, Section 4.2 proposes two generalization-based data enrichment methods.

4.1. Ontology-based generalization

Semantic reasoning from model-agnostic explanations (Stepišnik Perdih et al., 2021a) introduces a way of generalizing sets of terms using a domain ontology represented as a directed graph. It uses relations within the ontology (edges in the graph) that connect terms to more general ones. Each term is generalized relation by relation (in steps) until found generalization(s) are too connected to terms of other sets we are generalizing. This way the resulting sets contain more general terms but remain specific because we control the allowed intersection between terms of different sets during the process of generalization.
We have modified the mentioned approach so that, instead of generalizing sets of terms that represent model explanations, it generalizes individual terms found in the financial sentiment classification data set. Each resulting set contains all found generalizations of a single term.
The search for generalizations can be **constrained** or a **full** search of the ontology. The constrained setting only considers found generalizations that also satisfy the condition of being specific for the given term, meaning that generalizations common to multiple terms (to more than 1% of terms) are not considered, while the full ontology search generalizes each term to its top-level generalizations.

4.2. Data set enrichment

In this section, we describe ways in which we enrich the data set using acquired generalizations with the aim of improving the performance of prediction models. We try swapping terms we have successfully generalized with their generalizations as described in 4.2.1 and concatenating found generalizations of terms present in a sentence at the end of the sentence as described in 4.2.2. Both methods support the constrained and the full ontology-based generalization search.
Before any of the two approaches is employed we lemmatize the sentences with Lemmagen3 (pyp, 2021) so that we can recognize the terms in sentences for which generalizations have been found.

4.2.1. Term swapping

With term swapping, we augment the train subset with new samples. We acquire the new samples by swapping terms in sentences with their generalizations. This is done by iterating over terms that have been generalized and creating t new samples from each sentence that contains at least one occurrence of the term, where t is the number of found generalizations for that term. These new samples are immediately added to the subset so that other terms can be generalized in the next

iteration. We also keep the original sample in the subset. In each iteration, we get $n \cdot t$ new samples, where n is the number of samples in the subset containing the term we are swapping.
Because in this way the number of samples increases very quickly we introduce the parameter k which serves as a target factor of upscaling the number of samples in the train subset. If after any iteration, the number of samples in the subset is larger than $k \cdot N$, where N is the number of original samples in the subset before the swapping, the swapping stops.
Let us look at an example of a financial sentiment classification text after lemmatization:

- through real-time information and visualisation, *USA* help reduce business waste

and two of the new training instances acquired using term swapping with the constrained search of FIBO generalizations:

- through real-time information and visualisation, *united states of america* help reduce business waste
- through real-time information and visualisation, *geographic region identifier* help reduce business waste

4.2.2. Generalization concatenation

Generalization concatenation keeps the number of instances but appends all possible generalizations for FIBO terms found in a sentence to the end of the sentence of a training set.
An example of this approach is:

- through real-time information and visualisation, USA help reduce business waste, *code element, united states of america, geographic region identifier*

5. Experiments

In this section, we evaluate our method of enriching the data sets used for model training. First, we describe the train and test split of the evaluation data sets (Section 5.1). Next we present the models used in our experiments (section 5.2), followed by presenting the experimental setting (Section 5.3), and finally describing the results (Section 5.4).

5.1. Evaluation data sets

We split the data set of 5994 into train and test subsets with a random 10% of samples being included in the test subset. The proposed methods were benchmarked in both high- and low-data settings. In the high-data setting, the methods were benchmarked using the whole training data set (train_{ALL}). In the low-data setting, we have reduced the training data set to the 10% of the size of the original training data (train_{LOW}) while keeping the class distribution intact. The test set was kept the same in both experimental settings. Class distribution of the two subsets is presented in Table 2.

subset	positive	neutral	negative	total
train_{ALL}	1991	2731	672	5394
train_{LOW}	199	273	67	539
test	203	302	95	600

Table 2: Class distribution of train and test subsets. The number of training instances differs in the high- and low-data setting experiments, while the test set is the same.

A total of **818** different terms were generalized and the train subset contains an average of **11.04** occurrences of these terms per sentence. Table 3 shows examples of frequently generalized terms and their generalizations.

term	generalization
group	collection
report	document
executive	agent in role
customer	agent in role
shareholder	agent in role
future	agreement

Table 3: Examples of some of the most frequently generalized terms and one of their possible generalizations. Generalizations were found using the constrained search of the ontology.

5.2. Models

For the evaluation of our method we use the following models: logistic regression with doc2vec (*lr-doc2vec*) (Le and Mikolov, 2014), linear regression using character features (*lr-char*), linear regression using word features (*lr-word*), Support Vector Machine classifier using "all-mpnet-base-v2" representations from Simple Transformers (*svm-mpnet*), Support Vector Machine classifier using character features (*svm-char*), Support Vector Machine classifier using word features (*svm-word*) and TPOT (*tpot*) - an AutoML tool based on genetic programming which learns to normalize and model the data based on an internal validation procedure (Le et al., 2020). Because this approach is not able to preprocess raw text data, word features are extracted from the input documents using TF-IDF.
Additionally, we test our oversampling method in combination with the fine-tuning technique for transformer-based language models. For this purpose, we use two monolingual language models based on the BERT architecture, namely the original base version of the BERT language model (Devlin et al., 2019) and the finBERT language model (Araci, 2019) which was additionally trained on a corpus of unlabeled financial texts. For fine-tuning a classifier based on the language model, we added a linear layer with a softmax activation function at the output to serve as the classification layer. As input to the classifier, we took the

representation of the special (CLS) token from the last layer of the language model. The whole model was then jointly trained on the downstream task of financial sentiment classification. During training, we split the original training set into training and validation subsets in 90%-10% ratio. We used the Adam optimizer with the learning rate of $2e - 5$ and learning rate warmup over the first 10% of the training instances. We used a weight decay set to 0.01 for regularization. All models were trained for maximum of 3 epochs with batch size 32. We performed the training of the models using the HuggingFace Transformers library (Wolf et al., 2019). We tokenized the textual input for the neural models with the respective language model's tokenizer. For performing matrix operations efficiently, all inputs were adjusted to the same length, which is a standard procedure. After tokenizing all inputs, their maximum length was set to 256 tokens. Longer sequences were truncated, while shorter sequences were zero-padded.

5.3. Evaluation setting

Models described in 5.2 were trained on the unchanged training set that we use as a baseline (*baseline*) and subsets enriched with term swapping *(swp)* introduced in Section 4.2.1 or generalization concatenation (*cnct*) introduced in Section 4.2.2. When using term swapping for data enrichment we used different values of the k parameter: 2 and 10. Every model in all of the settings was evaluated on the original test set without any modifications.

As we consider term swapping as a data oversampling approach, we additionally compared our methods with two simple and widely used oversampling techniques in natural language processing. The first method is *random* oversampling where the original training set was oversampled by duplicating random instances in the training set so that the original class distribution remained the same. The second, more widely used technique, was the minority class oversampling. In this method, at each iteration, an instance from the current *minority* class is chosen at random and duplicated. This way the final oversampled training set has an approximately balanced class distribution. To control for the effect of the size of the data set on model performance, each baseline oversampling technique oversampled the original data set to the sizes of the proposed term swapping method.

Methods that employ ontology-based generalization search on the low-data setting are tested using both the *constrained* and *full* generalization search (see Section 4.1). While testing on the high-data setting we only explored the constrained generalization search due to longer model training times.

We measure the performance of the models using macro-F1 score, which is defined as the harmonic mean between recall and precision scores averaged across all classes. Formally, it is defined as follows:

$$F1 = \frac{1}{N}\sum_{i=1}^{N}\frac{2 * P_i * R_i}{P_i + R_i}$$

where i represents the class label, N represents the number of classes, P_i represents the i-th class precision score and R_i represents the i-th class recall score. We use this standard metric because it is shown to be more robust for problems with a highly unbalanced distribution of classes.

5.4. Evaluation results

5.4.1. High-data setting results

Table 4 shows F1-scores of the trained models described in Section 5.2 on the full data set.

All simpler models using logistic regression or SVM show increased performance by at least one of the data enrichment or oversampling methods, but the differences are rather small. The main difference (5 percentage points) can be observed when using term swapping generalization (parameter $k = 2$) with doc2vec.

For language models fine-tuned end-to-end (BERT and finBERT), the oversampling methods (swp, random, minority) seem to generally degrade the performance of the final model when the model is trained on the full data set. The results for the original BERT model show worse performance when oversampling methods are utilized, while for finBERT model only results with minority and random oversampling stay comparable with the baseline. This result indicates that oversampling in general is not a viable method for improving performance of language model-based classifiers when ample training data is already available. The language models also do not seem to gain enough additional information by introducing background knowledge from financial ontologies through concatenation of generalized terms at the end of the sentences (cnct). The performance of the BERT-based language model stays the same as without the introduction of background knowledge while a slight drop in performance is observed with the finBERT-based model. This effect might be explained by the fact that language models trained with self-attention and relatively long context windows weight every part of the input in relation to one another to construct the final representations. For this reason, these models are robust to minor perturbances in textual input, especially when the textual input is shorter than the input window.

5.4.2. Low-data setting results

The results of the trained models in terms of F1 scores on the downsized training set (where only 10% of the original training data is used) are presented in Table 5. In contrast to the high-data setting (see Section 5.4.1, the results on the downsized training data show that generalization and oversampling techniques help in improving the performance of all of the classifiers. In terms of our proposed methods, we see that the most

		lr-doc2vec	lr-char	lr-word	svm-mpnet	svm-char	svm-word	tpot	BERT	finBERT
baseline		0.45	0.46	0.47	0.58	0.47	0.46	**0.54**	**0.60**	**0.57**
cnct (constr.)		0.44	**0.49**	**0.49**	**0.59**	0.45	0.46	0.47	**0.60**	0.56
swp (constr.)	k2	**0.50**	0.44	0.48	0.57	0.42	**0.47**	0.42	0.59	0.55
	k10	0.49	0.44	0.48	0.57	0.42	**0.47**	0.41	0.53	0.51
minority	k2	0.38	**0.49**	0.43	0.57	0.48	**0.47**	0.46	0.57	**0.57**
	k10	0.32	**0.49**	0.47	0.56	**0.50**	**0.47**	0.26	0.54	0.55
random	k2	0.40	0.44	0.45	0.54	0.43	0.45	0.45	0.59	**0.57**
	k10	0.40	0.37	0.45	0.54	0.40	0.45	0.36	0.58	0.56

Table 4: Test set results of all models trained in **high data setting,** on the baseline data set (no generalizations or oversampling), the enriched training subsets with concatenation (*cnct*) and term swapping oversampling (*swp*), as well as the oversampled data using *minority* and *random* oversampling methods. Generalizations are obtained with the constrained ontology-based search. The models are evaluated with the F1-score. Bold results represent the best result for individual models.

		lr-doc2vec	lr-char	lr-word	svm-mpnet	svm-char	svm-word	tpot	BERT	finBERT
baseline		0.33	0.22	0.39	0.53	0.34	0.39	0.37	0.26	0.22
cnct (constr.)		0.27	0.22	0.38	0.53	0.36	0.38	0.38	0.22	0.30
cnct (full)		0.31	0.22	0.38	**0.56**	0.36	0.38	0.38	0.22	0.30
swp (constr.)	k2	0.33	0.22	0.39	0.37	0.34	0.39	0.37	0.35	0.31
	k10	0.35	0.33	0.34	0.51	0.34	0.30	0.34	0.38	0.36
swp (full)	k2	0.40	0.38	0.36	0.52	0.37	0.38	**0.41**	0.43	0.41
	k10	**0.44**	**0.42**	0.39	0.51	0.41	0.39	0.36	0.50	0.46
minority	k2	0.41	0.41	**0.44**	0.55	**0.42**	**0.44**	0.23	**0.52**	0.43
	k10	0.36	**0.42**	0.42	0.54	**0.42**	0.42	0.23	0.49	**0.49**
random	k2	0.35	0.37	0.38	0.53	0.37	0.38	0.31	0.36	0.27
	k10	0.36	0.35	0.38	0.53	0.36	0.38	0.31	0.24	0.29

Table 5: Test set results of all models trained in **low data setting**, on the baseline data set (no generalizations or oversampling), the enriched training subsets with concatenation (*cnct*) and term swapping oversampling (*swp*), as well as the oversampled data using *minority* and *random* oversampling methods. Generalizations are obtained with both constrained and full ontology-based searches. The models are evaluated with the F1-score. Bold results represent the best result for individual models.

consistent improvements are obtained using *full* search of the ontology. Overall, the best results are obtained using *svm-mpnet* model with our proposed background knowledge-enriched method *cnct(full)*; in this case the performance in low-data setting nearly reaches the performance of the finBERT model in high-data setting (see Table 4). We also see that term swapping (*swp*) leads to several large improvements, although *minority* oversampling is a very competitive approach (most frequently improving the individual classifier's performance).

In contrast to the high-data setting, for language model-based classifiers the performance can be increased using oversampling. Using our proposed term-swapping approach, we generally observe an increase in the final model performance as the size of the data set increases (k=10 vs. k=2), even though the highest improvements for BERT-based models are obtained with minority oversampling approach. The fine-tuned language models trained in low-data regimes generally lag behind the same models trained in high-data regimes, they however surpass other machine learning models in high-data settings.

6. Conclusion and future work

In our paper, we propose two generalization methods using the FIBO ontology as background knowledge. In the first one generalized terms are concatenated to the original training set instances, while in the second one, generalized terms are used in the oversampling setting, creating new generalized instances of the training set. We evaluate the potential of these methods in high- and low-data settings, and also more generally assess the potential of oversampling for financial sentiment analysis.

The results show that while in high-data setting best results are obtained using fine-tuned BERT-based models, where generalizations and oversampling do not lead to any improvement, simpler models using logistic regression or SVMs can be improved when integrating background knowledge (however improvements are rather small). More interestingly, we show that in low-data scenarios, large improvements can be obtained by our generalizations, as well as with simpler oversampling methods, leading to performances similar to those when 90% more data is available.

In future work, we aim to proceed in the following way. First, we will apply our method to other classification problems using annotations of our data set (relevance for corporate business, subjectivity, sustainability issues relevance). Next, we aim to test our methods on other financial sentiment data sets (e.g. SemEval 2017 data for fine-grained sentiment analysis of financial microblog posts and news headlines (Cortis et al., 2017a)). Next, as in our paper (Stepišnik Perdih et al., 2021a), we have already shown that generalizations can be used for model explainability, we will continue this line of research, which would lead to improved interpretability of financial sentiment classification models for financial domain experts. Last but not least, we plan to use our sentiment classifiers to annotate a larger corpus of annual reports, where correlation analysis of financial indicators and text sentiment will be assessed, continuing and improving over our work in (Smailović et al., 2017b).

7. Reproducibility and reusability

The code of all our experiments is publicly available at the following GitLab repository: `https://gitlab.com/Andrazp/sentiment_classification_with_financial_ontologies.git`. The data identifying the sentences of annual reports that we used in our experiments and their sentiment annotations is available at `http://kt.ijs.si/data/sentences_financial_sentiment.zip`. The FIBO ontology is public and accessible at (fib, 2021a).

Acknowledgements

This work was supported by the Slovenian Research Agency (ARRS) grants for the core programme Knowledge technologies (P2-0103) and the project quantitative and qualitative analysis of the unregulated corporate financial reporting (J5-2554). B.S. was funded through the ARRS junior researcher grant. We also want to thank Matthew Purver and Aljosa Valentincic for their help in data set preparation, as well as students of the School of Business and Economics for their effort in data annotation.

8. References

Amel-Zadeh, A. and Faasse, J. (2016). The information content of 10-K narratives: Comparing MD&A and footnotes disclosures. 01.

Araci, D. (2019). Finbert: Financial sentiment analysis with pre-trained language models. *arXiv preprint arXiv:1908.10063.*

Balakrishnan, R., Qiu, X. Y., and Srinivasan, P. (2010). On the predictive ability of narrative disclosures in annual reports. *European Journal of Operational Research*, 202(3):789–801.

Bertin, M. and Atanassova, I. (2012). Semantic enrichment of scientific publications and metadata. *D-lib Magazine*, 18(7/8).

Bobicev, V. and Sokolova, M. (2017). Inter-annotator agreement in sentiment analysis: Machine learning perspective.

Buehlmaier, M. and Whited, T. M. (2015). Looking for risk in words: A narrative approach to measuring the pricing implications of financial constraints. In *Annual Conference of the Western Finance Association (WFA)*.

Butler, M. and Kešelj, V. (2009). Financial forecasting using character n-gram analysis and readability scores of annual reports. In *Canadian Conference on Artificial Intelligence*, pages 39–51. Springer.

Chang, S., Han, W., Tang, J., Qi, G.-J., Aggarwal, C. C., and Huang, T. S. (2015). Heterogeneous network embedding via deep architectures. In *Proceedings of the 21th ACM SIGKDD International Conference on Knowledge Discovery and Data Mining*, KDD '15, pages 119–128, New York, NY, USA. ACM.

Chen, C., Liu, C., Chang, Y., and Tsai, H. (2013). Opinion mining for relating subjective expressions and annual earnings in US financial statements. *Journal of Information Science and Engineering*, 29(4):743–764.

Cortis, K., Freitas, A., Daudert, T., Huerlimann, M., Zarrouk, M., Handschuh, S., and Davis, B. (2017a). SemEval-2017 task 5: Fine-grained sentiment analysis on financial microblogs and news. In *Proceedings of the 11th International Workshop on Semantic Evaluation (SemEval-2017)*, pages 519–535, Vancouver, Canada, August. Association for Computational Linguistics.

Cortis, K., Freitas, A., Daudert, T., Huerlimann, M., Zarrouk, M., Handschuh, S., and Davis, B. (2017b). SemEval-2017 task 5: Fine-grained sentiment analysis on financial microblogs and news. In *Proceedings of the 11th International Workshop on Semantic Evaluation (SemEval-2017)*, pages 519–535, Vancouver, Canada, August. Association for Computational Linguistics.

Day, M.-Y. and Lee, C.-C. (2016). Deep learning for financial sentiment analysis on finance news providers. In *2016 IEEE/ACM International Conference on Advances in Social Networks Analysis and Mining (ASONAM)*, pages 1127–1134. IEEE.

Devlin, J., Chang, M.-W., Lee, K., and Toutanova, K. (2019). BERT: Pre-training of deep bidirectional transformers for language understanding. In *Proceedings of the 2019 Conference of the North American Chapter of the Association for Computational Linguistics: Human Language Technologies, Volume 1 (Long and Short Papers)*, pages 4171–4186, Minneapolis, Minnesota. Association for Computational Linguistics.

Dong, S. and Liu, C. (2021). Sentiment classification for financial texts based on deep learning. *Computational Intelligence and Neuroscience*, 2021.

El-Haj, M., Rayson, P. E., Young, S. E., Walker, M., Moore, A., Athanasakou, V., and Schleicher, T. (2016). Learning tone and attribution for financial text mining.

Feldman, R., Govindaraj, S., Livnat, J., and Segal, B. (2008). The incremental information content of tone change in management discussion and analysis. *Available at SSRN 1126962.*

(2021a). The Financial Industry Business Ontology. `https://spec.edmcouncil.org/fibo/`, December.

(2021b). Visualising FIBO. `https://datalanguage.com/blog/visualising-fibo`, December.

Freeman, L. C. (2017). *Research Methods in Social Network Analysis.* Routledge.

Goel, S. and Uzuner, O. (2016). Do sentiments matter in fraud detection? estimating semantic orientation of annual reports. *Intelligent Systems in Accounting, Finance and Management*, 23(3):215–239.

Gupta, A., Simaan, M., and Zaki, M. J. (2016). When positive sentiment is not so positive: Textual analytics and bank failures. *Available at SSRN 2773939.*

Hájek, P. and Olej, V. (2013). Evaluating sentiment in annual reports for financial distress prediction using neural networks and support vector machines. In *International Conference on Engineering Applications of Neural Networks*, pages 1–10. Springer.

Hajek, P., Olej, V., and Myskova, R. (2014). Forecasting corporate financial performance using sentiment in annual reports for stakeholders' decision-making. *Technological and Economic Development of Economy*, 20(4):721–738.

Halterman, A. and Radford, B. J. (2021). Few-shot upsampling for protest size detection. *arXiv preprint arXiv:2105.11260.*

Hu, M. and Liu, B. (2004). Mining and summarizing customer reviews. In *Proceedings of the Tenth ACM SIGKDD International Conference on Knowledge Discovery and Data Mining*, KDD '04, page 168–177, New York, NY, USA. Association for Computing Machinery.

Jin, Z., Yang, Y., and Liu, Y. (2019). Stock closing price prediction based on sentiment analysis and lstm. *Neural Computing and Applications*, pages 1–17.

Kim, C., Yin, P., Soto, C. X., Blaby, I. K., and Yoo, S. (2018). Multimodal biological analysis using NLP and expression profile. In *2018 New York Scientific Data Summit (NYSDS)*, pages 1–4, Aug.

Kogan, S., Levin, D., Routledge, B. R., Sagi, J. S., and Smith, N. A. (2009). Predicting risk from financial reports with regression. In *Proceedings of Human Language Technologies: The 2009 Annual Conference of the North American Chapter of the Association for Computational Linguistics*, pages 272–280. Association for Computational Linguistics.

Koloski, B., Perdih, T., Pollak, S., and Škrlj, B. (2021). Identification of covid-19 related fake news via neural stacking. In *Combating Online Hostile Posts in Regional Languages during Emergency Situation: First International Workshop, CONSTRAINT 2021, Collocated with AAAI 2021, Virtual Event, February 8, 2021, Revised Selected Papers*, page 177. Springer Nature.

Kothari, S., Li, X., and Short, J. E. (2009). The effect of disclosures by management, analysts, and business press on cost of capital, return volatility, and analyst forecasts: A study using content analysis. *The Accounting Review*, 84(5):1639–1670.

Krippendorff, K. (2018). *Content Analysis, An Introduction to its methodology.* Sage Publications, Thousand Oaks, CA, USA, 4th edition.

Le, Q. and Mikolov, T. (2014). Distributed representations of sentences and documents. In *International conference on machine learning*, pages 1188–1196.

Le, T. T., Fu, W., and Moore, J. H. (2020). Scaling tree-based automated machine learning to biomedical big data with a feature set selector. *Bioinformatics*, 36(1):250–256.

Lee, H., Surdeanu, M., MacCartney, B., and Jurafsky, D. (2014). On the importance of text analysis for stock price prediction. In *LREC*, pages 1170–1175.

Lee, S. S. (2021). Feature investigation for stock returns prediction using xgboost and deep learning sentiment classification.

Li, F. (2010). The information content of forward-looking statements in corporate filings—a naïve bayesian machine learning approach. *Journal of Accounting Research*, 48(5):1049–1102.

Loughran, T. and McDonald, B. (2011a). Barron's red flags: Do they actually work? *Journal of Behavioral Finance*, 12(2):90–97.

Loughran, T. and McDonald, B. (2011b). When is a liability not a liability? textual analysis, dictionaries, and 10-ks. *The Journal of Finance*, 66(1):35–65.

Lu, X., Zheng, B., Velivelli, A., and Zhai, C. (2006). Enhancing text categorization with semantic-enriched representation and training data augmentation. *Journal of the American Medical Informatics Association*, 13(5):526–535.

Man, X., Luo, T., and Lin, J. (2019). Financial sentiment analysis (fsa): A survey. In *2019 IEEE International Conference on Industrial Cyber Physical Systems (ICPS)*, pages 617–622. IEEE.

Pelicon, A., Pranjić, M., Miljković, D., Škrlj, B., and Pollak, S. (2020). Zero-shot learning for cross-lingual news sentiment classification. *Applied Sciences*, 10(17):5993.

(2021). Lemmagen3. `https://pypi.org/project/lemmagen3/#description`, December.

Qiu, X. Y., Srinivasan, P., and Street, N. (2006). Exploring the forecasting potential of company annual reports. *Proceedings of the American Society for Information Science and Technology*, 43(1):1–15.

Santos, J. S., Bernardini, F., and Paes, A. (2021). Measuring the degree of divergence when labeling tweets in the electoral scenario. In *Anais do X Brazilian*

Workshop on Social Network Analysis and Mining, pages 127–138. SBC.

Schneider, N., Schneider, L., Pinggera, P., Franke, U., Pollefeys, M., and Stiller, C. (2016). Semantically guided depth upsampling. In *German conference on pattern recognition*, pages 37–48. Springer.

Smailović, J., Grčar, M., Lavrač, N., and Žnidaršič, M. (2014). Stream-based active learning for sentiment analysis in the financial domain. *Information Sciences*, 285:181–203.

Smailovic, J., Znidarsic, M., Valentincic, A., Loncarski, I., Pahor, M., Martins, P., and Pollak, S. (2017a). Automatic analysis of annual financial reports: A case study. *Computación y Sistemas*, 21(4).

Smailović, J., Žnidaršič, M., Valentinčič, A., Lončarski, I., Pahor, M., Martins, P. T., and Pollak, S. (2017b). Automatic analysis of annual financial reports: A case study. *Computación y Sistemas*, 21(4):809–818.

Stepišnik Perdih, T., Lavrač, N., and Škrlj, B. (2021a). Semantic reasoning from model-agnostic explanations. In *2021 IEEE 19th World Symposium on Applied Machine Intelligence and Informatics (SAMI) [Elektronski vir]: on-line conference*, 2021 IEEE 19th World Symposium on Applied Machine Intelligence and Informatics (SAMI) [Elektronski vir]: online conference, page 105–110. Nasl. z nasl. zaslona Opis vira z dne 23. 3. 2021 Bibliografija: str. 10.

Stepišnik Perdih, T., Pollak, S., and Škrlj, B. (2021b). Jsi at the finsim-2 task: ontology-augmented financial concept classification. In Jurij Leskovec, et al., editors, *The Web Conference [Elektronski vir]: companion of the World Wide Web conference (WWW 2021): [30th edition, Ljubljana, 19th - 23rd April, 2021]*, The Web Conference [Elektronski vir]: companion of the World Wide Web conference (WWW 2021): [30th edition, Ljubljana, 19th - 23rd April, 2021], page 298–301. Association for Computing Machinery. Soavtorji: Vlado Dimovski, Judita Peterlin, Maja Meško, Vasja Roblek Opis vira z dne 14. 6. 2021 Nasl. z nasl. zaslona Bibliografija: str. 299-301 Abstract.

Tsai, M.-F. and Wang, C.-J. (2012). Visualization on financial terms via risk ranking from financial reports. In *COLING (Demos)*, pages 447–452.

Wang, W. Y. and Yang, D. (2015). That's so annoying!!!: A lexical and frame-semantic embedding based data augmentation approach to automatic categorization of annoying behaviors using# petpeeve tweets. In *Proceedings of the 2015 conference on empirical methods in natural language processing*, pages 2557–2563.

Wang, C.-J., Tsai, M.-F., Liu, T., and Chang, C.-T. (2013). Financial sentiment analysis for risk prediction. In *IJCNLP*, pages 802–808.

Wilson, T., Wiebe, J., and Hoffmann, P. (2009). Articles: Recognizing contextual polarity: An exploration of features for phrase-level sentiment analysis. *Computational Linguistics*, 35(3):399–433, September.

Wolf, T., Debut, L., Sanh, V., Chaumond, J., Delangue, C., Moi, A., Cistac, P., Rault, T., Louf, R., Funtowicz, M., Davison, J., Shleifer, S., von Platen, P., Ma, C., Jernite, Y., Plu, J., Xu, C., Scao, T. L., Gugger, S., Drame, M., Lhoest, Q., and Rush, A. M. (2019). HuggingFace's Transformers: State-of-the-art Natural Language Processing. *ArXiv*, abs/1910.03771.

Wu, X., Lv, S., Zang, L., Han, J., and Hu, S. (2019). Conditional bert contextual augmentation. In *International Conference on Computational Science*, pages 84–95. Springer.

Xing, F. Z., Cambria, E., and Welsch, R. E. (2018). Natural language based financial forecasting: a survey. *Artificial Intelligence Review*, 50(1):49–73.

Xing, F., Malandri, L., Zhang, Y., and Cambria, E. (2020). Financial sentiment analysis: an investigation into common mistakes and silver bullets. In *Proceedings of the 28th International Conference on Computational Linguistics*, pages 978–987.

Zhang, X., Zhao, J., and LeCun, Y. (2015). Character-level convolutional networks for text classification. *Advances in neural information processing systems*, 28.

Zhang, L., Xiao, K., Zhu, H., Liu, C., Yang, J., and Jin, B. (2018). Caden: A context-aware deep embedding network for financial opinions mining. In *2018 IEEE International Conference on Data Mining (ICDM)*, pages 757–766. IEEE.

Škrlj, B., Martinc, M., Kralj, J., Lavrač, N., and Pollak, S. (2020). tax2vec: Constructing interpretable features from taxonomies for short text classification. *Computer Speech Language*, page 101104.

Proceedings of the 4th Financial Narrative Processing Workshop @ LREC 2022, pages 27–35
Marseille, 24 June 2022

Detecting Causes of Stock Price Rise and Decline by Machine Reading Comprehension with BERT

Gakuto Tsutsumi, Takehito Utsuro
Graduate School of Science and Technology, University of Tsukuba,
1-1-1, Tennodai, Tsukuba, Ibaraki, 305-8573, Japan

Abstract

In this paper, we focused on news reported when stock prices fluctuate significantly. The news reported when stock prices change is a very useful source of information on what factors cause stock prices to change. However, because it is manually produced, not all events that cause stock prices to change are necessarily reported. Thus, in order to provide investors with information on those causes of stock price changes, it is necessary to develop a system to collect information on events that could be closely related to the stock price changes of certain companies from the Internet. As the first step towards developing such a system, this paper takes an approach of employing a BERT-based machine reading comprehension model, which extracts causes of stock price rise and decline from news reports on stock price changes. In the evaluation, the approach of using the title of the article as the question of machine reading comprehension performs well. It is shown that the fine-tuned machine reading comprehension model successfully detects additional causes of stock price rise and decline other than those stated in the title of the article.

Keywords: Machine Reading Comprehension, BERT, Finance News

1. Introduction

Factors that cause stock prices to fluctuate include IR announcements, in which a company communicates its business results and future business plans to shareholders and investors, and news reports on events that are closely related to the companies. When such information is delivered, as shown in Figure 1, the stock price can fluctuate significantly due to an increase in volume, which represents the volume of stock transactions in which the company's shares are sold or bought. When large fluctuations in stock prices occur in this way, news media related to finance on the Web may report on the fluctuations in stock prices as well as their causes as shown in Figure 2. In this paper, we focused on news reported when stock prices fluctuate significantly. The news reported when stock prices change is a very useful source of information on what factors cause stock prices to change, but because it is manually produced, not all events that cause stock prices to change are necessarily reported. Thus, in order to provide investors with information on those causes of stock price changes, it is necessary to develop a system to collect information on events that could be closely related to the stock price changes of certain companies from the Internet.

As the first step towards developing such a system, this paper takes an approach of employing a BERT (Devlin et al., 2019)-based machine reading comprehension model (Pranav et al., 2016), which extracts causes of stock price changes from news reports on stock price changes (Figure 3). Those extracted causes are intended to be further used to train a system to collect information on events that could be closely related to the stock price changes of certain companies from the Internet.

In the evaluation results, overall, the approach of using the title of the article as the question Q of the machine reading comprehension performs well. We also compare the performance of two models, where one is fine-tuned with stock price rise examples, while the other is fine-tuned with stock price decline examples. The former model performs well when evaluated against stock price rise examples and so does the latter model when evaluated against stock price decline examples. It is shown that, however, the former (stock price rise) model performs worse when evaluated against stock price decline examples. It is also the case that the latter (stock price decline) model performs worse when evaluated against stock price rise examples. These results are mainly because words within stock price rise examples and decline examples are somehow different from each other as we describe in section 2. Based on these results, it is also shown that the model fine-tuned with the mixture of stock price rise and decline examples is the most appropriate for the general use where the stock price rise or decline is unknown.

We also examine whether the answer span predicted by the fine-tuned model actually includes additional information other than the question (i.e., the title of the article) or not. The rate of including additional information other than the title of the article is about 70% for the stock price decline and about 50% for the stock price rise[1]. Here, as we describe in section 4, most of them actually do not overlap with the title of the article and hence the fine-tuned model detects causes of stock price rise and decline that are not stated in the title of the article. Thus, this result indicates that the fine-tuned model successfully detects additional causes of stock price rise and decline other than those stated in the title of the article.

The method proposed and the evaluation results of this paper are summarized as below:

[1]Their rates of exact and partial match with the reference answer are over 60% in the total of rise and decline.

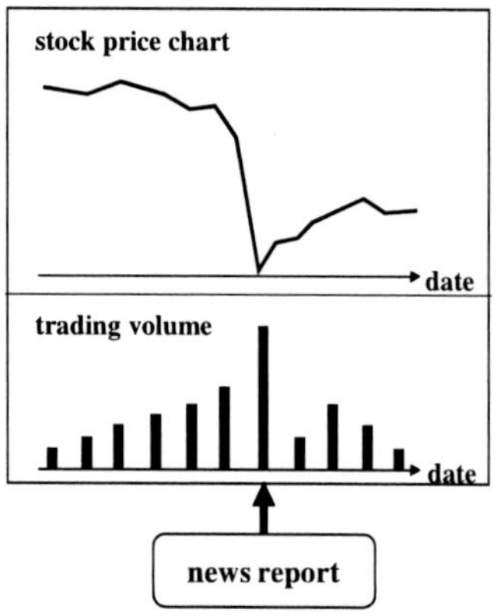

Figure 1: Relation of Stock Price Changes and Trading Volume per Day and News Report

Table 1: Statistics of the Categories of 100 Articles delivered from "MINKABU"

category	# of articles
news on stock price changes and their causes	28
news on companies such as the announcements on new products	13
news on domestic equities	21
news on foreign equities	9
news on exchange market	3
news on bond market	3
news for individual investors	23
total	100

- A BERT-based machine reading comprehension model extracts causes of stock price rise and decline from news reports on stock price changes.
- The approach of using the title of the article as the question Q of the machine reading comprehension performs well.
- The rate of including additional information other than the title of the article is about 70% for the stock price decline and about 50% for the stock price rise.

2. Stock Price News of "MINKABU"

In this paper, the news site from which we collect the stock price news is `minkabu.jp`[2], where we used 23,989 articles[3] delivered from "MINKABU".

Table 2: # of Occurrences and their Ratio (%) of Individual Words representing Rise in Stock Prices among 627 Examples of Machine Reading Comprehension of Causes of Stock Price Changes

word	#	ratio
反発 (correction)	176	19.7
続伸 (continued to rise)	172	19.3
高値 (high price)	115	12.9
カイ気配 (bid price)	87	9.7
大幅高 (large rise)	66	7.4
上昇 (rise)	56	6.3
ストップ高 (hit limit high)	54	6.0
急伸 (rise rapidly)	49	5.5
連騰 (winning streak)	40	4.5
堅調 (increase steadily)	38	4.3
急騰 (sharp rise)	35	3.9
other	5	0.5
total	893	100

Table 3: # of Occurrences and their Ratio (%) of Individual Words representing Decline in Stock Prices among 777 Examples of Machine Reading Comprehension of Causes of Stock Price Changes

word	#	ratio
嫌気 (discouraged)	430	22.7
反落 (reactionary fall)	316	16.7
続落 (continued to decline)	221	11.7
赤字 (deficit)	206	10.9
急落 (fall rapidly)	137	7.2
減益 (decrease in profit)	99	5.2
出尽くし感 (material exhaustion)	70	3.7
転落 (fall)	56	3.0
下落 (decline)	44	2.3
下振れ (downside)	40	2.1
大幅安 (large decline)	40	2.1
引き下げ (reduction)	34	1.8
other	202	10.7
total	1,895	100

`minkabu.jp` includes about 290,000 articles (as of November 2021) that are delivered from "MINKABU". Table 1 shows the statistics of the categories (manually classified by the author of the paper) of 100 articles randomly sampled from the collected 23,989 articles. Based on this statistics, out of the overall 290,000 articles delivered from "MINKABU", it is estimated that the number of articles on "news on stock price changes and their causes" amount to 81,200 (28%). Thus, "MINKABU" can be considered as a resource with a sufficient number of articles for devel-

[2] `https://minkabu.jp/`

[3] Out of 23,989 articles, 15,300 are delivered from June 30th to December 3rd, 2020, while 8,689 are delivered from March 5th to June 1st, 2021.

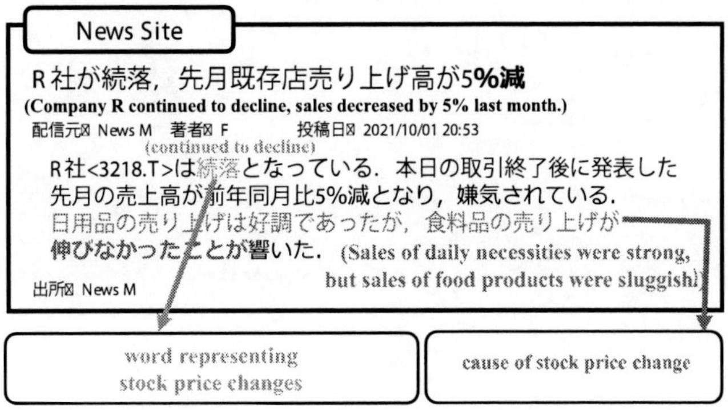

Figure 2: The Word representing Stock Price Changes and a Cause of Stock Price Change: an Example

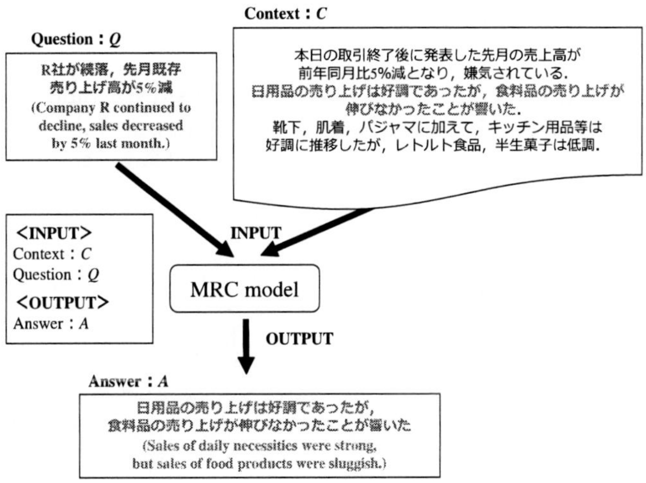

Figure 3: The Framework of Machine Reading Comprehension of Causes of Stock Price Changes

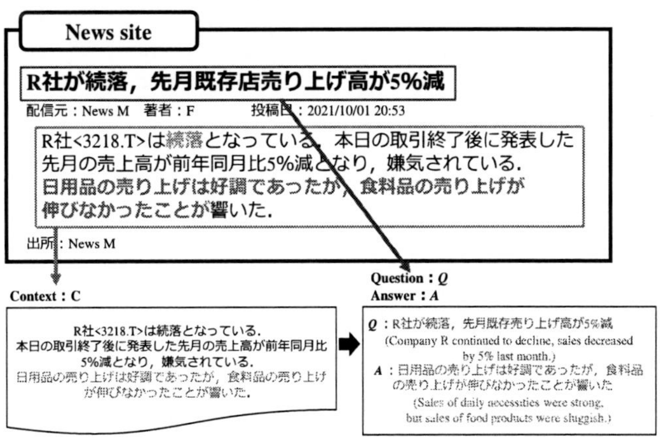

Figure 4: The Procedure of Developing an Example of Machine Reading Comprehension of Causes of Stock Price Changes

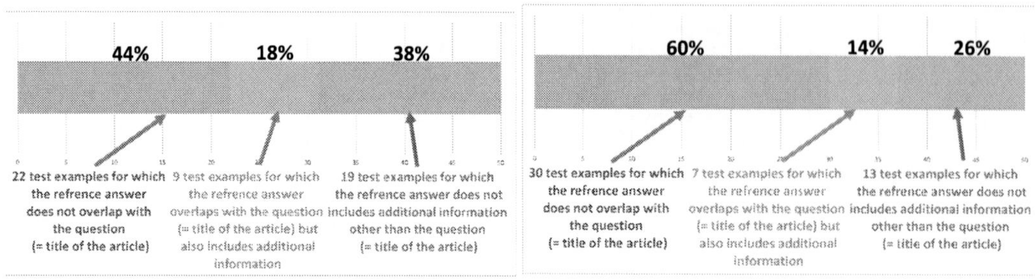

(a) 50 rise examples

(b) 50 decline examples

Figure 5: Statistics on whether the refrence answer includes additional information other than the question (= the title of the article) or not

oping a dataset for the examples of machine reading comprehension of causes of stock price changes.

There are two major types of fluctuations in stock prices: rise and decline. First, we focus on the rise in stock prices and created a dataset of examples of machine reading comprehension of causes of stock price rise. Here, we first selected more than 11 kinds of words listed in Table 2 representing "rise" in stock prices. Then, in the procedure of collecting candidates of example articles of machine reading comprehension of causes of stock price rise, we collect articles containing at least one of those words of Table 2. In the case of the evaluation in this paper, we used randomly selected 627 articles containing at least one of those words listed in Table 2, from 3,300 articles[4] of the distributor "MINKABU". This is the result of discarding 14 articles that are not appropriate for developing examples of machine reading comprehension of causes of stock price changes. This is also the result of discarding 35 articles including another 13 words[5] representing "decline" in stock prices.

Next, we focus on the decline in stock prices and created a dataset of examples of machine reading comprehension of causes of stock price decline. The general procedure of collecting candidates of example articles of machine reading comprehension of causes of stock price decline is almost the same as the case of the rise in stock prices. We first selected more than 12 kinds of words listed in Table 3 representing "decline" in stock prices. Then, we simply collect articles containing those individual words of Table 3. In the case of the evaluation in this paper, we obtained 2,117 articles from 23,988 articles from distributor "MINKABU" that contained at least one of more than 12 kinds of words listed in Table 3 representing "decline" in stock prices. From the 2,117 articles retrieved, finally, randomly selected 777 datasets of examples of machine reading comprehension of causes of stock price decline were created.

3. The Procedure of Developing Machine Reading Comprehension Examples: Comprehending Causes of Stock Price Changes from Stock Price News Articles

We developed 627 examples of machine reading comprehension of causes of stock price changes for rise and 777 for decline, as shown in the procedure of Figure 4. As the context C, the full text of the article that is delivered from "MINKABU" is used. As the question text Q, the title of the stock price change news is used as it is. The title of the stock price change news includes the company name and the word "continued to decline", which indicates the change of the stock price, such as in "Company R continued to decline, sales decreased by 5% last month." So, this information would be useful for extracting the cause of the stock price change from the context C. It is also useful in that the cost of manually developing the question Q is reduced by using the title of the stock price change news as the question Q[6].

Here, it is important to examine whether the reference answer span actually includes additional information other than the question (i.e., the title of the article) or not[7]. Figure 5 shows this statistics, where Figure 5(a) shows the statistics of the stock price rise examples, while Figure 5(b) shows that with stock price decline examples. It is very interesting to see that, for the stock price decline examples, the reference answer does not overlap with the title of the article for 60% cases and

[4]Delivered from October 30th to December 3rd, 2020.

[5]Those 13 words include "反落 (reactionary fall)", "下落 (decline)", "続落 (continued to decline)", "急落 (fall rapidly)", "売りに押され (drop)", and "安値 (low price)".

[6]The dataset including the span of the stock price changes is represented in the character level, where those input texts are segmented into a morpheme sequence in the evaluation.

[7]This additional information is manually examined, where we ignore the cases of just a fragmental difference of a few functional words. We judge that there exists additional information only when the difference of the information is more than a few functional words.

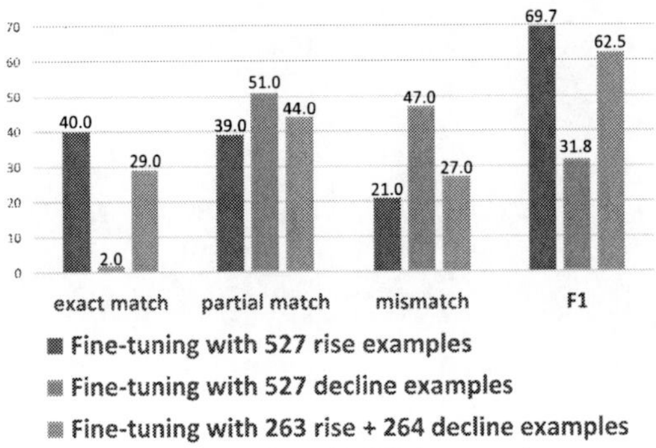

(a) Evaluation with 100 rise examples

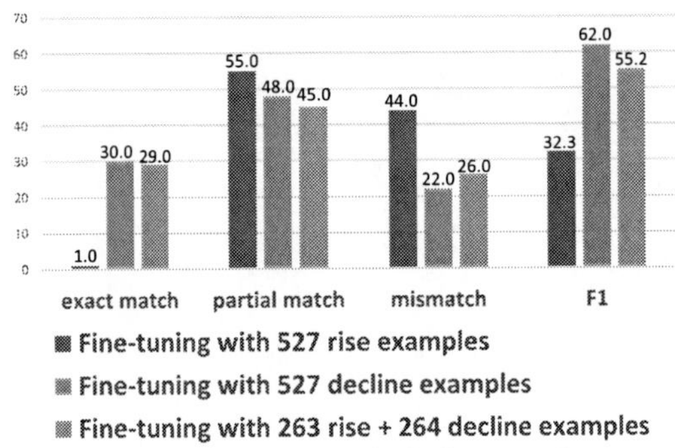

(b) Evaluation with 100 decline examples

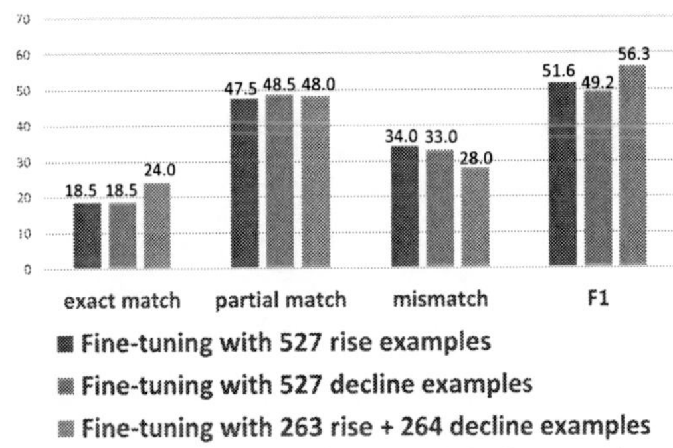

(c) Evaluation with 100 rise + 100 decline examples

Figure 6: Evaluation Results

it does overlap with the title but still has additional information for 14% cases. For the stock price rise examples, on the other hand, the reference answer does not overlap with the title of the article for just 44% cases (less than the decline examples) and it does overlap with the title but still has additional information for 18% cases. Thus, it is important to examine whether the fine-tuned model does actually successfully detect those additional causes information other than those stated in the title of the article.

As for the issue of the difference between stock price decline and rise, the difference of 60% and 44% (the rates of the articles where the reference answer does not overlap with the title of the article) can be interpreted as below: the title of those stock price news articles do not tend to include the detailed causes of the stock price decline, while they tend to include the detailed causes of the stock price rise.

4. Evaluation

4.1. Evaluation Procedure

As the version of BERT (Devlin et al., 2019) implementation which can handle a text in Japanese, the TensorFlow version[8] was used as the Japanese implementation, and the NICT BERT Japanese pre-trained model[9] was adopted. Before applying BERT modules, MeCab[10] was applied with mecab-ipadic-NEologd dictionary[11] and the Japanese text was segmented into a morpheme sequence. Then, within the BERT fine-tuning module, the WordPiece module with 110k shared WordPiece vocabulary was applied, and the Japanese text was further segmented into a subword unit sequence. Finally, the BERT fine-tuning module for machine reading comprehension[12] was applied. In the fine-tuning procedure, the BERT pre-trained model was fine-tuned with the training examples of machine reading comprehension of causes of stock price changes developed in the previous section.

4.2. Evaluation Results

In the evaluation, the following three types of training examples for fine-tuning are examined.

(a) Randomly selected 527 examples of stock price rise, excluding the 100 examples of stock price rise used in the evaluation.

(b) Randomly selected 527 examples of stock price decline, excluding the 100 examples of stock price decline used in the evaluation.

(c) Randomly selected 263 examples of stock price rise and 264 examples of stock price decline, excluding the 200 examples of stock price rise and decline (100 each) used in the evaluation.

Figure 6 shows the evaluation results[13], where Figure 6(a) shows that with 100 examples of causes of stock price rise, Figure 6(b) that with 100 examples of

[8] `https://github.com/google-research/bert`

[9] `https://alaginrc.nict.go.jp/nict-bert/index.html`

[10] `http://taku910.github.io/mecab/` (in Japanese)

[11] `https://github.com/neologd/mecab-ipadic-neologd`

[12] `run_squad.py`, with the number of epochs as 2, batch size as 8, and learning rate as 0.00003.

[13] "Exact match" is defined as the reference answer span and that predicted by the model being identical. "Partial match" is defined as those two being not identical but overlapping. "Mismatch" is defined as those two being not overlapping, which corresponds to false positive. F1 is computed on the level of input sets of tokens (i.e., morphemes).

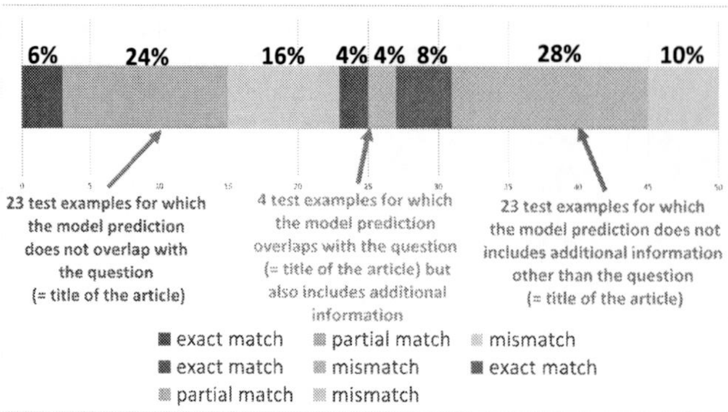

(a) 50 rise examples

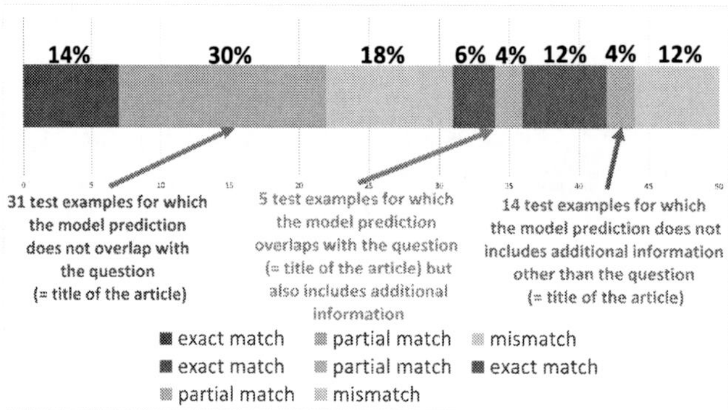

(b) 50 decline examples

Figure 7: Results on whether the model prediction includes additional information other than the question (= the title of the article) or not

causes of stock price decline, and Figure 6(c) that with 200 examples of causes of stock price rise and decline (100 each). Overall, the best performance of evaluation with stock price rise examples is achieved by the model fine-tuned with stock price rise examples (Figure 6(a)). Similarly, the best performance of evaluation with stock price decline examples is achieved by the model fine-tuned with stock price decline examples (Figure 6(b)). These are simply because words representing stock price rise and decline are mostly different from each other. The model fine-tuned with the mixture of stock price rise and decline examples (total number of training examples are fixed as 527 for all the models) performs the best in the evaluation with the mixture of stock price rise and decline examples (Figure 6(c)). This model fine-tuned with the mixture training examples performs relatively high in Figure 6(a) compared with the best performing model, even though the number of stock price rise training examples is just half of the best performing model. This is also the case in Figure 6(b). Thus, it can be claimed that the model with the mixture training examples is the most appropriate for the general use where the stock price rise or decline is unknown.

As described in section 3, in the procedure of developing the question of machine reading comprehension, we use the title of the stock price change news as the question Q as it is. Thus, it is important to examine whether the answer span predicted by the model actually includes additional information other than the question (i.e., the title of the article) or not. Figure 7 shows this evaluation result, where Figure 7(a) shows the result of the evaluation with stock price rise examples, while Figure 7(b) shows that with stock price decline examples. It is very interesting to see that, for the stock price decline examples, the model prediction includes additional information other than the title of the article for about 72% of the cases[14], where for 62% of them, model prediction does not overlap with the title of the article, and for the remaining 10%, model prediction overlaps with the title but still has additional information. For the stock price rise examples, on the other hand, this rate is for about 54% of the cases[15], where

[14]The exact match and the partial match rate for those about 72% cases is (14+30+6+4)/72%=54%/72%=75.0%. The remaining 25.0% are mismatch and irrelevant to the question.

[15]The exact match and the partial match rate for those 54%

Table 4: Stock Price Rise Examples (trained with 263 rise + 264 decline examples, evaluation with 100 rise + 100 decline examples)

(a) the model prediction (= reference answer) overlaps with the title of the article but also includes additional information

title of the article	context = full text of the article (the text below is simpified for ease of reference)	model prediction = reference answer (additional information is underlined)
N 社が大幅続伸、T 建物の商業施設で駐車場満空把握ソリューションの活用を開始 (= Company N began using the solution to monitor parking lot occupancy at T Construction company's commercial facilities, and its stock price has continued to rise.)	N 社 <4056.T>が大幅高で 3 日続伸している。午前 9 時ごろ、商業施設「スマーク伊勢崎」(群馬県伊勢崎市) で、T 建物 <8804.T>の運営する商業施設では初の試みとなる、人工知能 (AI) 技術を活用した大型平面駐車場の満空把握・管制ソリューションの活用を開始したと発表しており、これが好感されている。今回の「スマーク伊勢崎」における導入は、人手不足による誘導員の確保の難しさを解消するのが狙い。(= N Corp's stock price<4056.T>has continued to rise. The company announced that it has begun using an AI-based solution to monitor parking lot occupancy for the first time at T Construction company's<8804.T>commercial facility S, which has been favorable impression. The introduction of the system to Commercial Facility S is aimed at alleviating labor shortages.)	人工知能 (AI) 技術を活用した大型平面駐車場の満空把握・管制ソリューションの活用を開始した (= it has begun using an AI-based solution to monitor parking lot occupancy)

(b) the model prediction (= reference answer) does not overlap with the title of the article

title of the article	context = full text of the article (the text below is simpified for ease of reference)	model prediction = reference answer
<注目銘柄 >= I 社、DX 時代の変身株に (= <Stocks to Watch>= Company I has become a hot stock in the DX era.)	I 社 <4056.T>は IT 系を中心としたニュースサイトを運営するほか、非 I T系メディアの育成も進めている。ネット上「見込み顧客」を発掘して営業機会の創出を支援する事業が好調である。(= Company I operates a news website related to IT and is also in the process of developing non-IT media. Its business of finding "customers" on the Internet and supporting their sales activities is performing well.)	ネット上「見込み顧客」を発掘して営業機会の創出を支援する事業が好調 (= Its business of finding "customers" on the Internet and supporting their sales activities is performing well)

Table 5: Stock Price Decline Examples (trained with 263 rise + 264 decline examples, evaluation with 100 rise + 100 decline examples)

(a) the model prediction (= reference answer) overlaps with the title of the article but also includes additional information

title of the article	context = full text of the article (the text below is simpified for ease of reference)	model prediction = reference answer (additional information is underlined)
S 社が急落、第 2 工場の償却費発生で 21 年 7 月期は大幅減益へ (= Company S falls rapidly, posting sharply decrease profit in July '20 due to depreciation costs incurred at its second plant.)	S 社 <9262.T>が急落している。主力の高齢者向け弁当販売で、フランチャイズ店が約 60 店舗の増加を見込むが、第 2 工場の稼働に伴い人件費が増加するほか、減価償却費が発生することが利益を圧迫する。(= S Corp's stock price<9262.T>falls rapidly. The company expects an increase of about 60 franchise stores in its mainstay boxed lunch sales to the elderly, but labor costs will increase with the start of operations at the second plant, and depreciation costs expense will pressure profits.)	第 2 工場 の稼働に伴い 人件費が増加するほか、減価償 却 費 が 発 生 す る こ と が利益を圧迫する(= labor costs will increase with the start of operations at the second plant, and depreciation costs expense will pressure profits)

(b) the model prediction (= reference answer) does not overlap with the title of the article

title of the article	context = full text of the article (the text below is simpified for ease of reference)	model prediction = reference answer
O 社が続落、20 年 10 月期業績は計画下振れで着地 (= Company O has continued to decline, and its performance in October '20 was lower than previously planned.)	O 社 <7827.T>が続落している。17 日の取引終了後、集計中の 20 年 10 月期業績について、売り上げが下振れて着地したようだと発表しており、これが嫌気されている。新型コロナウイルス感染症の影響で、一定の営業制限を余儀なくされたことや、梱包用材などの受注が低迷したことが響いた。(= O Corp's stock price<7827.T>has continued to decline. After the close of trading on October 17, the company announced that sales for October '20, which are still being compiled, were down, and the market discouraged about it. The company's sales activities were limited due to COVID-19, and orders for packaging materials and other products were sluggish.)	新型コロナウイルス感染症の影響で、一定の営業制限を余儀なくされたことや、梱包用材などの受注が低迷したことが響いた (= The company's sales activities were limited due to COVID-19, and orders for packaging materials and other products were sluggish)

for 46% of them, model prediction does not overlap with the title of the article, and for the remaining 8%, model prediction overlaps with the title but still has additional information. Compared with the statistics on whether the reference answer span actually includes additional information other than the question (i.e., the title of the article) or not in Figure 5, these rates are sufficiently high and it can be claimed that the model prediction does include additional information other than the title of the article. This result indicates that the fine-tuned model successfully detects additional causes of stock price rise and decline other than those stated in the title of the article.

Table 4 and Table 5 show the examples of the articles of those stock price rise and decline cases, respectively. In those examples, the model prediction is exact match with the reference answer. Table 4(a) and Table 5(a) show the cases where the model prediction (= reference answer) overlaps with the title of the article but also includes additional information (underlined), while Table 4(b) and Table 5(b) show the cases where the model prediction (= reference answer) does not overlap with the title of the article. As we described in the discussion on the statistics of Figure 7, those cases of detecting fully additional information other than the title of the article are majority cases. Thus, it can be claimed that the model prediction (= the reference answer) successfully includes additional information other than the title of the article in those cases.

5. Related Work

As a related work, Liu et al. (2020) studied the issue of pre-trained financial language model for financial text mining. The task studied is FiQA[16] Task 2 "Opinion-based QA over financial data". This task is closer to general question answering in the financial domain, compared to our task of answering the causes of the stock price rise and decline. As another related work, Mariko et al. (2020) organized the Financial Document Causality Detection Shared Task (FinCausal 2020), where the tasks such as detection of causes and effects in the general financial domain are studied (Becquin, 2020; Imoto and Ito, 2020; Ionescu et al., 2020; Pielka et al., 2020; Kao et al., 2020; Szántó and Berend, 2020; Özenir and Karadeniz, 2020; Chakravarthy et al., 2020). This paper, on the other hand, concentrates on the issue of answering the causes of rise and decline of stock price. Zhu et al. built a large-scale QA dataset containing both tabular and textual data (Zhu et al., 2021). They also proposed a QA model which is capable of reasoning over both tables and text. Liu et al. (2018) also proposed an interface that highlights risk-related sentences in the financial reports based on sentence embedding techniques, where it provides the function of visualization of financial time-series data for a corresponding company.

cases is (6+24+4+4)/54%=34%/54%=63.0%. The remaining 37.0% are mismatch and irrelevant to the question.

[16]`https://sites.google.com/view/fiqa/home`

6. Conclusion

This paper took an approach of employing a BERT (Devlin et al., 2019)-based machine reading comprehension model (Pranav et al., 2016), which extracts causes of stock price rise and decline from news reports on stock price changes. In the evaluation results, overall, the approach of using the title of the article as the question Q of the machine reading comprehension performed well. It is also shown that the model fine-tuned with the mixture of stock price rise and decline examples is the most appropriate for the general use where the stock price rise or decline is unknown. Future work includes scaling up into beyond the machine reading comprehension setting where only the question Q is available and the candidates of context C have to be automatically collected from a large pool of documents (Chen et al., 2017; Lee et al., 2019).

7. Bibliographical References

Becquin, G. (2020). GBe at FinCausal 2020, task 2: Span-based causality extraction for financial documents. In *Proc. 1st Joint Workshop on Financial Narrative Processing and MultiLing Financial Summarisation*, pages 40–44.

Chakravarthy, S., Kanakagiri, T., Radhakrishnan, K., and Umapathy, A. (2020). Domino at FinCausal 2020, task 1 and 2: Causal extraction system. In *Proc. 1st Joint Workshop on Financial Narrative Processing and MultiLing Financial Summarisation*, pages 90–94.

Chen, D., Fisch, A., Weston, J., and Bordes, A. (2017). Reading Wikipedia to answer open-domain questions. In *Proc. 55th ACL*, pages 1870–1879.

Devlin, J., Chang, M.-W., Lee, K., and Toutanova, K. (2019). BERT: Pre-training of deep bidirectional Transformers for language understanding. In *Proc. NAACL-HLT*, pages 4171–4186.

Imoto, T. and Ito, T. (2020). JDD @ FinCausal 2020, task 2: Financial document causality detection. In *Proc. 1st Joint Workshop on Financial Narrative Processing and MultiLing Financial Summarisation*, pages 50–54.

Ionescu, M., Avram, A.-M., Dima, G.-A., Cercel, D.-C., and Dascalu, M. (2020). UPB at FinCausal-2020, tasks 1 & 2: Causality analysis in financial documents using pretrained language models. In *Proc. 1st Joint Workshop on Financial Narrative Processing and MultiLing Financial Summarisation*, pages 55–59.

Kao, P.-W., Chen, C.-C., Huang, H.-H., and Chen, H.-H. (2020). NTUNLPL at FinCausal 2020, task 2:improving causality detection using Viterbi decoder. In *Proc. 1st Joint Workshop on Financial*

Narrative Processing and MultiLing Financial Summarisation, pages 69–73.

Lee, K., Chang, M.-W., and Toutanova, K. (2019). Latent retrieval for weakly supervised open domain question answering. In *Proc. 57th ACL*, pages 6086–6096.

Liu, Y.-W., Liu, L.-C., Wang, C.-J., and Tsai, M.-F. (2018). RiskFinder: A sentence-level risk detector for financial reports. In *Proc. NAACL: Demonstrations*, pages 81–85.

Liu, Z., Huang, D., Huang, K., Li, Z., and Zhao, J. (2020). FinBERT: A pre-trained financial language representation model for financial text mining. In *Proc. 29th IJCAI*, pages 4513–4519.

Mariko, D., Abi-Akl, H., Labidurie, E., Durfort, S., De Mazancourt, H., and El-Haj, M. (2020). The financial document causality detection shared task (FinCausal 2020). In *Proc. 1st Joint Workshop on Financial Narrative Processing and MultiLing Financial Summarisation*, pages 23–32.

Özenir, G. and Karadeniz, İ. (2020). ISIKUN at the FinCausal 2020: Linguistically informed machine-learning approach for causality identification in financial documents. In *Proc. 1st Joint Workshop on Financial Narrative Processing and MultiLing Financial Summarisation*, pages 85–89.

Pielka, M., Ramamurthy, R., Ladi, A., Brito, E., Chapman, C., Mayer, P., and Sifa, R. (2020). Fraunhofer IAIS at FinCausal 2020, tasks 1 & 2: Using ensemble methods and sequence tagging to detect causality in financial documents. In *Proc. 1st Joint Workshop on Financial Narrative Processing and MultiLing Financial Summarisation*, pages 64–68.

Szántó, Z. and Berend, G. (2020). ProsperAMnet at FinCausal 2020, task 1 & 2: Modeling causality in financial texts using multi-headed transformers. In *Proc. 1st Joint Workshop on Financial Narrative Processing and MultiLing Financial Summarisation*, pages 80–84.

8. Language Resource References

Pranav, R., Jian, Z., Konstantin, L., and Percy, L. (2016). SQuAD: 100,000+ questions for machine comprehension of text. In *Proc. EMNLP*, pages 2383–2392. Holt, Rinehart & Winston.

Zhu, F., Lei, W., Huang, Y., Wang, C., Zhang, S., Lv, J., Feng, F., and Chua, T.-S. (2021). TAT-QA: A question answering benchmark on a hybrid of tabular and textual content in finance. In *Proc. 59th ACL*, pages 3277–3287.

Proceedings of the 4th Financial Narrative Processing Workshop @ LREC 2022, pages 36–42
Marseille, 24 June 2022

XLNET-GRU Sentiment Regression Model for Cryptocurrency News in English and Malay

Nur Azmina Mohamad Zamani[1,2], Jasy Liew Suet Yan[1], Ahmad Muhyiddin Yusof[3]
[1]School of Computer Sciences, Universiti Sains Malaysia, 11800 USM, Penang, Malaysia.
[2]Faculty of Computer and Mathematical Sciences, Universiti Teknologi MARA Perak Branch, Tapah Campus, 35400 Tapah Road, Perak, Malaysia.
[3]Academy of Language Studies, Universiti Teknologi MARA Perak Branch, Seri Iskandar Campus, 32610 Seri Iskandar, Perak, Malaysia.

namz.ina@gmail.com, jasyliew@usm.my, ahmadmuhyiddin4@uitm.edu.my

Abstract

Contextual word embeddings such as the transformer language models are gaining popularity in text classification and analytics but have rarely been explored for sentiment analysis on cryptocurrency news particularly on languages other than English. Various state-of-the-art (SOTA) pre-trained language models have been introduced recently such as BERT, ALBERT, ELECTRA, RoBERTa, and XLNet for text representation. Hence, this study aims to investigate the performance of using Gated Recurrent Unit (GRU) with Generalized Autoregressive Pretraining for Language (XLNet) contextual word embedding for sentiment analysis on English and Malay cryptocurrency news (Bitcoin and Ethereum). We also compare the performance of our XLNet-GRU model against other SOTA pre-trained language models. Manually labelled corpora of English and Malay news are utilized to learn the context of text specifically in the cryptocurrency domain. Based on our experiments, we found that our XLNet-GRU sentiment regression model outperformed the lexicon-based baseline with mean adjusted R2 = 0.631 across Bitcoin and Ethereum for English and mean adjusted R2 = 0.514 for Malay.

Keywords: sentiment analysis, deep learning, pre-trained language models, cryptocurrency news

1. Introduction

Cryptocurrency is a new form of digital currency designed to achieve transparency, decentralization, and immutability by utilising blockchain technology and cryptographic functions (Pintelas et al., 2020). As cryptocurrencies can be traded in coin exchanges, cryptocurrency price prediction models assist cryptocurrency investors in making investment decisions either to buy, sell or hold to maximise earnings, as well as policymakers and financial scholars in analysing the behaviour of cryptocurrency markets. Sentiment has shown to play a crucial role in cryptocurrency price prediction since the changing aspects of the cryptocurrency market is determined by sentiment from various sources such as online news and social media (Karalevicius et al., 2018; Rognone et al., 2020). Therefore, developing models that can accurately detect sentiment signals from text sources and measure the sentiment strength is an important first step to ensure reliability of the cryptocurrency price prediction in the downstream task.

The lexicon-based (Gurdgiev & O'Loughlin, 2020; Karalevicius et al., 2018; Loughran & Mcdonald, 2014; Mai et al., 2015) and machine learning methods utilising classic representations such as bag-of-words (BoW) or TF-IDF (Georgoula et al., 2015; Lamon et al., 2017) remain the most popular computational methods used to extract sentiment features for cryptocurrency price prediction. However, the sentiment prediction models that are often used as an intermediate component to generate sentiment features within the cryptocurrency price prediction pipeline are often not evaluated thoroughly and this has caused the effect of leveraging sentiment features in cryptocurrency price prediction models to be mixed in existing studies. Also, these sentiment analysis methods most often do not take context or relationship between words into account, and thus do not provide the best results when classifying or scoring text for sentiment.

Recently, word embedding has gained traction due to its enhanced functionality and performance (Li et al., 2017). From the vectors produced by the word embeddings, machine learning or deep learning methods such as Long Short-Term Memory (LSTM) and Gated Recurrent Unit (GRU) have shown to yield good performance (Attila, 2017; Devika et al., 2016). One of the most popular word embeddings used in prior studies is Word2Vec coupled with LSTM to generate the sentiment score from tweets and news as sentiment features (Mohanty et al., 2018; Vo et al., 2019). Sentiment features produced by the Word2Vec deep learning models have yet to show any significant effect on the cryptocurrency price prediction models. Furthermore, dynamic embeddings or pre-trained language models have also been scarcely explored in the realm of sentiment analysis for cryptocurrency news especially in more than one language.

Thus, the goal of this paper is to explore the development and evaluation of a deep learning sentiment model, GRU with the latest transformer language model, Generalized Autoregressive Pretraining for Language (XLNet) for sentiment detection and scoring in English and Malay cryptocurrency news. XLNet is chosen because it has shown to yield better performance than BERT as XLNet considers all possible permutations of the factorisation order instead of the fixed forward-backward factorisation order in BERT and thus can avoid the pretrain-finetune discrepancy faced in BERT (Devlin et al., 2019; Yang et al., 2020).

First, we present the architecture of our XLNet-GRU model for sentiment analysis in English and Malay news respectively. Second, we evaluate the performance of our XLNet-GRU model against VADER (i.e., the most commonly used lexicon-based sentiment scoring method) and currently the most popular transformer language model (i.e., Bidirectional Encoder Representations or BERT). In addition, we also compare our results with other three state-of-the-art (SOTA) pre-trained language models including A Lite BERT (ALBERT) (Lan et al., 2020), Pre-training Text Encoders as Discriminators Rather Than Generators (ELECTRA) (Clark et al., 2020), and Robustly Optimized BERT Pre-training Approach (RoBERTa) (Liu et al., 2019). To our knowledge, this is the first study investigating sentiment analysis from Malay news sources (resource poor language) in addition to English news. Second, we review and compare the overall performance of the XLNet-GRU model across English and Malay languages.

We also contribute by creating two news sentiment corpora specifically on the topic of Bitcoin and Ethereum, one corpus in English and the second corpus in Malay. Both news sentiment corpora are manually labeled and carefully curated to serve as training and test sets for the XLNet-GRU sentiment model to perform sentiment regression. The cryptocurrency domain has given birth to a rich set of terminologies and jargons, making its news vocabulary to be significantly different from general, financial and economic news. As such, sentiment models trained using general or financial news may not generalize well on cryptocurrency news. Therefore, our cryptocurrency news sentiment corpora make an important contribution to advance the development of sentiment models particularly in the new but growing cryptocurrency domain.

2. Related Work

A majority of prior studies applying the lexicon-based approach focused on VADER and Textblob for sentiment scoring and classification. Stenqvist & Lönnö (2017) applied VADER to first score the sentiment of each tweet and then determined the sentiment class (positive or negative). The sentiment labels were then aggregated based on time series intervals to be used as features in cryptocurrency price prediction. Similarly, Valencia et al. (2019) also used VADER to extract positive, negative, neutral and compound scores from tweets. Prajapati (2020) applied VADER, Textblob and Flair to obtain multiple sentiment views on English news for cryptocurrency price prediction while Chin & Omar (2020) utilized the NTUSD dictionary (Chen et al., 2018). However, these studies did not directly evaluate the performance of the sentiment scoring method before feeding the sentiment feature into the cryptocurrency price prediction model. Instead, the cryptocurrency price prediction results (i.e., the downstream task) is used as a proxy to assess the effectiveness of the sentiment features.

More recent studies have also ventured into applying static word embeddings such as Word2Vec and FastText as the representation on cryptocurrency-related texts, but mainly in English language. Mohanty et al. (2018) and Vo et al. (2019) first labeled news with sentiment based on the rise and fall of the cryptocurrency prices (i.e., increasing price represented positive sentiment and decreasing price represented negative sentiment). The news with the sentiment labels were then transformed into sentiment feature vectors using the Word2Vec embeddings in both studies. These studies also did not evaluate the accuracy of the sentiment feature extraction method and used the cryptocurrency price prediction results as an indirect measure to assess the effectiveness of the sentiment features.

The use of contextual word embeddings such as BERT and ULMFiT language models to perform sentiment analysis for cryptocurrency price prediction is currently still limited. Cerda (2021) performed two types of experiments, one for sentiment analysis and the second for stance detection. For sentiment analysis, SentiWordNet was used to generate the sentiment score (continuous label ranging from -1 to 1) while for stance detection, the pre-trained Universal Language Model Fine-tuning (ULMFiT) and BERT models were fine-tuned individually as the features to perform the sentiment classification task. Then, the features were fed into an Extreme Gradient Boosting (XGBoost) model. Both ULMFiT and BERT applied with the XGBoost model produced positive results with F1-scores of 0.62 and 0.67 respectively in classifying sentiment. ULMFiT was good in identifying positive and neutral tweets but performed badly in classifying negative tweets as it had the tendency to misclassify the negative ones as positive. On the contrary, BERT was reported to show better classification performance for positive, neutral and negative tweets compared to ULMFiT.

Newer pre-trained language models have been introduced since BERT but have yet to be explored in sentiment analysis for cryptocurrency news. Prior studies are even rarer in the Malay language. In this paper, we propose a news sentiment regression model applying XLNet as the text representation to be fed into the GRU deep learning model for sentiment regression of English and Malay news. As BERT has shown good performance in sentiment classification, BERT is used as the comparison with our sentiment model together with ALBERT, ELECTRA and RoBERTa.

3. Data

3.1 Data Collection

Cryptocurrency news on Bitcoin and Ethereum in English and Malay were collected for a duration of one year from 1 January 2021 until 31 December 2021.

NewsAPI[1] was used to extract English cryptocurrency news from various sources such as Reuters, Forbes, Yahoo, and New York Times. Using NewsAPI, we extracted English online news based on the queries: "(Bitcoin OR BTC)" and "(Ethereum OR ETH)". Parsehub was utilised to extract Malay news from various Malay online news sites such as Intraday.my[2], Berita Harian[3], Utusan Malaysia[4], and Harian Metro[5] (i.e., local Malay news sites). Parsehub extracted Malay news from Intraday using the web page URLs. The data collection process is illustrated in Figure 1.

The raw data extracted was filtered by splitting into two different corpora: English news corpus and Malay news corpus. Table 1 shows the number of English and Malay news for Bitcoin and Ethereum. The purpose for the split

[1] https://newsapi.org/

[2] Intraday.my: https://intraday.my/

[3] Berita Harian: https://www.bharian.com.my/

[4] Utusan Malaysia: https://www.utusan.com.my/

[5] Harian Metro: https://www.hmetro.com.my/

was to allow sentiment analysis to be performed separately on each language.

Only the news headlines were included in our analysis as news headlines sufficiently capture the main points of the topic as opposed to the news content that may introduce unnecessary noise into the sentiment model. Any non-English and non-Malay instances were removed. Tokenization, lemmatization, and special characters removal were applied to each corpus using natural language processing tools appropriate for each language. Only the pre-processed text would then proceed with sentiment scoring.

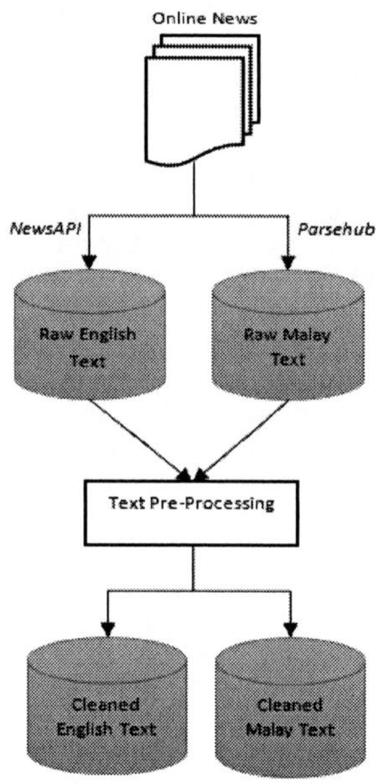

Figure 1: Data extraction and pre-processing.

News-Topic	English	Malay
Bitcoin	1518	1521
Ethereum	1205	1453

Table 1: Number of news documents by language and topic.

3.2 Data Annotation

To obtain training and test data for the sentiment model, manual annotation was performed by three annotators including the primary researcher. All three annotators worked on annotating both English and Malay news. The annotators were required to have basic understanding on the cryptocurrency topic and must be able to read and comprehend English and Malay languages. The annotation team was made up of one female and two male university students and lecturer between the age of 24 – 31. All annotators were well-versed in both English and Malay.

Each news headline was labelled with sentiment polarity scores ranging from -1 to +1 with one decimal place (-1: very negative, +1: very positive and 0: neutral). Sentiment scores within the range of 0.1 – 0.3 would be considered low positive, 0.4 – 0.6 to be moderately positive and 0.7 – 1 very positive. Similar ranges were applied to the negative sentiment scores. We chose a numeric scale as the sentiment output instead of discrete polarity classes to capture more nuanced sentiment expressions and features from the news headlines. The following shows examples of news headlines for Bitcoin being assigned with the positive and negative sentiment scores.

Example 1 – Positive Sentiment
Bitcoin: Tesla invests about $1.50 billion in bitcoin – Reuters.com
[Sentiment Score: 1]

Example 2 – Negative Sentiment
Bitcoin: Chinese local government auctions seized bitcoin mining machines
[Sentiment Score: -0.8]

A codebook describing the annotation task and examples was provided to the annotators. All annotators were trained using the same set of samples and disagreements were resolved through discussion to obtain the final sentiment score. Training was conducted for several rounds until the percentage agreement reached greater than 50%. Once the expected percentage agreement was achieved, each remaining news headline would be annotated by at least two annotators and the final sentiment score would be computed by taking the mean score across all annotators.

Inter-annotator reliability is computed using Krippendorff's alpha (Krippendorff, 2018) to measure the agreement between annotators for the continuous labels. Table 2 depicts the inter-annotator reliability measures achieved for English and Malay news headlines.

Inter-rater-Metric	English	Malay
Agreement %	63%	61%
Krippendorf's	0.58	0.56

Table 2: Inter-annotator reliability measures.

The alpha within the range of 0.56 to 0.58 indicates acceptable agreement between annotators given the subjectivity and complexity of the annotation task. We observed that the sentiment scores assigned by annotators most often only vary less than ±0.2.

4. Methodology

4.1 Deep Learning Architecture for Sentiment Regression

Figure 2 illustrates the XLNet encoding architecture to produce the vector representation. The news headlines were first tokenized using the XLNet pre-trained word embedding ('xlnet-base-cased'[6] for English text) and 'xlnet-base-bahasa-cased'[7] for Malay text) with 12 layers of transformer blocks, 768 hidden layers (dimensions), and 12 self-attention heads (Gong et al., 2019). Next, the encoding was performed with the use of attention mask where the permutation language modelling took place. This

[6] English XLNet: https://huggingface.co/xlnet-base-cased

[7] Malay XLNet: https://huggingface.co/malay-huggingface/xlnet-base-bahasa-cased

allowed bidirectional contexts to be captured for the positional encoding based on factorization order instead of the sequence order. Then, the context vector produced was utilised for the XLNet fine-tuning (training) process.

Fine-tuning was required to learn the context of the word with the newly assigned sentiment weights based on cryptocurrency-related sentiment from the labeled data. The fine-tuned XLNet model was then incorporated into the GRU sentiment deep learning model. The GRU sentiment deep learning architecture is shown in Figure 3.

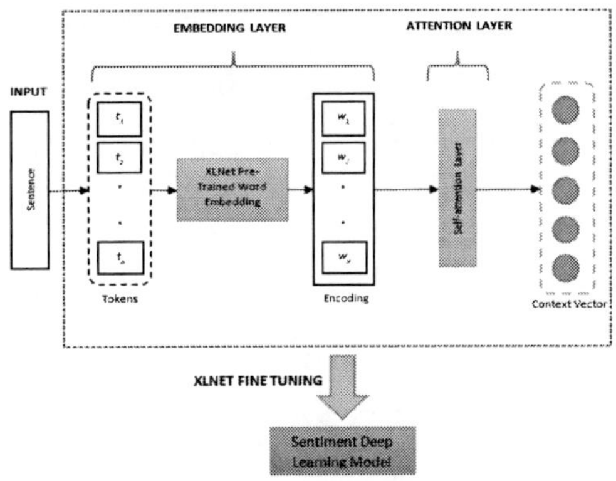

Figure 2: XLNet encoding architecture.

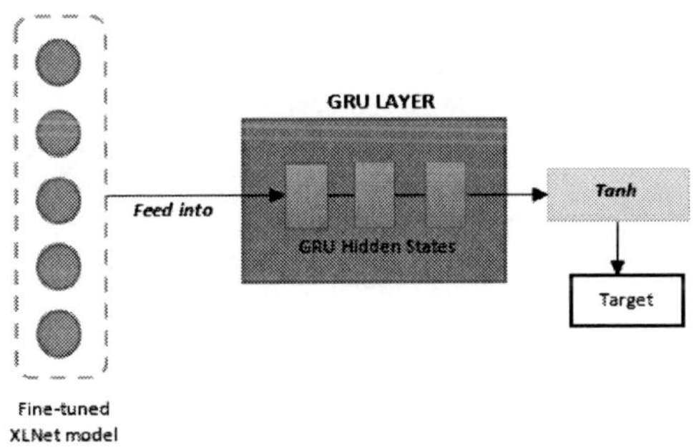

Figure 3: GRU Sentiment deep learning architecture.

From Figure 3, the pre-trained XLNet word embedding that had gone through finetuning was fed into the GRU layer consisting of 768 hidden nodes, one output layer and a dropout rate of 0.1. Tanh was used as the activation function as it is suitable for the sentiment regression output values of between -1 to +1.

Grid search with 5-fold cross validation was used to find the most optimized hyperparameter settings for the XLNet-GRU sentiment regression model. The range of hyperparameter values included in the grid search during the optimization process are listed as follows:

- Batch size: {8, 16, 32, 64}
- Learning rate: {2e-5, 3e-5, 3e-4}
- Number of epochs: {30, 40, 50}

Finally, a batch size of 8 was utilized for the AdamW optimizer with the learning rate of 2e-5 and 30 epochs for training.

Each labeled corpus was first split into 80% as the training (finetuning) set and 20% as the test set. From each corpus, 200 samples were reserved for the test set for each coin and the remaining samples were used for training and validation (~1500 instances). The training set was fed into the XLNet-GRU sentiment regression model for training.

Adjusted R^2 was used as the primary performance metric to measure how well the predicted values fit to the original values. The higher the value of adjusted R^2, the better the model performance. In addition, we also report RMSE and MAE as error measures (i.e., lower error means better model performance).

5. Results and Analysis

5.1 English Sentiment Models

The VADER compound score (lexicon-based approach) is used as a simple baseline for comparison in English news. VADER is chosen as the baseline for lexicon-based approach because it is the most common lexicon-based method encountered in existing studies.

We also set up the BERT, ALBERT, ELECTRA and RoBERTa pre-trained language models in our experiments for the English model as they served as SOTA language models found in existing studies (Farha & Magdy, 2021; Pranesh et al., 2020). BERT ('bert-base-cased')[8] was fine-tuned to learn word contexts from the English news sentiment corpus with the GRU deep learning model (BERT-GRU) We also fine-tune ALBERT ('albert-base-v2')[9], ELECTRA ('google/electra-small-discriminator')[10], and RoBERTa ('roberta-base')[11] to be incorporated into the GRU deep learning model. Table 3 shows the results obtained for English VADER, BERT-GRU, ALBERT-GRU, ELECTRA-GRU, RoBERTa-GRU, and XLNet-GRU.

ENGLISH CRYPTOCURRENCY NEWS			
Bitcoin			
Model	RMSE	MAE	Adjusted R^2
VADER	0.483	0.388	0.081
BERT-GRU	0.346	0.219	0.527
ALBERT-GRU	0.527	0.428	-0.095
ELECTRA-GRU	0.356	0.229	0.499
RoBERTa-GRU	0.325	0.209	0.583
XLNet-GRU	**0.296**	**0.185**	**0.654**
Ethereum			
Model	RMSE	MAE	Adjusted R^2
VADER	0.423	0.324	-0.139
BERT-GRU	0.257	0.154	0.582
ALBERT-GRU	0.395	0.333	0.007
ELECTRA-GRU	0.292	0.162	0.459
RoBERTa-GRU	0.277	0.149	0.512
XLNet-GRU	**0.249**	**0.131**	**0.607**

Table 3: Model performance for English cryptocurrency news.

[8] English BERT: https://huggingface.co/bert-base-cased

[9] English ALBERT: https://huggingface.co/albert-base-v2

[10] English ELECTRA: https://huggingface.co/google/electra-small-discriminator

[11] English RoBERTa: https://huggingface.co/roberta-base

Based on Table 3, VADER achieved adjusted R^2 of 0.081 and -0.139 for Bitcoin and Ethereum respectively. The baseline results utilizing purely a lexicon-based approach indicate very low accuracy. The negative adjusted R^2 value is treated as 0, which signifies poor fit as sentiment words in the VADER dictionary is made up of common sentiment words in general and not catered specifically to handle cryptocurrency-related sentiment words. The same negative adjusted R^2 value is also observed for Bitcoin using ALBERT-GRU whereas, an adjusted R^2 of 0.007 is observed for Ethereum. Although a positive value was obtained for Ethereum, the performance is extremely low.

On the contrary, the adjusted R^2 in BERT-GRU, RoBERTa-GRU and XLNet-GRU models demonstrate more promising results. For Bitcoin, the RoBERTa-GRU model obtained an adjusted R^2 of 0.583, while our XLNet-GRU model achieved a higher score of 0.654. Similar observation applies to our XLNet-GRU model for Ethereum with an adjusted R^2 of 0.607. Surprisingly, BERT-GRU (adjusted $R^2 = 0.582$) manages to surpass RoBERTa-GRU for Ethereum.

The results clearly show that our XLNet-GRU model consistently yields the best performance in sentiment regression on English cryptocurrency news for both Bitcoin and Ethereum in comparison to VADER and the other SOTA pre-trained language models.

5.2 Malay Sentiment Models

VADER cannot be directly applied to Malay text as it only supports English. For Malay, we use the Open Multilingual WordNet[12] to first retrieve the English synonym to each Malay word in a news headline before feeding the English synonyms into VADER for sentiment scoring. WordNet-Bahasa[13] from the Open Multilingual WordNet is used to recognize the Malay words.

To set up the SOTA models for Malay, BERT ('bert-base-bahasa-cased')[14] and ALBERT ('malay-huggingface/albert-base-bahasa-cased')[15] pre-trained on Malay text were fine-tuned to learn the context words from the Malay sentiment corpus and then fed into a separate GRU deep learning model. VADER, BERT-GRU, and ALBERT-GRU were evaluated against our XLNet-GRU model for Malay cryptocurrency news. As there is no pre-trained language model available for ELECTRA and RoBERTa in Malay, both are excluded for comparison. The results on Malay cryptocurrency news are shown in Table 4.

From Table 4, VADER shows the poorest performance as indicated by the negative adjusted R^2 scores for both Bitcoin and Ethereum. Such low performance is attributed to the lack of reliable Malay sentiment lexicons, especially those containing words that are related to cryptocurrency. On the other hand, ALBERT-GRU shows improved performance than VADER but still yields a negative adjusted R^2 of -0.119 for Bitcoin.

BERT-GRU and XLNet-GRU fare better in scoring sentiment for Malay cryptocurrency news. The performance scores between BERT-GRU and XLNet-GRU for Malay cryptocurrency news show only a small difference, particularly for Ethereum. For Bitcoin, the XLNet-GRU model achieved better performance in RMSE (reduction in error) and adjusted R^2 (increase in fit between the predicted and actual scores) compared to BERT-GRU. While both BERT-GRU and XLNet-GRU reported MAE scores with a very slight difference, the larger RMSE score observed in BERT-GRU compared to XLNet-GRU indicate a greater variance in error. Therefore, we can conclude that XLNet-GRU still yields performance advantages in Bitcoin news.

MALAY CRYPTOCURRENCY NEWS			
Bitcoin			
Model	RMSE	MAE	Adjusted R^2
VADER	0.584	0.471	-0.590
BERT-GRU	0.364	**0.252**	0.383
ALBERT-GRU	0.490	0.458	-0.119
XLNet-GRU	**0.351**	0.255	**0.428**
Ethereum			
Model	RMSE	MAE	Adjusted R^2
VADER	0.598	0.485	-0.956
BERT-GRU	**0.271**	**0.144**	0.597
ALBERT-GRU	0.327	0.209	0.414
XLNet-GRU	**0.271**	0.168	**0.599**

Table 4: Model performance for Malay cryptocurrency news.

As for Ethereum, XLNet-GRU shows slightly higher MAE than BERT-GRU but the greater difference between RMSE and MAE of BERT-GRU indicates that BERT-GRU still suffers from a greater variance in error, which is consistent to our findings from Bitcoin. XLNet-GRU still achieved adjusted R^2 of 0.599, which is slightly better than BERT-GRU with adjusted R^2 of 0.597.

From the overall results, XLNet-GRU is still deemed the winner for Malay cryptocurrency news as it achieved the best RMSE and adjusted R^2 scores.

5.3 Comparing English and Malay Sentiment Models

To compare the XLNet-GRU in both Malay and English languages, the mean RMSE, MAE and adjusted R^2 are calculated across Bitcoin and Ethereum and shown in Table 5.

English XLNet-GRU			
	RMSE	**MAE**	**Adjusted R^2**
Bitcoin	0.296	0.185	0.654
Ethereum	0.249	0.131	0.607
Mean	**0.273**	**0.158**	**0.631**
Malay XLNet-GRU			
Bitcoin	0.351	0.255	0.428
Ethereum	0.271	0.168	0.599
Mean	**0.311**	**0.212**	**0.514**

Table 5: Comparison of results achieved for English and Malay texts using XLNet-GRU.

[12] Open Multilingual WordNet: http://globalwordnet.org/resources/wordnets-in-the-world/

[13] WordNet Bahasa: http://wn-msa.sourceforge.net/

[14] Malay BERT: https://huggingface.co/malay-huggingface/bert-base-bahasa-cased

[15] Malay ALBERT: https://huggingface.co/malay-huggingface/albert-base-bahasa-cased

Based on the comparable mean error and adjusted R^2 scores, we can conclude that XLNet-GRU shows fairly consistent performance across both English (mean adjusted $R^2 = 0.631$) and Malay (mean adjusted $R^2 = 0.514$) with only slightly better performance observed in the English model mainly due to the availability of more training data in the English news sentiment corpus. The results could also imply that the pre-trained English language model contains vocabulary that is more relevant to cryptocurrency terms in comparison to Malay. Thus, our method proves that it is possible to create a Malay sentiment model that is comparable in terms of performance to an English sentiment model despite the more limited language resources in Malay.

6. Conclusion

To conclude, we presented a XLNet-GRU model to perform sentiment regression for cryptocurrency news in English and Malay. Our XLNet-GRU sentiment regression model applies the latest XLNet transformer-based contextual word embedding for both English and Malay cryptocurrency news (Bitcoin and Ethereum). XLNet is a new pre-trained language model, which has not been explored in sentiment analysis of cryptocurrency news. Our experiment results show that XLNet-GRU outperforms BERT-GRU and other SOTA baselines as well as the naïve lexicon-based baseline, VADER. The performance of XL-Net-GRU is comparable in both English and Malay news.

To the best of our knowledge, this is the first study experimenting with a deep learning sentiment model for Malay cryptocurrency news. In addition, we also curated an English sentiment corpus and a Malay sentiment corpus specifically in the cryptocurrency news domain, which can serve as the benchmark to evaluate the quality of sentiment features extracted in the intermediate step within the cryptocurrency price prediction pipeline. We hope to release and share the cryptocurrency news sentiment corpora for the benefit of future research in the financial domain.

For future work, we hope that this cryptocurrency sentiment corpora will motivate further research through experimentation with other contextual word embeddings and deep learning methods particularly for Malay (i.e., the poor language resource). The XLNet-GRU model can be applied and evaluated on other domains and text sources such as tweets.

7. Acknowledgement

Acknowledgement to "Ministry of Higher Education Malaysia for Fundamental Research Grant Scheme with Project Code: FRGS/1/2020/ICT02/USM/02/3". This research was also made possible through the Academic Training Scheme (SLAB), a scholarship by the Ministry of Higher Education Malaysia. We would like to thank our annotators from Universiti Sains Malaysia (USM) and Universiti Teknologi MARA (UiTM) whose expertise and diligence have greatly assisted the research.

8. References

Attila, S. D. (2017). Impact of social media on cryptocurrency trading with deep learning. *Scientific Students' Conference*, 47.

Cerda, G. N. C. (2021). *Bitcoin price prediction through stimulus analysis: On the footprints of Twitter's crypto-influencers* [Master's Thesis, Pontificia Universidad Católica de Chile].

Chen, C.-C., Huang, H.-H., and Chen, H.-H. (2018). NTUSD-Fin: A market sentiment dictionary for financial social media data applications. *Proceedings of the 1st Financial Narrative Processing Workshop (FNP 2018)*, 37–43.

Chin, C. K., and Omar, N. (2020). Bitcoin price prediction based on sentiment of news article and market data with LSTM model. *Asia-Pacific Journal of Information Technology and Multimedia*, *9*(1), 1–16.

Clark, K., Luong, M.-T., and Le, Q. V. (2020). *ELECTRA: Pre-training Text Encoders as Discriminators Rather Than Generators*, 18.

Devika, M. D., Sunitha, C., and Ganesh, A. (2016). Sentiment Analysis: A Comparative Study on Different Approaches. *Procedia Computer Science*, *87*, 44–49.

Devlin, J., Chang, M.-W., Lee, K., and Toutanova, K. (2019). BERT: Pre-training of Deep Bidirectional Transformers for Language Understanding. *Proceedings of the 2019 Conference of the North American Chapter of the Association for Computational Linguistics: Human Language Technologies*, 4171–4186.

Farha, I. A., and Magdy, W. (2021). Benchmarking Transformer-based Language Models for Arabic Sentiment and Sarcasm Detection. *Proceedings of the 6th Arabic Natural Language Processing Workshop*, 21–31.

Georgoula, I., Pournarakis, D., Bilanakos, C., Sotiropoulos, D. N., and Giaglis, G. M. (2015). Using time-series and sentiment analysis to detect the determinants of Bitcoin prices. *SSRN Electronic Journal*.

Gong, X.-R., Jin, J.-X., and Zhang, T. (2019). Sentiment analysis using autoregressive language modeling and broad learning system. *2019 IEEE International Conference on Bioinformatics and Biomedicine (BIBM)*, 1130–1134.

Gurdgiev, C., and O'Loughlin, D. (2020). Herding and anchoring in cryptocurrency markets: Investor reaction to fear and uncertainty. *Journal of Behavioral and Experimental Finance*, *25*, 100271.

Karalevicius, V., Degrande, N., and De Weerdt, J. (2018). Using sentiment analysis to predict interday Bitcoin price movements. *The Journal of Risk Finance*, *19*(1), 56–75.

Krippendorff, K. (2018). *Content analysis: An introduction to its methodology* (Fourth). SAGE Publications.

Lamon, C., Nielsen, E., and Redondo, E. (2017). Cryptocurrency price prediction using news and social media sentiment. *SMU Data Science Review*, 1–22.

Lan, Z., Chen, M., Goodman, S., Gimpel, K., Sharma, P., and Soricut, R. (2020). *ALBERT: A Lite BERT for self-supervised learning of language representations*. 1–17.

Li, M., Lu, Q., Long, Y., and Gui, L. (2017). Inferring Affective Meanings of Words from Word Embedding. *IEEE Transactions on Affective Computing*, *8*(4), 443–456.

Liu, Y., Ott, M., Goyal, N., Du, J., Joshi, M., Chen, D., Levy, O., Lewis, M., Zettlemoyer, L., and Stoyanov, V. (2019). RoBERTa: A Robustly Optimized BERT Pretraining Approach. *ArXiv:1907.11692 [Cs]*.

Loughran, T., and Mcdonald, B. (2014). Measuring Readability in financial disclosures. *The Journal of Finance*, *69*(4), 1643–1671.

Mai, F., Bai, Q., and Shan, J. (2015). The impacts of social media on Bitcoin performance. *International Conference on Information Systems (ICIS)*, 1–16.

Mohanty, P., Patel, D., Patel, P., and Roy, S. (2018). Predicting fluctuations in cryptocurrencies' price using users' comments and real-time prices. *7th International Conference on Reliability, Infocom Technologies and Optimization (ICRITO)*, 6.

Pintelas, E., Livieris, I. E., Stavroyiannis, S., Kotsilieris, T., and Pintelas, P. (2020). Investigating the problem of cryptocurrency price prediction: A deep learning approach. In I. Maglogiannis, L. Iliadis, and E. Pimenidis (Eds.), *Artificial Intelligence Applications and Innovations* (Vol. 584, pp. 99–110). Springer International Publishing.

Prajapati, P. (2020). Predictive analysis of Bitcoin price considering social sentiments. *ArXiv:2001.10343 [Cs]*.

Pranesh, R., Kumar, S., and Shekhar, A. (2020). CLPLM: Character Level Pretrained Language Model for ExtractingSupport Phrases for Sentiment Labels. *Proceedings of the 17th International Conference on Natural Language Processing*, 475–480.

Rognone, L., Hyde, S., and Zhang, S. S. (2020). News sentiment in the cryptocurrency market: An empirical comparison with Forex. *International Review of Financial Analysis*, *69*, 101462.

Stenqvist, E., and Lönnö, J. (2017). *Predicting Bitcoin price fluctuation with Twitter sentiment analysis* [Degree Project]. KTH Royal Institute of Technology School of Computer Science and Communication.

Valencia, F., Gómez-Espinosa, A., and Valdés-Aguirre, B. (2019). Price movement prediction of cryptocurrencies using sentiment analysis and machine learning. *Entropy*, *21*(6), 589.

Vo, A.-D., Nguyen, Q.-P., and Ock, C.-Y. (2019). Sentiment analysis of news for effective cryptocurrency price prediction. *International Journal of Knowledge Engineering*, *5*(2), 47–52.

Yang, Z., Dai, Z., Yang, Y., Carbonell, J., Salakhutdinov, R. R., and Le, Q. V. (2020). XLNet: Generalized autoregressive pretraining for language understanding. *Advances in Neural Information Processing Systems (NeurIPS 2019)*, 1–11.

Proceedings of the 4th Financial Narrative Processing Workshop @ LREC 2022, pages 43–52
Marseille, 24 June 2022

The Financial Narrative Summarisation Shared Task (FNS 2022)

Mahmoud El-Haj[1], **Nadhem Zmandar**[1], **Paul Rayson**[1], **Ahmed AbuRa'ed**[2],
Marina Litvak[3], **Nikiforos Pittaras**[4], **George Giannakopoulos**[4,5], **Aris Kosmopoulos**[4,5],
Blanca Carbajo-Coronado[6], **Antonio Moreno-Sandoval**[6]
[1]Lancaster University, UK
[2]University of British Columbia, Canada
[3]Shamoon College of Engineering, Israel
[4]NCSR "Demokritos", Athens, Greece
[5]SciFY PNPC, Athens, Greece
[6]Universidad Autónoma Madrid, Spain
[1]{m.el-haj, n.zmandar, p.rayson}@lancaster.ac.uk
[2]ahmed.aburaed@upf.edu, [3]marinal@ac.sce.ac.il
[4,5]ggianna@iit.demokritos.gr, pittarasnikif@gmail.com, akosmo@scify.org
[6]{blanca.carbajo, antonio.msandoval}@uam.es

Abstract

This paper presents the results and findings of the Financial Narrative Summarisation Shared Task on summarising UK, Greek and Spanish annual reports. The shared task was organised as part of the Financial Narrative Processing 2022 Workshop (**FNP 2022 Workshop**). The Financial Narrative summarisation Shared Task (FNS-2022) has been running since 2020 as part of the Financial Narrative Processing (FNP) workshop series (El-Haj et al., 2022; El-Haj et al., 2021; El-Haj et al., 2020b; El-Haj et al., 2019c; El-Haj et al., 2018). The shared task included one main task which is the use of either abstractive or extractive automatic summarisers to summarise long documents in terms of UK, Greek and Spanish financial annual reports. This shared task is the third to target financial documents. The data for the shared task was created and collected from publicly available annual reports published by firms listed on the Stock Exchanges of UK, Greece and Spain. A total number of 14 systems from 7 different teams participated in the shared task.

1. What are financial narratives

Companies produce a variety of reports containing both narrative and numerical information at various times during their financial year, including annual financial reports. This creates vast amounts of financial information which can be impossible to navigate, handle and keep track of. This shows the vital need for automatic summarisation systems in order to reduce the time and effort of both the shareholders and investors.

2. Related Work

The increased availability of financial reports data has been met with research interest for applying automatic summarisation methods. The task of automatic text summarisation aims to produce a condensed, informative and non-redundant summaries from a single or multiple input texts (Nenkova and McKeown, 2011). This is achieved by either identifying and ranking subsets of the input text (i.e. extractive approaches ((Gupta and Lehal, 2010)), or by generating the summary from scratch (i.e. abstractive methods (Moratanch and Chitrakala, 2016; Zmandar et al., 2021)). Extractive methods have been a popular venue for summarising text due to their relative simplicity and the comparatively high requirements of abstractive methods for computational resources and available data.
Extractive summarisation utilises scoring approaches to identify and reorder parts of the input (e.g. sentences, phrases and/or passages), using a variety of feature extraction and evaluation methods (Luhn, 1958; Baxendale, 1958; Edmundson, 1969; Mori, 2002; McCargar, 2004; Giannakopoulos et al., 2008). Where adequate data is available, machine learning methods have been employed, such as Hidden Markov Models (Fung and Ngai, 2006), topic-based modelling (Aries et al., 2015), genetic algorithms (Litvak et al., 2010) and clustering methods (Radev et al., 2000; Liu and Lindroos, 2006; Kruengkrai and Jaruskulchai, 2003).

The employment of summarisation and natural language processing techniques in general has promising applications in the financial domain (El-Haj et al., 2019b). The SummariserPort system (de Oliveira et al., 2002) has been used to produce summaries for financial news, where it utilized lexical cohesion (Flowerdew and Mahlberg, 2009), using sentence linkage heuristics to generate the output summary. A summarisation system for financial news was proposed in (Filippova et al., 2009) generating query-based company-tailored summaries. This was done through using unsupervised sentence ranking with simple frequency-based features. Recently, statistical features with heuristic approaches have been used to summarise financial textual disclosures (Cardinaels et al., 2019), generating summaries with reduced positive bias, leading to more conservative valuation judgements by investors that receive them. Further, the Financial Narrative Summarisation task (El-Haj, 2019) of the Multiling 2019 workshop (Giannakopoulos, 2019) involved the generation of structured summaries from financial narrative disclosures. Considering this body of work, the Financial Narrative Summarisation task (FNS 2020 (El-Haj et al., 2020a)) task resulted in the first large scale experimental results and state-of-the-art summarisation methods applied to financial data. The task focused on annual reports produced by UK firms listed on the London Stock Exchange (LSE). The shared task was held as part of the 1st Joint Workshop on Financial Narrative Processing and MultiLing Financial Summarisation (FNP-FNS 2020) (El-Haj et al., 2020c). The participating systems used a variety of techniques and methods ranging from rule based extraction methods (Litvak et al., 2020; Vhatkar et al., 2020; Arora and Radhakrishnan, 2020; Azzi and Kang, 2020) to traditional machine learning methods (Suarez et al., 2020; Vhatkar et al., 2020; Arora and Radhakrishnan, 2020) and high performing deep learning models (Agarwal et al., 2020; Singh, 2020; La Quatra and Cagliero, 2020; Vhatkar et al., 2020; Arora and Radhakrishnan, 2020; Azzi and Kang, 2020; Zheng et al., 2020).

One of the main challenges and limitations reported by the participants was the average length of annual reports (around 60,000 words), which made the training process difficult as it requires powerful resources (e.g. GPUs) to avoid long training time. In addition, participants argued that extracting both text and structure from PDF files with numerous tables, charts, and numerical data resulted in noisy data being extracted. Such feedback highlights interesting aspects and challenging components of Financial Narrative Summarisation, which presents a high-difficulty task and an interesting research problem that is worth investigating. The 2022 Financial Narrative summarisation task (FNS 2022) promotes this effort by providing such a shared task in the FNP 2022 workshop[1].

3. Data Description

The Financial Narrative Summarisation (FNS 2022) aims to demonstrate the value and challenges of applying automatic text summarisation to financial text written in English, Spanish and Greek, usually referred to as financial narrative disclosures. The task dataset has been extracted from UK, Greek and Spanish annual reports published in PDF file format.

3.1. English Dataset

In the Financial Narrative Summarisation task we focus on annual reports produced by UK firms listed on The London Stock Exchange (LSE).

In the UK and elsewhere, annual report structure is much less rigid than those produced in the US. Companies produce glossy brochures with a much looser structure, which makes automatic summarisation of narratives in UK annual reports a challenging task.

[1]Main workshop: http://wp.lancs.ac.uk/cfie/fnp2022/

For the FNS 2022 Shared task[2] we use approximately 4,000 UK annual reports for firms listed on LSE, covering the period between 2002 and 2017 (El-Haj et al., 2014; El-Haj et al., 2019a).

We divided the full text within annual reports into *training*, *testing* and *validation* sets providing both the full text of each annual report along with gold-standard summaries.

In total there are 3,863 annual reports divided into training, testing and validation sets. Table 1 shows the dataset details.

Data Type	Train	Validate	Test
Report full text	3,000	363	500
Gold summaries	9,873	1,250	1,673

Table 1: FNS 2022 Shared Task Dataset

3.2. Greek Dataset

The Greek dataset is composed by the annual reports of years 2019 and 2020. These reports are in PDF format and can be from 100 to 300 pages long. The Greek reports can be less structured compared to the English ones.

Although the reports seem to follow some pattern, we can observe at several occasions that the structure can differ greatly. For example the "highlights" section can be found in most of the reports but it is not always located at the same sections. Furthermore some of the reports were problematic during the dataset creation process and that reason they were not used. Common problems were the language used (some were in English), the specific variation of PDF format used or the very weird structure used by the authors of the report. The initial documents were around 300, while the final dataset was composed by 262 documents.

Data Type	Train	Validate	Test
Report full text	162	50	50
Gold summaries	324	100	100

Table 2: FNS 2022 Shared Task Greek Dataset

The full text was also divided into training, testing and validation sets in a similar way as with the other datasets. Table 2 shows the dataset details. The golden summaries were extracted from the statement of the "chairman/board" and the annual report of "management board".

3.3. Spanish Dataset

The Spanish dataset is taken from the FinT-esp corpus (Moreno-Sandoval et al., 2020) and consists of 262 documents with a distribution utterly similar to the Greek dataset (see Table 3).

[2]http://wp.lancs.ac.uk/cfie/fns2022/

The dates of the annual reports range from 2014 to 2018. The source is in PDF format, with a total number of pages between 40 and 400. In plain text, the files have an average of 36,285 words.

Data Type	Train	Validate	Test
Report full text	162	50	50
Gold summaries	324	100	100

Table 3: FNS 2022 Shared Task Spanish Dataset

The originals were carefully edited by hand, and fragments not containing the narrative (tables, footnotes, headers, etc.) were removed. In addition, the letters from the chairpersons were removed from the reports, as they have been used to make the summaries. Several linguists edited each letter to simplify and reduce the length of the Gold Summaries to 1000 word tokens.

4. Data Availability

For the shared task we first provide the training and validation sets, which include the full text of each annual report along with the gold-standard summaries. On average, there are at least three gold-standard summaries for each annual report with some reports containing up to seven gold-standard summaries. The full test set is available only to organisers who evaluate the participating systems. The gold-standard summaries for the test set were not provided to participants in advance.

5. Task Description

For the purpose of this task each team was asked to produce one summary for each annual report. The summary length should not exceed **1000** words. We advised that the summary is generated/extracted based on the narrative sections.

Only one summary was allowed for each report, but participating teams were welcome to participate with more than one system. The participants were asked to follow a standard file naming process to aid the automatic evaluation process. Also, for standardisation and consistency all output summary files were required to be in UTF-8 file format.

Regarding generated outputs from a participant system, the following criteria were requested for each language:

- Each team should produce a no more than 1000 words summary for each annual report in the testing set.
- One summary should be provided for each report.
- Each summary should be named following the pattern **ID_summary**. Example: 25082_summary.
- All outputs should be in UTF-8 file format.
- All output summaries should be compressed following the pattern *<TeamName>_Summaries.tar.gz*.

5.1. Evaluation

To evaluate the generated system summaries against the human gold-standard summaries we used the Java Rouge (JRouge)[3] package for ROUGE, using multiple variants (i.e. ROUGE-1, ROUGE-2, ROUGE-L and ROUGE-SU4) (Ganesan, 2018).

The team with the best ROUGE-2 scores for all three languages was selected as the winner of the competition. The scores are weighted as follows: English (50%), Spanish (25%) and Greek (25%) as later shown in Table 5.

6. Data Sample

```
Financial Narrative Dataset
|------training
        |------annual_reports
        |------gold_summaries
|------validation
        |------annual_reports
        |------gold_summaries
|------testing
        |------annual_reports
```

Figure 1: Dataset Structure

Figure 1 shows the structure of the Financial Narrative Summarisation dataset for all three languages: English, Greek and Spanish. At the beginning of the shared task we provided the participants with two directories, corresponding to "training" and "validation" sets. Each contained the full text of the annual reports and the gold standard summaries.

The data was provided in plain text format in a directory structure as in Figure 1. Each annual report has a unique ID and it is used across in order to link the full text from an annual report to its gold-standard summaries.

For example, the gold standard summaries for the file called **19** in the *training/annual_reports* directory can be located in the *training_gold_summaries* as files with the same ID (19) as a prefix: **19_1** to **19_3**.

7. Participants and Systems

In total, 14 summarisation systems by 7 different teams have participated and submitted their system summaries to FNS 2022, the teams are presented in Table 4.

AO-Lancs team produced a hybrid summariser using TF-IDF and clustering methodology. Utilising statistical methods to combine the TF-IDF Sentence score with the Clustering Euclidean distance for each sentence, producing new hybrid sentence rankings. A

[3]https://github.com/kavgan/ROUGE-2.0

Team	Affiliation
LSIR	École Polytechnique Fédérale de Lausanne (EPFL)
SSC-AI-RG	State Street Corporation
IIC	Instituto de Ingeniería de Conocimiento
TREDENCE	Tredence Inc.
LIPI	Fidelity Investments, Jadavpur University
MACQUARIE	Macquarie University
AO-LANCS	Lancaster University

Table 4: FNS 2022 participating teams and their affiliations

60/40 weighting in favour of clustering was applied when combining the scores (Ogden and El-Haj, 2022).

LSIR team participated with two systems; the first uses a pre-trained multilingual abstractive summarisation model (mT5) that was fine-tuned on the downstream task to generate the start of the summaries, while the second system approaches the problem as an extractive summariser in which a similarity search is performed on the trained span embeddings to find good candidates for a summary start. The language models were fine-tuned on a financial document collection of three languages; English, Spanish and Greek, and aim to identify the beginning of the summary narrative part of the document. The system based on mT5 achieves the highest performance in the given task, ranked 1st on Rouge scores over the three languages (Foroutan et al., 2022).

Tredence team submitted a multi-lingual long document summarisation system. They developed task-specific summarisation methods for all three languages: English, Spanish and Greek. The solution is divided into two parts, where a RoBERTa model was fine tuned to identify and extract summarising segments from English documents and T5 based models were used for summarising Spanish and Greek documents. An mT5 model was fine-tuned to identify potential narrative sections for Greek and Spanish, followed by fine tuning mT5 and T5 (Spanish version) for abstractive summarisation task. This system also features a novel approach for generating summarisation training dataset using long document segmentation and the semantic similarity across segments (Pant and Chopra, 2022).

SSC_AI_RG team created an algorithm called K-Maximal Word Allocation which allocates K words i.e. 1000 words in narrative sections or areas according to their weights as amount of words to be generated from a section. For extraction we experimented with Top-K, Bert and Bart extractive summarisers. To identify key narrative sections in English reports, they built a section classification system which classifies if the section should be in summary or not. They extracted TOC, section names and applied lookup in summaries to annotate section names. Clusters were created around narrative sentences based on following assumptions: Language Independence, Structure Independence and Neighbourhood Assumption. Top M Narrative Sections according to their weights were translated to Spanish and Greek. Keywords were extracted from these with weights later to be used to identify narrative sentences and areas and calculate weights (Shukla et al., 2022).

LIPI team has used the system provided by last year's winning team (Orzhenovskii, 2021), the original summariser provided by Orzhenovskii relies on T5 in order to perform the summarisation.

IIC team developed a summariser based on a sequence classification task whose objective was to find the sentence where the summary begins in the English dataset. For the reports in Spanish and Greek they used an abstractive strategy creating an Encoder-Decoder architecture in Spanish, MariMari, based on an existing Encoding-only model; they also trained multilingual Encoder-Decoder models for this task. As for the Greek dataset, they created a translation-summary-translation system in which the reports were translated into English and summarised, and then the summaries were translated back to Greek (Vaca et al., 2022).

Finally, **Macquarie team** used Longformer-Encoder-Decoder (LED) (Beltagy et al., 2020) model to generate the summaries. They also investigated the multi-stage fine-tuning approach to explore if it helps the model to generate better on the financial domain and avoids the problem of forgetting (Khanna et al., 2022).

8. Results and Discussion

The participating systems used a variety of techniques and methods ranging from fine tuning pre-trained transformers to using high performing deep learning models and word embeddings.

In addition, the participating teams used methods to investigate the hierarchy of the annual reports to try and detect structure and extract the narrative sections, in order to identify the parts in the report from which the gold summaries were extracted.

The majority of the applied techniques were extractive, since the dataset is highly structured with discrete sections.

Team	En	ES	EL	Score
LSIR-1	0.37	0.16	0.14	0.26
SSC-AI-RG-1	0.33	0.15	0.19	0.25
SSC-AI-RG-3	0.32	0.15	0.19	0.24
IIC	0.37	0.13	0.10	0.24
SSC-AI-RG-2	0.30	0.15	0.19	0.23
TREDENCE-2	0.32	0.13	0.14	0.23
TREDENCE-1	0.32	0.13	0.14	0.23
LIPI	0.38	0.07	0.05	0.22
TREDENCE-3	0.32	0.13	0.07	0.21
LSIR-3	0.28	0.14	0.13	0.21
MACQUARIE-1	0.30	0.00	0.00	0.15
MACQUARIE-3	0.30	0.00	0.00	0.15
MACQUARIE-2	0.30	0.00	0.00	0.15
AO-LANCS	0.14	0.13	0.13	0.14

Table 5: FNS 2022 results
EN: English, ES: Spanish, EL: Greek

The results in Table 5 show the ROUGE-2 F measure score for each language. The systems are ranked according to the final score which is weighted as follows: English (50%), Spanish (25%) and Greek (25%). The results shows that Team LSIR ranked first using the first run of their module. Please note that we use *0.00* to indicate a no-participation for a given language.

The complete evaluation results including ROUGE 1, 2, L and SU4 are show in tables 6, 7, 8, 9,10 and 11. Such results will be used as a comparison line in the future, by incorporating them into a venue of results, techniques and approaches, which we hope will be useful to researchers working on Financial Text Summarisation.

9. Bibliographical References

Agarwal, R., Verma, I., and Chatterjee, N. (2020). Langresearchlab_nc at fincausal 2020, task 1: A knowledge induced neural net for causality detection. In *Proceedings of the 1st Joint Workshop on Financial Narrative Processing and MultiLing Financial Summarisation*, pages 33–39.

Aries, A., Zegour, D. E., and Hidouci, K. W. (2015). Allsummarizer system at multiling 2015: Multilingual single and multi-document summarization. In *Proceedings of the 16th Annual Meeting of the Special Interest Group on Discourse and Dialogue*, pages 237–244. The Association for Computer Linguistics.

Arora, P. and Radhakrishnan, P. (2020). Amex ai-labs: An investigative study on extractive summarization of financial documents. In *Proceedings of the 1st Joint Workshop on Financial Narrative Processing and MultiLing Financial Summarisation*, pages 137–142.

Azzi, A. A. and Kang, J. (2020). Extractive summarization system for annual reports. In *Proceedings of the 1st Joint Workshop on Financial Narrative Processing and MultiLing Financial Summarisation*, pages 143–147.

Baxendale, P. B. (1958). Machine-made index for technical literature—an experiment. *IBM Journal of research and development*, 2(4):354–361.

Beltagy, I., Peters, M. E., and Cohan, A. (2020). Longformer: The long-document transformer. *arXiv preprint arXiv:2004.05150.*

Cardinaels, E., Hollander, S., and White, B. J. (2019). Automatic summarization of earnings releases: attributes and effects on investors' judgments. *Review of Accounting Studies*, 24(3):860–890.

de Oliveira, P. C. F., Ahmad, K., and Gillam, L. (2002). A financial news summarization system based on lexical cohesion. In *Proceedings of the International Conference on Terminology and Knowledge Engineering, Nancy, France.*

Edmundson, H. P. (1969). New methods in automatic extracting. *Journal of the ACM (JACM)*, 16(2):264–285.

El-Haj, M., Rayson, P., Young, S., and Walker, M. (2014). Detecting document structure in a very large corpus of uk financial reports. In *European Language Resources Association (ELRA).*

El-Haj, M., Rayson, P., and Moore, A. (2018). The first financial narrative processing workshop (fnp 2018). In *Proceedings of the LREC 2018 Workshop.*

El-Haj, M., Rayson, P., Alves, P., Herrero-Zorita, C., and Young, S. (2019a). Multilingual financial narrative processing: Analysing annual reports in english, spanish and portuguese. *World Scientific Publishing.*

El-Haj, M., Rayson, P., Walker, M., Young, S., and Simaki, V. (2019b). In search of meaning: Lessons, resources and next steps for computational analysis of financial discourse. *Journal of Business Finance & Accounting*, 46(3-4):265–306.

Mahmoud El-Haj, et al., editors. (2019c). *Proceedings of the Second Financial Narrative Processing Workshop (FNP 2019)*, Turku, Finland, September. Linköping University Electronic Press.

El-Haj, M., AbuRa'ed, A., Litvak, M., Pittaras, N., and Giannakopoulos, G. (2020a). The financial narrative summarisation shared task (FNS 2020). In *Proceedings of the 1st Joint Workshop on Financial Narrative Processing and MultiLing Financial Summarisation*, pages 1–12, Barcelona, Spain (Online), December. COLING.

Mahmoud El-Haj, et al., editors. (2020b). *Proceedings of the 1st Joint Workshop on Financial Narrative Processing and MultiLing Financial Summarisation*, Barcelona, Spain (Online), December. COLING.

El-Haj, M., Athanasakou, V., Ferradans, S., Salzedo, C., Elhag, A., Bouamor, H., Litvak, M., Rayson, P., Giannakopoulos, G., and Pittaras, N. (2020c). Proceedings of the 1st joint workshop on financial narrative processing and multiling financial summarisation. In *Proceedings of the 1st Joint Workshop on Fi-*

nancial Narrative Processing and MultiLing Financial Summarisation.

Mahmoud El-Haj, et al., editors. (2021). *Proceedings of the 3rd Financial Narrative Processing Workshop*, Lancaster, United Kingdom, 15-16 September. Association for Computational Linguistics.

Mahmoud El-Haj, et al., editors. (2022). *Proceedings of the 4th Financial Narrative Processing Workshop*, Marseille, France, 24 June. The 13th Language Resources and Evaluation Conference, LREC 2022.

El-Haj, M. (2019). Multiling 2019: Financial narrative summarisation. In *Proceedings of the Workshop MultiLing 2019: Summarization Across Languages, Genres and Sources*, pages 6–10.

Filippova, K., Surdeanu, M., Ciaramita, M., and Zaragoza, H. (2009). Company-oriented extractive summarization of financial news. In *Proceedings of the 12th Conference of the European Chapter of the ACL (EACL 2009)*, pages 246–254.

Flowerdew, J. and Mahlberg, M. (2009). *Lexical cohesion and corpus linguistics*, volume 17. John Benjamins Publishing.

Foroutan, N., Romanou, A., Massonnet, S., Lebret, R., and Aberer, K. (2022). Multilingual text summarization on financial documents. In *Proceedings of the 4th Financial Narrative Processing Workshop*, Marseille, France, 24 June. The 13th Language Resources and Evaluation Conference, LREC 2022.

Fung, P. and Ngai, G. (2006). One story, one flow: Hidden markov story models for multilingual multidocument summarization. *ACM Transactions on Speech and Language Processing (TSLP)*, 3(2):1–16.

Ganesan, K. (2018). Rouge 2.0: Updated and improved measures for evaluation of summarization tasks. *arXiv preprint arXiv:1803.01937*.

Giannakopoulos, G., Karkaletsis, V., Vouros, G., and Stamatopoulos, P. (2008). Summarization system evaluation revisited: N-gram graphs. *ACM Transactions on Speech and Language Processing (TSLP)*, 5(3):1–39.

Giannakopoulos, G. (2019). Proceedings of the workshop multiling 2019: Summarization across languages, genres and sources. In *Proceedings of the Workshop MultiLing 2019: Summarization Across Languages, Genres and Sources*.

Gupta, V. and Lehal, G. S. (2010). A survey of text summarization extractive techniques. *Journal of emerging technologies in web intelligence*, 2(3):258–268.

Khanna, U., Ghodratnama, S., Moll´a, D., and Beheshti, A. (2022). Transformer-based models for long document summarisation in financial domain. In *Proceedings of the 4th Financial Narrative Processing Workshop*, Marseille, France, 24June. The 13th Language Resources and Evaluation Conference, LREC 2022.

Kruengkrai, C. and Jaruskulchai, C. (2003). Generic text summarization using local and global properties of sentences. In *Proceedings IEEE/WIC International Conference on Web Intelligence (WI 2003)*, pages 201–206. IEEE.

La Quatra, M. and Cagliero, L. (2020). End-to-end training for financial report summarization. In *Proceedings of the 1st Joint Workshop on Financial Narrative Processing and MultiLing Financial Summarisation*, pages 118–123.

Litvak, M., Last, M., and Friedman, M. (2010). A new approach to improving multilingual summarization using a genetic algorithm. In *Proceedings of the 48th annual meeting of the association for computational linguistics*, pages 927–936.

Litvak, M., Vanetik, N., and Puchinsky, Z. (2020). Sce-summary at the fns 2020 shared task. In *Proceedings of the 1st Joint Workshop on Financial Narrative Processing and MultiLing Financial Summarisation*, pages 124–129.

Liu, S. and Lindroos, J. (2006). Experiences from automatic summarization of imf staff reports. *Practical Data Mining: Applications, Experiences and Challenges*, page 43.

Luhn, H. P. (1958). The automatic creation of literature abstracts. *IBM Journal of research and development*, 2(2):159–165.

McCargar, V. (2004). Statistical approaches to automatic text summarization. *Bulletin of the American Society for Information Science and Technology*, 30(4):21–25.

Moratanch, N. and Chitrakala, S. (2016). A survey on abstractive text summarization. In *2016 International Conference on Circuit, power and computing technologies (ICCPCT)*, pages 1–7. IEEE.

Moreno-Sandoval, A., Gisbert, A., and Montoro, H. (2020). Fint-esp: a corpus of financial reports in spanish. In Fuster, et al., editors, *Multiperspectives in analysis and corpus design*, pages 89–102, Granada. Comares.

Mori, T. (2002). Information gain ratio as term weight: the case of summarization of ir results. In *COLING 2002: The 19th International Conference on Computational Linguistics*.

Nenkova, A. and McKeown, K. (2011). *Automatic summarization*. Now Publishers Inc.

Ogden, A. and El-Haj, M. (2022). Financial narrative summarisation using a hybrid tf-idf and clustering summariser: Ao-lancs system at fns 2022. In *Proceedings of the 4th Financial Narrative Processing Workshop*, Marseille, France, 24 June. The 13th Language Resources and Evaluation Conference, LREC 2022.

Orzhenovskii, M. (2021). T5-LONG-EXTRACT at FNS-2021 shared task. In *Proceedings of the 3rd Financial Narrative Processing Workshop*, pages 67–69, Lancaster, United Kingdom, 15-16 September. Association for Computational Linguistics.

Pant, M. and Chopra, A. (2022). Multilingual financial

documentation summarization by team_tredence for fns2022. In *Proceedings of the 4th Financial Narrative Processing Workshop*, Marseille, France, 24 June. The 13th Language Resources and Evaluation Conference, LREC 2022.

Radev, D., Jing, H., and Budzikowska, M. (2000). Centroid-based summarization of multiple documents: Clustering, sentence extraction, and evaluation. In *Proceedings of the ANLP/NAACL-2000 Workshop on Summarization*.

Shukla, N. K., Vaid, A., Katikeri, R. C., Keeriyadath, S., and Raja, M. (2022). Dimsum: Distributed and multilingual summarization of financial narratives. In *Proceedings of the 4th Financial Narrative Processing Workshop*, Marseille, France, 24 June. The 13th Language Resources and Evaluation Conference, LREC 2022.

Singh, A. (2020). Point-5: Pointer network and t-5 based financial narrative summarisation. In *Proceedings of the 1st Joint Workshop on Financial Narrative Processing and MultiLing Financial Summarisation*, pages 105–111.

Suarez, J. B., Martínez, P., and Martínez, J. L. (2020). Combining financial word embeddings and knowledge-based features for financial text summarization uc3m-mc system at fns-2020. In *Proceedings of the 1st Joint Workshop on Financial Narrative Processing and MultiLing Financial Summarisation*, pages 112–117.

Vaca, A., Segurado, A., Betancur, D., and Jiménez, A. B. (2022). Extractive and abstractive summarization methods for financial narrative summarization in english, spanish and greek. In *Proceedings of the 4th Financial Narrative Processing Workshop*, Marseille, France, 24June. The 13th Language Resources and Evaluation Conference, LREC 2022.

Vhatkar, A., Bhattacharyya, P., and Arya, K. (2020). Knowledge graph and deep neural network for extractive text summarization by utilizing triples. In *Proceedings of the 1st Joint Workshop on Financial Narrative Processing and MultiLing Financial Summarisation*, pages 130–136.

Zheng, S., Lu, A., and Cardie, C. (2020). Sumsum@ fns-2020 shared task. In *Proceedings of the 1st Joint Workshop on Financial Narrative Processing and MultiLing Financial Summarisation*, pages 148–152.

Zmandar, N., Singh, A., El-Haj, M., and Rayson, P. (2021). Joint abstractive and extractive method for long financial document summarization. In *Proceedings of the 3rd Financial Narrative Processing Workshop*, pages 99–105, Lancaster, United Kingdom, 15-16 September. Association for Computational Linguistics.

Appendix A - English Task Results

Model	R-1 / R	R-1 / P	R-1 / F	R-2 / R	R-2 / P	R-2 / F
LIPI	0.587	0.451	0.496	0.472	0.326	0.374
IIC	0.566	0.472	0.497	0.438	0.337	0.366
LSIR-1	0.583	0.443	0.489	0.464	0.317	0.365
SSC-AI-RG-1	0.551	0.482	0.495	0.455	0.272	0.327
TREDENCE-2	0.49	0.461	0.462	0.346	0.323	0.322
TREDENCE-3	0.49	0.461	0.462	0.346	0.323	0.322
SSC-AI-RG-3	0.524	0.483	0.484	0.421	0.274	0.319
TREDENCE-1	0.428	0.503	0.447	0.305	0.363	0.317
MACQUARIE-1	0.48	0.438	0.443	0.334	0.302	0.303
MACQUARIE-3	0.48	0.435	0.442	0.333	0.301	0.302
MACQUARIE-2	0.476	0.434	0.441	0.33	0.297	0.301
SSC-AI-RG-2	0.472	0.491	0.462	0.358	0.282	0.3
LSIR-3	0.49	0.442	0.451	0.355	0.241	0.275
AO-LANCS	0.372	0.292	0.317	0.184	0.126	0.143

Table 6: ROUGE-1 and ROUGE-2 on English dataset ordered by R2 F1 score

Model	R-L / R	R-L / P	R-L / F	R-SU4 / R	R-SU4 / P	R-SU4 / F
LIPI	0.559	0.449	0.487	0.515	0.369	0.417
IIC	0.547	0.455	0.484	0.483	0.368	0.402
SSC-AI-RG-1	0.523	0.465	0.478	0.499	0.241	0.312
SSC-AI-RG-3	0.497	0.459	0.464	0.469	0.243	0.307
LSIR-1	0.552	0.439	0.479	0.508	0.36	0.409
TREDENCE-1	0.45	0.47	0.45	0.347	0.412	0.362
TREDENCE-2	0.477	0.437	0.448	0.394	0.37	0.368
TREDENCE-3	0.477	0.437	0.448	0.394	0.37	0.368
SSC-AI-RG-2	0.457	0.457	0.444	0.408	0.247	0.293
MACQUARIE-1	0.471	0.413	0.431	0.384	0.35	0.352
MACQUARIE-3	0.467	0.41	0.428	0.384	0.347	0.351
MACQUARIE-2	0.466	0.408	0.427	0.381	0.345	0.349
LSIR-3	0.461	0.41	0.425	0.411	0.213	0.27
AO-LANCS	0.312	0.227	0.257	0.253	0.155	0.185

Table 7: ROUGE-L and ROUGE-SU4 on English dataset ordered by ROUGE-L F1 score

Appendix B - Greek Task Results

Model	R-1 / R	R-1 / P	R-1 / F	R-2 / R	R-2 / P	R-2 / F
SSC-AI-RG-3	0.34	0.442	0.381	0.14	0.296	0.185
SSC-AI-RG-1	0.34	0.442	0.381	0.14	0.296	0.185
SSC-AI-RG-2	0.34	0.442	0.381	0.14	0.296	0.185
LSIR-1	0.297	0.421	0.346	0.112	0.203	0.141
TREDENCE-1	0.154	0.574	0.234	0.097	0.321	0.138
TREDENCE-2	0.154	0.574	0.234	0.097	0.321	0.138
AO-LANCS	0.284	0.448	0.344	0.091	0.276	0.131
LSIR-3	0.26	0.404	0.315	0.106	0.177	0.13
LSIR-2	0.246	0.42	0.309	0.089	0.174	0.115
LSIR-4	0.248	0.418	0.309	0.09	0.169	0.115
IIC	0.215	0.473	0.294	0.063	0.215	0.095
TREDENCE-3	0.068	0.683	0.119	0.043	0.415	0.072
LIPI	0.101	0.625	0.17	0.026	0.33	0.046

Table 8: ROUGE-1 and ROUGE-2 on Greek dataset ordered by R2 F1 score

Model	R-L / R	R-L / P	R-L / F	R-SU4 / R	R-SU4 / P	R-SU4 / F
SSC-AI-RG-3	0.247	0.348	0.284	0.177	0.328	0.226
SSC-AI-RG-1	0.247	0.348	0.284	0.177	0.328	0.226
SSC-AI-RG-2	0.247	0.348	0.284	0.177	0.328	0.226
LSIR-1	0.234	0.319	0.267	0.151	0.253	0.186
AO-LANCS	0.208	0.341	0.252	0.134	0.31	0.182
LSIR-3	0.205	0.293	0.238	0.145	0.202	0.167
LSIR-4	0.185	0.299	0.225	0.134	0.205	0.16
LSIR-2	0.183	0.3	0.224	0.132	0.207	0.159
IIC	0.165	0.353	0.222	0.106	0.247	0.146
TREDENCE-1	0.138	0.641	0.217	0.105	0.351	0.15
TREDENCE-2	0.138	0.641	0.217	0.105	0.351	0.15
TREDENCE-3	0.084	0.672	0.144	0.046	0.439	0.077
LIPI	0.081	0.509	0.137	0.046	0.402	0.08

Table 9: ROUGE-L and ROUGE-SU4 on Greek dataset ordered by ROUGE-L F1 score

Appendix C - Spanish Task Results

Model	R-1 / R	R-1 / P	R-1 / F	R-2 / R	R-2 / P	R-2 / F
LSIR-1	0.54	0.425	0.466	0.177	0.147	0.157
SSC-AI-RG-3	0.505	0.419	0.449	0.167	0.136	0.146
SSC-AI-RG-1	0.505	0.419	0.449	0.167	0.136	0.146
SSC-AI-RG-2	0.505	0.419	0.449	0.167	0.136	0.146
LSIR-3	0.511	0.429	0.454	0.158	0.129	0.138
AO-LANCS	0.503	0.425	0.448	0.15	0.128	0.134
TREDENCE-2	0.445	0.506	0.438	0.134	0.149	0.131
TREDENCE-1	0.445	0.506	0.438	0.134	0.149	0.131
TREDENCE-3	0.445	0.506	0.438	0.134	0.149	0.131
LSIR-2	0.497	0.418	0.443	0.149	0.122	0.131
LSIR-4	0.501	0.421	0.449	0.144	0.118	0.128
IIC	0.396	0.488	0.407	0.122	0.155	0.125
LIPI	0.142	0.58	0.217	0.045	0.196	0.07

Table 10: ROUGE-1 and ROUGE-2 on Spanish dataset ordered by R2 F1 score

Model	R-L / R	R-L / P	R-L / F	R-SU4 / R	R-SU4 / P	R-SU4 / F
LSIR-1	0.259	0.226	0.238	0.264	0.222	0.236
TREDENCE-2	0.192	0.238	0.2	0.212	0.24	0.208
TREDENCE-1	0.192	0.238	0.2	0.212	0.24	0.208
TREDENCE-3	0.192	0.238	0.2	0.212	0.24	0.208
LSIR-3	0.183	0.162	0.168	0.249	0.201	0.217
SSC-AI-RG-3	0.178	0.167	0.168	0.25	0.201	0.218
SSC-AI-RG-1	0.178	0.167	0.168	0.25	0.201	0.218
SSC-AI-RG-2	0.178	0.167	0.168	0.25	0.201	0.218
LSIR-2	0.178	0.163	0.167	0.241	0.195	0.21
AO-LANCS	0.194	0.147	0.164	0.238	0.199	0.211
IIC	0.143	0.204	0.159	0.194	0.236	0.197
LSIR-4	0.171	0.152	0.159	0.238	0.192	0.209
LIPI	0.098	0.325	0.146	0.069	0.291	0.107

Table 11: ROUGE-L and ROUGE-SU4 on Spanish dataset ordered by ROUGE-L F1 score

Proceedings of the 4th Financial Narrative Processing Workshop @ LREC 2022, pages 53–58
Marseille, 24 June 2022

Multilingual Text Summarization on Financial Documents

Negar Foroutan*, Angelika Romanou*, Stéphane Massonnet, Rémi Lebret, Karl Aberer
École Polytechnique Fédérale de Lausanne (EPFL)
firstname.lastname@epfl.ch

Abstract

This paper proposes a multilingual Automated Text Summarization (ATS) method targeting the Financial Narrative Summarization Task (FNS-2022). We developed two systems; the first uses a pre-trained abstractive summarization model that was fine-tuned on the downstream objective, the second approaches the problem as an extractive approach in which a similarity search is performed on the trained span representations. Both models aim to identify the beginning of the continuous narrative section of the document. The language models were fine-tuned on a financial document collection of three languages (English, Spanish, and Greek) and aim to identify the beginning of the summary narrative part of the document. The proposed systems achieve high performance in the given task, with the sequence-to-sequence variant ranked 1st on ROUGE-2 F1 score on the test set for each of the three languages.

Keywords: multilingual text summarization, language models, natural language processing

1. Introduction

Machine Learning and Natural Language Processing have seen a tremendous increase in applications in the financial sector, mainly due to the need for automated approaches addressing financial tasks on both qualitative and quantitative data. Financial narrative summarization is a task that has drawn the attention of academia over the past couple of years with works regarding financial reports summarization (Suarez et al., 2020; Abdaljalil and Bouamor, 2021; Orzhenovskii, 2021) or financial news summarization (Passali et al., 2021). This is mainly because these computer-aided techniques could have an actual impact by saving considerable human manual annotation time and effort.

In this paper, we present our system regarding the Financial Narrative Summarization Shared Task [1] which aims to summarize the annual financial reports from international firms in three different languages: English, Greek, and Spanish. The input datasets are comprised of annual reports along with a set of human-curated summaries for each report, made by different annotators. Based on data statistics that will be presented in detail in Section 3, the summaries are created based on both extractive and abstractive approaches. This, along with the multilingual nature of the provided data, poses an additional level of difficulty on this specific task and paves the way for more sophisticated and holistic approaches to tackle these challenges.

We propose two distinct approaches to tackle the problem of Financial Narrative Summarization. Based on these, we implemented four systems that were tested and submitted to the shared task. All of the submitted systems leverage the fact that in the provided use case, the sentences that comprise the summary are usually extracted from the initial document in consecutive order. Therefore, we formulate the problem to identify the beginning of the summary in the document's corpus, following one abstractive and one extractive approach. In summary:

- **Sequence-to-sequence approach**: We use a pre-trained abstractive summarization model that is fine-tuned on the downstream task and aims to generate the start of the summaries.
- **Template-based approach**: We learn span representations from the financial documents in an unsupervised manner, and we apply similarity search on them to find suitable candidates for the summary start by building an index of summary templates.

The rest of the document is structured in the following manner: Section 2 presents the related work around text summarization and multilingual text representations. Section 3 describes the dataset used in this work. Section 4 presents the system created to deal this task. Section 5 presents the experiments and the results for each implemented model. Finally, Section 6 summarises the results and prompts for a discussion about future work and further applications.

2. Related Work

This section reviews the recent developments in Automated Text Summarization (ATS) and multilingual sentence embeddings and highlights the connection between our approach and the related literature.

2.1. Text summarization

There are two types of Automatic Text Summarization: Abstractive Summarization and Extractive Summarization. Automatic Text Summarization via the Extractive method constructs a summary by selecting the most pertinent sentences from the text and concatenating them. State-of-the-art extractive summarization methods use transformer based approaches modifying the

*Both authors contributed equally to this work.
[1] http://wp.lancs.ac.uk/cfie/fns2022/

BERT model (Liu and Lapata, 2019), proposing hierarchical encoder architectures (Liu and Lapata, 2019), as well as using summary-level representations (Zhong et al., 2020), leveraging the semantics of the entire summary. Automatic Text Summarization via the abstractive method consists of forming a summary inspired by human cognitive processes, understanding the text and writing a condensed version of it with minimal semantic loss. Important works around abstractive summarization involve the use of the encoder-decoder architecture for generating summaries in an auto-regressive manner (Liu and Lapata, 2019) and text generation (Lewis et al., 2019; Zhang et al., 2020). ATS has been applied in various use cases and domains with interesting academic work around news summarization (Sethi et al., 2017), biomedical document summarization (Azadani et al., 2018), legal document (Anand and Wagh, 2019) and scientific paper summarization (Alampalli Ramu et al., 2019). In this work, we use both extractive and abstractive summarization inspired by the literature, and we apply a custom filtering preprocessing procedure to the input data.

2.2. Multilingual Sentence Representations

Language models and transfer learning have become one of the cornerstones of natural language processing in recent years, especially in the context of machine translation and multilingual text representations. While some approaches were built for a single language or several languages separately, there is recent literature that demonstrates models trained on datasets that contain sentences from various languages, outperforming monolingual models in various multilingual benchmarks. Notable works propose methods to handle low-resource languages through zero-shot or few-shot cross-lingual transfer (Pfeiffer et al., 2020; Cao et al., 2020), as well as massive multilingual pretraining (Devlin et al., 2018; Xue et al., 2020) for both auto-encoder and auto-regressive models. Additionally, there has been a recent growing interest in using individual raw sentences for self-supervised constructive learning on top of pre-trained language models (Liu et al., 2021; Gao et al., 2021). In our case, we also use constructive learning in a multilingual setting to acquire multilingual representations of the summaries.

3. Dataset

The provided datasets included documents of financial reports along with a set of human-curated summaries. The corpora of the reports were extracted through Optical Character Recognition (OCR) from the original PDF documents. Each report in the English dataset had from three to seven respective gold summaries, whereas both the Greek and the Spanish reports had two respective gold summaries each. As presented in Table 1, the number of data samples for the English documents is far more than for the other two languages. This could pose a challenge when it comes to the fine-tuning of monolingual approaches. Motivated by this, instead of using a monolingual approach exclusively for each language, we also tested multilingual approaches on both the high resource language, English, and low resource languages, Greek and Spanish.

Language	**Split**	**Number of Documents**	
		Report	*Summary*
English	Train	3000	9873
	Validation	363	1250
	Test	500	1673
Greek	Train	162	324
	Validation	50	100
	Test	50	100
Spanish	Train	162	324
	Validation	50	100
	Test	50	100

Table 1: Datasets split sizes per language.

The lengths of the reports follow the same distribution in all languages with an average size of around 46500 tokens. However, the size of the gold summaries varies a lot among the three languages with the English and the Spanish datasets following the same distribution with a median size of around 775 tokens, and the Greek dataset around 1500 tokens.

Exploratory analysis was also made regarding the existence of the gold summary's sentences in the corresponding report as well as the position of the summary in the document. Based on these descriptive results, we found that for the English dataset, the summaries are extracted from the document in a continuous fashion. This signals that not only the summarization method was an extractive one, but also finding the start of the summary in the document and taking consecutive sentences someone can construct the gold summary with high accuracy performance. While this finding hints at an extractive way of formulating this text summarization problem, the rest of the datasets follow a different approach. For both the Greek and the Spanish cases, in more than 85% of the samples, the gold summary could not be found in the document which means that they are not a sequential subset of the reports and therefore an abstractive method might be more well suited. To tackle this heterogeneity of the datasets, we decided to apply different experiments that leverage the power of both sequence-to-sequence models as well as auto-encoding ones and apply them to the task of identifying the start of the summary in the documents.

4. System

In this section, we present in detail the two approaches that the submitted systems are based on and explain the methodology behind them.

4.1. Sequence-to-sequence approach

In this abstractive summarization approach, we used a pre-trained sequence-to-sequence model, fine-tuned on the provided dataset on the task of start-of-summary prediction (Orzhenovskii, 2021). To achieve this, at the inference time, the model performs a similarity search between the output generated from the model and each sentence of the document. It then locates the span that is the closest match in terms of token similarity and selects it as the beginning of the summary. Having this selected start point in the document, it constructs the summary by taking the 1000 consecutive words. We submitted two flavours of this approach; one that utilizes the multilingual power of the used sequence-to-sequence model and keeps the input data in its original format, and one that translates the Greek and Spanish data into English, runs inference and then translates back the generated summaries to their original languages.

4.2. Template-based approach

We also propose an extractive summarization using an unsupervised summary generation method to find the best start candidate in a report to begin the summary with. The motivation behind this approach is the assumption that the start of the golden summaries can be clustered into different templates, and for each report, we want to start the generated summary with a block of tokens similar to the existing templates in our training dataset. We achieve this by mapping the span representations of the reports and the start block of the summaries in the same embedding space using BERT-like models. First, we compute the representations of the first 64 tokens of each summary, and we cluster them using the k-means algorithm. Next, we extract all 64-token blocks of each report with a 32-token window and compute their representations. For each report, we then find the block with the highest cosine similarity to all the clusters' centroids and consider it the beginning of the summary. Similarly, as with the sequence-to-sequence approach, having the selected span representation as the start of the summary, we take 1000 consecutive words (in addition to the start-of-summary span) and construct the predicted summary for the document. Once again, we submitted two variants of this method, having as input the original data format as well as their translations (for Greek and Spanish).

5. Experiments & Results

We first evaluate the proposed template-based approach with different models to get span representations. Then, we compare the best template-based model with the pre-trained abstractive summarization model fine-tuned on the given task.

Lang	Model	Rouge-1	Rouge-2	Rouge-L
EN	mBERT	**0.4059**	**0.2570**	**0.3875**
	mDeBERTa	0.4012	0.2544	0.3824
	MAD-X^{mBERT}	**0.4059**	0.2548	0.3872
	Mirror-mBERT	0.4016	0.2525	0.3827
GR	mBERT	**0.1337**	0.0363	0.1259
	mDeBERTa	0.1267	0.0348	0.1179
	MAD-X^{mBERT}	0.1335	**0.0373**	**0.1264**
	Mirror-mBERT	0.1320	0.0360	0.1247
ES	mBERT	**0.2354**	**0.0984**	**0.2068**
	mDeBERTa	0.2180	0.0838	0.1900
	MAD-X^{mBERT}	0.2317	0.0978	0.2030
	Mirror-mBERT	0.2300	0.0968	0.2017

Table 2: Rouge F1 scores on the validation sets between the constructed summaries and the golden summaries for each language dataset using different backbone models for the template-based approach. Scores in bold are the best model for each language.

5.1. Unsupervised summary generation using span representations

5.1.1. Zero-shot setting

For the unsupervised summary generation case, we first used mBERT (Devlin et al., 2018) and mDeBERTa (He et al., 2021) as baseline models for the span representations. These are transformer-based models, pre-trained on a large corpus of multilingual data in a self-supervised fashion. Both of them are trained on the Mask Language Model objective, meaning that the model is asked to predict a masked token in a given text input. Consequently, they manage to learn bi-directional representations of the input sentences. We used these pre-trained models on all languages without any fine-tuning on the datasets. We used the average of the text's tokens output embeddings as span representations. For the k-means algorithm, we ran experiments with $k = 1, 3, 5, 10$ and reported the results with the highest validation Rouge F1 score, which were obtained with $k = 10$.

5.1.2. Fine-tuned setting

Additionally, we fined-tuned and tested two transformer-based models: Mirror-BERT (Liu et al., 2021) and MAD-X (Pfeiffer et al., 2020). Mirror-BERT leverages the contrastive learning technique and is trained on fully identical or slightly modified text span pairs as positive fine-tuning examples while maximizing their similarity during identity fine-tuning. In our experiments, we used the same implementation and training setup introduced by the authors of the Mirror-BERT paper[2] (Liu et al., 2021), using mBERT. MAD-X is an adapter-based framework that enables high parameter-efficient transfer to arbitrary tasks and languages by learning modular language and task representations. In our experiments, we used the

[2] https://github.com/cambridgeltl/mirror-bert

mBERT version of the MAD-X, and we fine-tuned a separate adapter for each language. We used the same training setup suggested by AdapterHub [3]. We used both of the models to get the span representations and then applied the method proposed in Section 4.

5.1.3. Experimental Results

Results for the unsupervised extractive summarization approach can be found in Table 2. There is no a significant difference in terms of Rouge scores between the different models to get the span representations. We can however notice that the scores for English are much higher than the two other languages. That could be explained by the limited number of samples provided for both Greek and Spanish. As noticed in Section 3, the distribution of the summaries in Greek is slightly different from the other two. Such a singularity could potentially explained why the performance in Greek are the lowest. As the performance obtained with mBERT are marginally better than with the other models, we decided to select that model for the shared task.

5.2. Unsupervised vs supervised learning

For the sequence-to-sequence modeling, we used the mT5 (Xue et al., 2020) model, which is a massively multilingual pre-trained text-to-text transformer model. mT5 is a multilingual extension of T5 (Raffel et al., 2020) that was pre-trained on a new Common Crawl-based dataset covering 101 (mC4). In our experiments, we used the same data preparation pipeline and training setup as (Orzhenovskii, 2021). The only difference is the maximum source length, which is set to 3900 due to limited GPU memory. In Table 3, we compare the performance of fine-tuned mT5 with the best unsupervised model, which is obtained with mBERT. The supervised approach significantly outperforms the unsupervised approach in English, but we can see that both approaches obtained similar performance in Greek and Spanish. Such a result is a good indicator that the unsupervised approach is a promising alternative to the computationally expensive sequence-to-sequence modeling approach when the number of training samples is quite limited. As the results with mT5 on English were however significantly better, we decided to submit this system to the shared task.

Further experiments were conducting following a slightly different approach by formulating the problem as a span classification task. In this case, we select a beginning span from the summaries and spans from documents that are not present in the respective summaries, and perform span classification on whether the span is a start-of-summary or not. For this classification task, we used a monolingual BERT-like model that is trained on the respective language of the dataset. Therefore, we used BERT (Devlin et al., 2018), Greek-BERT (Koutsikakis et al., 2020) and BETO (Canete et al., 2020) for the English, Greek and Spanish respectively. These approaches were not the final submission to the task since their performance was substantially inferior that the rest of the implemented systems.

[3]https://github.com/Adapter-Hub/adapter-transformers

Lang	Model	Rouge-1	Rouge-2	Rouge-L
EN	mBERT	0.4059	0.2570	0.3875
	mT5	**0.4402**	**0.3014**	**0.4236**
GR	mBERT	**0.1337**	0.0363	**0.1259**
	mT5	0.1336	**0.0367**	0.1258
ES	mBERT	**0.2354**	**0.0984**	**0.2068**
	mT5	0.2259	0.0921	0.1970

Table 3: Rouge F1 scores on the validation sets between the sequence-to-sequence approach (mT5) and the proposed unsupervised generation approach based on mBERT. Scores in bold are the best obtained for each language.

Lang	Model	Rouge-1	Rouge-2	Rouge-L
EN	mBERT	0.451	0.275	0.425
	mT5	**0.489**	**0.365**	**0.479**
GR	mBERT	0.315	0.130	0.238
	mT5	**0.346**	**0.141**	**0.267**
	English-based model with translation			
	mBERT	0.309	0.115	0.225
	mT5	0.309	0.115	0.224
ES	mBERT	0.454	0.138	0.168
	mT5	**0.466**	**0.157**	**0.238**
	English-based model with translation			
	mBERT	0.449	0.128	0.159
	mT5	0.443	0.131	0.167

Table 4: Rouge F1 scores on the test sets between the constructed summaries and the golden summaries for each language dataset. Scores in bold are the best obtained for each language.

5.3. Results on the Shared Task

On the test set from the shared task, the results reported in Table 4 show that the mT5 outperforms our proposed unsupervised approach in all the provided languages. Given the fact that mT5 is a supervised model trained on a massive multilingual dataset and later fine-tuned on the task's training dataset, its superiority was expected. However, our unsupervised approach shows a promising performance considering that the models in this approach do not have any understanding of the summarization task. Such a method can be a practical solution in a data-limited scenario. Additionally, as expected, using the translation of Greek and Spanish reports as the inputs is inferior to using the original form. This observation could be explained by the fact that translation from these languages to English and then from English back to them introduce a new error to the problem, especially since the extracted text from the pdf documents can be quite noisy. Also, as Greek and Spanish contributed to the pre-training phase of both mBERT and mT5, it was expected for these models to perform better compared to the translated ones on the original data.

6. Conclusion & Future work

In this paper, we submitted an automated document summarization solution for multilingual financial reports. We proposed two approaches: one based on the multilingual sequence-to-sequence model mT5 and one using unsupervised summary generation by identifying the templates of the beginning of the summaries. Experiments have shown that overall, this task heavily relies on the way summarization is happened by the dataset curators and aims for dataset-dependent preprocessing mechanisms. The presented results also made apparent the trade-off between the monolingual and the multilingual approaches showing that in low resource datasets, it might be better to employ transfer learning from a pre-trained multilingual model that relies on fine-tuning.

A potential extension to our work is to formulate this setting as a multi-task problem and deploy a method that can be extended beyond the modeling of the beginning of the narrative section. Additionally, a challenge that remains to be tackled is to find a more efficient way to remove the OCR noise from the datasets at the preprocessing step. Moreover, an interesting application would be to use a hybrid model that can handle the extractive and abstractive fashion of the datasets. Lastly, it would be insightful to see experimental results on the Financial Narrative Summarization task with language model augmentation approaches that leverage both the entities and factuality of the input text.

7. Bibliographical References

Abdaljalil, S. and Bouamor, H. (2021). An exploration of automatic text summarization of financial reports. In *Proceedings of the Third Workshop on Financial Technology and Natural Language Processing*, pages 1–7.

Alampalli Ramu, N., Bandarupalli, M. S., Nekkanti, M. S. S., and Ramesh, G. (2019). Summarization of research publications using automatic extraction. In *International Conference on Intelligent Data Communication Technologies and Internet of Things*, pages 1–10. Springer.

Anand, D. and Wagh, R. (2019). Effective deep learning approaches for summarization of legal texts. *Journal of King Saud University-Computer and Information Sciences*.

Azadani, M. N., Ghadiri, N., and Davoodijam, E. (2018). Graph-based biomedical text summarization: An itemset mining and sentence clustering approach. *Journal of biomedical informatics*, 84:42–58.

Canete, J., Chaperon, G., Fuentes, R., Ho, J.-H., Kang, H., and Pérez, J. (2020). Spanish pre-trained bert model and evaluation data. *Pml4dc at iclr*, 2020:2020.

Cao, S., Kitaev, N., and Klein, D. (2020). Multilingual alignment of contextual word representations. *arXiv preprint arXiv:2002.03518*.

Devlin, J., Chang, M.-W., Lee, K., and Toutanova, K. (2018). Bert: Pre-training of deep bidirectional transformers for language understanding. *arXiv preprint arXiv:1810.04805*.

Gao, T., Yao, X., and Chen, D. (2021). Simcse: Simple contrastive learning of sentence embeddings. *arXiv preprint arXiv:2104.08821*.

He, P., Gao, J., and Chen, W. (2021). Debertav3: Improving deberta using electra-style pretraining with gradient-disentangled embedding sharing. *arXiv preprint arXiv:2111.09543*.

Koutsikakis, J., Chalkidis, I., Malakasiotis, P., and Androutsopoulos, I. (2020). Greek-bert: The greeks visiting sesame street. In *11th Hellenic Conference on Artificial Intelligence*, pages 110–117.

Lewis, M., Liu, Y., Goyal, N., Ghazvininejad, M., Mohamed, A., Levy, O., Stoyanov, V., and Zettlemoyer, L. (2019). Bart: Denoising sequence-to-sequence pre-training for natural language generation, translation, and comprehension. *arXiv preprint arXiv:1910.13461*.

Liu, Y. and Lapata, M. (2019). Text summarization with pretrained encoders. *arXiv preprint arXiv:1908.08345*.

Liu, F., Vulić, I., Korhonen, A., and Collier, N. (2021). Fast, effective, and self-supervised: Transforming masked language models into universal lexical and sentence encoders. *arXiv preprint arXiv:2104.08027*.

Orzhenovskii, M. (2021). T5-long-extract at fns-2021 shared task. In *Proceedings of the 3rd Financial Narrative Processing Workshop*, pages 67–69.

Passali, T., Gidiotis, A., Chatzikyriakidis, E., and Tsoumakas, G. (2021). Towards human-centered summarization: A case study on financial news. In *Proceedings of the First Workshop on Bridging Human–Computer Interaction and Natural Language Processing*, pages 21–27.

Pfeiffer, J., Vulić, I., Gurevych, I., and Ruder, S. (2020). Mad-x: An adapter-based framework for multi-task cross-lingual transfer. *arXiv preprint arXiv:2005.00052*.

Raffel, C., Shazeer, N., Roberts, A., Lee, K., Narang, S., Matena, M., Zhou, Y., Li, W., and Liu, P. J. (2020). Exploring the limits of transfer learning with a unified text-to-text transformer. *Journal of Machine Learning Research*, 21(140):1–67.

Sethi, P., Sonawane, S., Khanwalker, S., and Keskar, R. (2017). Automatic text summarization of news articles. In *2017 International Conference on Big Data, IoT and Data Science (BID)*, pages 23–29. IEEE.

Suarez, J. B., Martínez, P., and Martínez, J. L. (2020). Combining financial word embeddings and knowledge-based features for financial text summarization uc3m-mc system at fns-2020. In *Proceedings of the 1st Joint Workshop on Financial Narrative Processing and MultiLing Financial Summarisation*, pages 112–117.

Xue, L., Constant, N., Roberts, A., Kale, M., Al-Rfou, R., Siddhant, A., Barua, A., and Raffel, C. (2020). mt5: A massively multilingual pre-trained text-to-text transformer. *arXiv preprint arXiv:2010.11934*.

Zhang, J., Zhao, Y., Saleh, M., and Liu, P. (2020). Pegasus: Pre-training with extracted gap-sentences for abstractive summarization. In *International Conference on Machine Learning*, pages 11328–11339. PMLR.

Zhong, M., Liu, P., Chen, Y., Wang, D., Qiu, X., and Huang, X. (2020). Extractive summarization as text matching. *arXiv preprint arXiv:2004.08795*.

Proceedings of the 4th Financial Narrative Processing Workshop @ LREC 2022, pages 59–64
Marseille, 24 June 2022

Extractive and Abstractive Summarization Methods for Financial Narrative Summarization in English, Spanish and Greek

Alejandro Vaca, Alba Segurado, David Betancur, Álvaro Barbero*
IIC (Instituto de Ingeniería del Conocimiento)
* Universidad Autónoma de Madrid
{alejandro.vaca, alba.segurado, david.betancur, alvaro.barbero}@iic.uam.es

Abstract

This paper describes the three summarization systems submitted to the Financial Narrative Summarization Shared Task (FNS-2022). We developed a task-specific extractive summarization method for the reports in English. It was based on a sequence classification task whose objective was to find the sentence where the summary begins. On the other hand, since the summaries for the reports in Spanish and Greek were not extractive, we used an abstractive strategy for each of the languages. In particular, we created a new Encoder-Decoder architecture in Spanish, MariMari, based on an existing Encoding-only model; we also trained multilingual Encoder-Decoder models for this task. Finally, the summaries for the reports in Greek were obtained with a translation-summary-translation system in which the reports were translated to English and summarised, and then the summaries were translated back to Greek.

Keywords: Extractive Summarization, Abstractive Summarization, Multilingual Models, Encoder-Decoder

1. Introduction

Given the increasing availability and volume of financial information, the development of summarization algorithms that can provide short yet accurate information is of significant practical interest. To this end, the Financial Narrative Summarization (FNS)[1] challenge (Zmandar et al., 2022) intends to raise the quality of automated text summarization methods for the financial domain, for the Greek, English and Spanish languages. One of the main challenges for this task was the average length of the given annual reports (several dozens of pages), which made the training process extremely time consuming. In addition, the texts were extracted from PDF files with tables, charts, and numerical data, which resulted in poor, noisy inputs.

2. Past Work

The participating systems of previous editions of the challenge used techniques and methods ranging from rule-based extraction methods to high-performing deep learning models and word embeddings, including fine tuning pre-trained transformers models. Some teams investigated the hierarchy of the reports to select the narrative sections and identify the parts where the gold standard summaries were extracted. Participants applied techniques such as the Determinant Point Processes sampling algorithm (Kulesza and Taskar, 2012) or a combination of Pointer Network (Vinyals et al., 2015) and T5 (Raffel et al., 2019) algorithms. Others used word embeddings such as BERT embeddings (Devlin et al., 2018), word2vec, CBOW and skip grams ((Mikolov et al., 2013b), (Mikolov et al., 2013a)).

The best method in the previous edition (Orzhenovskii, 2021) was based on T5 (Raffel et al., 2019). The model was fine-tuned to generate the beginning of an abstractive summary and find the closest match of the output in the report's full text. The author also found intelligent insights in the data which simplified the problem, and much of our data treatment was based on those ideas.

3. Methodology

In this section we describe the different methodologies for each of the proposed languages. First, a preliminary analysis regarding the summaries with respect to the original reports they come from is presented, together with some considerations from the data analysis and exploration. Then, summarization models are explained for all three languages.

3.1. Previous Analysis and Considerations

We begin our analysis with the reports in English. In this case, as the summaries were extractive, a proper analysis was performed to detect where they began. For each report, a sentence tokenization was implemented using nltk's (Bird et al., 2009) *sent_tokenize* module. After the tokenization, the summaries were compared to the gold standard and the position where the gold included the sentence was saved. A few gold standards were given in the task but only the first one was used following the results on last year's competition (Orzhenovskii, 2021). In Figure 1 we can observe that very few reports start their summary after the 150-200th sentence. We performed this analysis based on the insights obtained by (Orzhenovskii, 2021). This can be used to optimize further processes as summaries usually start before the 250th sentence. The mean of the beginnings was between sentence 39 and 40.

[1]The FNS challenge is part of the 4th Financial Narrative Processing Workshop

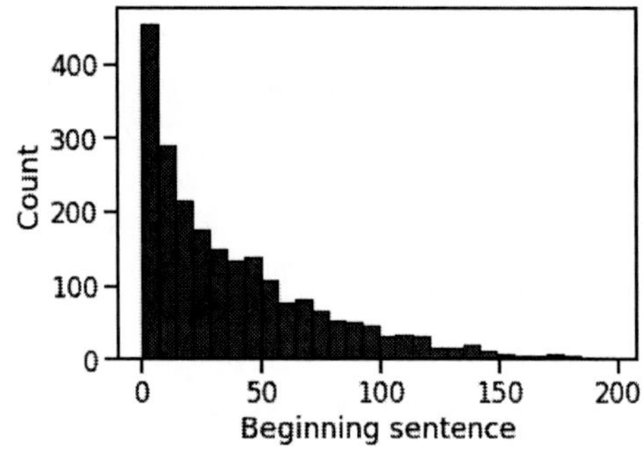

Figure 1: Histogram of beginnings of summaries for the English task.

As Spanish and Greek summaries were abstractive, no further analysis and considerations were taken into account.

3.2. Models

In this section we introduce the summarization models we used for this task, separately for each language.

3.2.1. English

For the English language, financial summaries are mostly CEO letters explaining the general results of the company as stated in the financial report. This means that summaries are literally contained in the original text, therefore the solution to this task could be extractive. This greatly simplifies the problem of generating the summaries, as no abstractive generative model is needed. The task is therefore reduced to finding where the summary (the CEO letter) starts and ends. Before this, a simpler approach was tried, based on classifying whether each sentence is part of the summary or not. This, however, proved to be too simplistic, therefore the alternative strategy was used.

There are various approaches to finding the start and end of the summary in the original text. One possible approach is to frame the summarization problem as a token classification task, where all tokens are null except for summary start and end tokens. This, however, poses a difficult learning problem. The learning signal becomes too sparse, since only one start and one end token are present in each document.

In this work we propose solving this task as a sequence classification problem, where the objective is to find the sentence where the summary starts. Given the distribution of real summaries in the train set, where it was observed that many of them were longer than 1000 words, and the workshop restriction of 1000 words per summary, the end of summaries was heuristically selected by taking the next 1000 words after the start of the beginning sentence predicted by our model.

The following procedure was used to build the training dataset for our model. The objective was to provide the model not only with the sentence to analyze, but also with the surrounding ones, in order to give the model more context to decide whether that sentence is the start of the summary or not. To this end, we picked surrounding sentences (both preceding and following the sentence being processed) until the token limit of our model (512 tokens) is reached.

A special `[SEP]` token is added to mark the boundaries of the sentence that should be classified by the model, thus producing a text in the form "Sentences previous to the query. All sentences we can fit. `[SEP]` Sentence being processed `[SEP]` Sentences following the sentence to analyze. Can also be more than one; All sentences we can fit". This way, the model can contextualize the sentence being processed at the moment.

The model used for this task was Deberta-V3-large (He et al., 2021), as it performs significantly better than the rest of the Encoder-based large models (the ones most suitable for a classification task like this one). In (He et al., 2021), a comparative table for GLUE tasks against BERT (Devlin et al., 2018), RoBERTa (Liu et al., 2019), XLNET (Yang et al., 2019), ELECTRA (Clark et al., 2020) and DeBERTa (He et al., 2020) is presented, showing that it is the best performing model in 7 out of 8 tasks.

To easen the classification task, some heuristics based on the preliminary analysis of the data were also applied. As it was identified that summaries start mostly between sentences 7 and 200, only the first 250 sentences from each financial report were considered, both on the training and testing sets. This greatly accelerated training time and reduced the time needed for generating predictions. This was especially relevant, given the size of the original financial reports. Moreover, this avoided predictions of starting positions beyond the 250th sentence and therefore unlikely according to the distribution observed in the training and validation splits.

Regarding the hyperparameters used to train the model, we performed preliminary experiments using the hyperparameter spaces from (He et al., 2021), and then launched the final run with the best configuration found.

3.2.2. Spanish

In the case of Spanish, summaries were not extractive, and that made the task much harder than in English. Original texts were of similar length as English ones, but in this case no classification model could be used. As, given the existing technology, it was not possible to use whole financial reports to learn to generate whole CEO letters, a full transfer learning approach was followed. This procedure consisted of using the Spanish portion of a multilingual summaries dataset to train different models. Details about the training data and results will be specified in the Experiments section.

For abstractive summarization tasks, an Encoder-Decoder architecture such as BART (Lewis et al., 2019), Pegasus (Zhang et al., 2019), Prophetnet (Yan

Hyperparameter	Values
Learning Rate	(3e-5, 7e-5, log)
Num Train Epochs	7
Train Batch Size	{32, 64, 128}
Warmup Steps	{50, 100, 500, 1000}
Weight Decay	(0.0, 0.1)

Table 1: Hyperparameter space for abstractive summarization models in Spanish.

et al., 2020) or T5 (Raffel et al., 2019) is needed. However, there are no such models trained in Spanish, therefore other approaches were tried. On the one hand, two multilingual Encoder-Decoder models were trained. On the other hand, a new Encoder-Decoder model was created from an existing Encoder-only model.
As for the hyperparameters, Optuna (Akiba et al., 2019) was used for finding the best hyperparameter set. For each model, the hyperparameter space in table 1 was used for looking for the best setting.

3.2.2.1 MT5

MT5 (Xue et al., 2020) is a multilingual variant of T5 (Raffel et al., 2019) that was pre-trained on a new Common Crawl-based dataset covering 101 languages, on multiple tasks, including abstractive text summarization. We fine-tuned the MT5 model on the Spanish portion of the MLSUM dataset (Scialom et al., 2020), to predict the concatenation of the title and the summary of each item in the dataset. We made the fine-tuned model available[2] at the huggingface hub.

3.2.2.2 XLM-Prophetnet

XLM-Prophetnet (Yan et al., 2020) is a cross-lingual version of ProphetNet, pretrained on wiki100 xGLUE dataset (Liang et al., 2020). Prophetnet is an Encoder-Decoder architecture suitable for sequence-to-sequence tasks. In English, it is able to perform similarly to BART (Lewis et al., 2019), T5 (Raffel et al., 2019), or Pegasus (Zhang et al., 2019) on abstractive summarization tasks, therefore its multilingual version is expected to work decently for the task proposed in this work. In this work, a fine-tuned version on the Spanish portion of MLSUM dataset[3] was made publicly available.

3.2.2.3 MariMari

(Rothe et al., 2019) propose to use already trained only-Encoder language models to create new Encoder-Decoder architectures from them. Their hypothesis is that much of the knowledge of such models could be reused for NLG tasks, given their great language modeling results and their good performance in NLU tasks. For that, two Encoder models are used, one as the Encoder and the other as the Decoder, including some cross-attention weights from one to the other.
Although there are no high-performing, openly available Encoder-Decoder models in Spanish, there are several Encoder-only models. After studying the different alternatives, which were compared in (Gutiérrez-Fandiño et al., 2021), we decided to use the Roberta-base from (Gutiérrez-Fandiño et al., 2021), also known as *MarIA*. Since our model is made up of two *MarIA* models, we decided to name it in a befitting way as *MariMari*. Moreover, Encoder-Decoder versions of BETO (Cañete et al., 2020), a Spanish BERT, had already been published, therefore we had a model to compare our own results against.
In (Rothe et al., 2019) the authors tested different configurations for their Encoder-Decoder models. Authors report the best configuration is to tie weights of the Encoder and the Decoder, which also has the advantage of saving GPU memory; therefore we followed this recommended configuration when training MariMari. We also made this model [4] openly available in the Huggingface Hub.

3.2.3. Greek

For the Greek language, the challenge was the lack of models available and the short time to train a big, state-of-the-art Greek language model. Also the debugging of the models posed an additional challenge, as no member of the team was a Greek speaker.
In order to tackle this, our approach consisted of a translation-summary-translation system that uses an existing Greek-English translation novel model (Tiedemann and Thottingal, 2020) based on MarianMT framework (Junczys-Dowmunt et al., 2018) and an English BART (Lewis et al., 2019) model which is particularly effective on summarization, translation and text generation in general. The checkpoint of the BART model used was fine-tuned on CNN Daily Mail, a large collection of text-summary pairs which suits our need on this specific task.
The last step on the task is the translation back to Greek. For this task, the DeepL API (DeepL, 2022) was used as the transformers-based solution by (Tiedemann and Thottingal, 2020) generated poor quality outputs such as continuously repeated or non-existing words.

4. Experiments and Results.

This section focuses mainly on the systems for English and Spanish, as these were the two languages for which experiments were carried out. For Greek, as explained in previous section, we decided to use already available methods without further training.

[2]https://huggingface.co/IIC/mt5-spanish-mlsum

[3]https://huggingface.co/IIC/xprophetnet-spanish-mlsum

[4]https://huggingface.co/IIC/marimari-r2r-mlsum

model	rouge1	rouge2	rougeL	rougeLsum
MT5	21.98	6.52	17.74	18.98
XML-Prophetnet	25.12	8.48	20.62	19.65
Mari-Mari	**28.78**	**10.67**	**23.04**	**25.78**
beto2beto	25.86	8.91	21.24	21.59

Table 2: Results on the test set of MLSUM for the MT5, XML-Prophetnet and Mari-Mari models presented in this work and the exisiting beto2beto model. Higher is better.

model	rouge1	rouge2	rougeL	rougeLsum
Mari-Mari	30.85	**10.36**	**14.92**	**29.35**
XLM-Prophetnet	**31.67**	10.10	14.74	27.51
MT5	30.38	9.12	14.31	28.03
beto2beto	31.50	9.97	14.56	27.69

Table 3: Results on the Spanish validation set of FNS for the MT5, XML-Prophetnet and Mari-Mari models presented in this paper and the exisiting beto2beto model. Higher is better.

4.1. Abstractive Summarization on MLSUM for Spanish

Our summarization models were trained on the Spanish portion of MLSUM (Scialom et al., 2020), since it is a large collection of text-summary pairs. We show the results of our models, and also of the model beto2beto-mlsum[5], on the test set of MLSUM, in Table 2.

We first report results on the test set of MLSUM, and then present results for the validation set of the FNS in Spanish.

We proceeded as follows. Once all three models were trained on MLSUM (Scialom et al., 2020), we split the reports into shorter segments that we could input in the models and produced summaries of each of the segments. If the concatenation of the resulting summaries was too long, we repeated the procedure with the summaries.

The summaries were also postprocessed, since the models had learnt certain sentences that were repeated throughout the MLSUM dataset.

Finally, we chose the Mari-Mari model, since the resulting summaries had higher scores on the validation set.

Table 3 shows the results of the three fine-tuned models on the Spanish validation set.

4.2. Binary Classification for Summary Start Detection in English.

The task for the English model is a binary classification task, of whether the current sentence starts or not the summary, therefore it is highly unbalanced, as only one sentence per report has label 1. For this reason, f1-macro (Opitz and Burst, 2019) is the metric selected to evaluate this model. Note that even when the model fails to detect the summary start correctly, if the start sentence predicted and the real one are close enough the resulting Rouge metric (Lin, 2004) on the summary will not be too penalized.

Table 4 shows results for Deberta-V3-large (He et al., 2021) on the validation set of FNS, in terms of F1-macro in detecting the start of the summaries.

[5]https://huggingface.co/LeoCordoba/beto2beto-mlsum

Metric	Deberta-v3-large
F1-Macro	**0.6989**

Table 4: F1-Macro for Deberta-v3-large on validation set of FNS.

	English	Spanish	Greek
ROUGE 2	36.6	12.5	9.5

Table 5: Results (ROUGE 2 F1 scores) on the test sets of our models, provided by the FNS organizers. Higher is better.

4.3. Results on the test sets

Table 5 shows the results (ROUGE 2 F1 scores) of our three models on the test sets (provided by the FNS organizers).

5. Conclusions

In this work we present several solutions for the FNS task of FNP 2022. First, extractive summarization models were trained in English. For that, most relevant Encoder-only language models in English were reviewed, selecting Deberta-v3-large in the end due to its effectiveness in English benchmarks.

A different approach was followed for Spanish and Greek. For Spanish, three different abstractive summarization models were trained, and their results are reported, both on the test set of MLSUM and the validation set of FNS. They are also compared against beto2beto, an existing model of similar size and architecture as the ones presented. Finally, for Greek, pretrained summarization models in English were used, together with automatic translation.

6. Acknowledgements

We would like to acknowledge the Cátedra of Computational Linguistics from Universidad Autónoma de Madrid [6] for letting us use their machines to train the extractive and abstractive summarization models.

7. Bibliographical References

Akiba, T., Sano, S., Yanase, T., Ohta, T., and Koyama, M. (2019). Optuna: A next-generation hyperparameter optimization framework. *CoRR*, abs/1907.10902.

[6]http://catedras.iic.uam.es/catedra-linguistica-computacional/

Bird, S., Klein, E., and Loper, E. (2009). *Natural language processing with Python: analyzing text with the natural language toolkit.* " O'Reilly Media, Inc.".

Cañete, J., Chaperon, G., Fuentes, R., Ho, J.-H., Kang, H., and Pérez, J. (2020). Spanish pre-trained bert model and evaluation data. In *PML4DC at ICLR 2020*.

Clark, K., Luong, M., Le, Q. V., and Manning, C. D. (2020). ELECTRA: pre-training text encoders as discriminators rather than generators. *CoRR*, abs/2003.10555.

DeepL. (2022). Deepl api. `https://www.deepl.com/es/docs-api`. Accessed: 2022-04-13.

Devlin, J., Chang, M., Lee, K., and Toutanova, K. (2018). BERT: pre-training of deep bidirectional transformers for language understanding. *CoRR*, abs/1810.04805.

Gutiérrez-Fandiño, A., Armengol-Estapé, J., Pàmies, M., Llop-Palao, J., Silveira-Ocampo, J., Carrino, C. P., Gonzalez-Agirre, A., Armentano-Oller, C., Penagos, C. R., and Villegas, M. (2021). Spanish language models. *CoRR*, abs/2107.07253.

He, P., Liu, X., Gao, J., and Chen, W. (2020). Deberta: Decoding-enhanced BERT with disentangled attention. *CoRR*, abs/2006.03654.

He, P., Gao, J., and Chen, W. (2021). Debertav3: Improving deberta using electra-style pre-training with gradient-disentangled embedding sharing. *CoRR*, abs/2111.09543.

Junczys-Dowmunt, M., Grundkiewicz, R., Dwojak, T., Hoang, H., Heafield, K., Neckermann, T., Seide, F., Germann, U., Aji, A. F., Bogoychev, N., Martins, A. F. T., and Birch, A. (2018). Marian: Fast neural machine translation in C++. In *Proceedings of ACL 2018, System Demonstrations*, pages 116–121, Melbourne, Australia, July. Association for Computational Linguistics.

Kulesza, A. and Taskar, B. (2012). *Determinantal Point Processes for Machine Learning*. Now Publishers Inc., Hanover, MA, USA.

Lewis, M., Liu, Y., Goyal, N., Ghazvininejad, M., Mohamed, A., Levy, O., Stoyanov, V., and Zettlemoyer, L. (2019). BART: denoising sequence-to-sequence pre-training for natural language generation, translation, and comprehension. *CoRR*, abs/1910.13461.

Liang, Y., Duan, N., Gong, Y., Wu, N., Guo, F., Qi, W., Gong, M., Shou, L., Jiang, D., Cao, G., Fan, X., Zhang, B., Agrawal, R., Cui, E., Wei, S., Bharti, T., Qiao, Y., Chen, J., Wu, W., Liu, S., Yang, F., Majumder, R., and Zhou, M. (2020). XGLUE: A new benchmark dataset for cross-lingual pre-training, understanding and generation. *CoRR*, abs/2004.01401.

Lin, C.-Y. (2004). ROUGE: A package for automatic evaluation of summaries. In *Text Summarization Branches Out*, pages 74–81, Barcelona, Spain, July. Association for Computational Linguistics.

Liu, Y., Ott, M., Goyal, N., Du, J., Joshi, M., Chen, D., Levy, O., Lewis, M., Zettlemoyer, L., and Stoyanov, V. (2019). Roberta: A robustly optimized BERT pretraining approach. *CoRR*, abs/1907.11692.

Mikolov, T., Chen, K., Corrado, G., and Dean, J. (2013a). Efficient estimation of word representations in vector space. *CoRR*, abs/1301.3781.

Mikolov, T., Sutskever, I., Chen, K., Corrado, G., and Dean, J. (2013b). Distributed representations of words and phrases and their compositionality. In *Proceedings of the 26th International Conference on Neural Information Processing Systems - Volume 2*, NIPS'13, page 3111–3119, Red Hook, NY, USA. Curran Associates Inc.

Opitz, J. and Burst, S. (2019). Macro F1 and macro F1. *CoRR*, abs/1911.03347.

Orzhenovskii, M. (2021). T5-LONG-EXTRACT at FNS-2021 shared task. In *Proceedings of the 3rd Financial Narrative Processing Workshop*, pages 67–69, Lancaster, United Kingdom, 15-16 September. Association for Computational Linguistics.

Raffel, C., Shazeer, N., Roberts, A., Lee, K., Narang, S., Matena, M., Zhou, Y., Li, W., and Liu, P. J. (2019). Exploring the limits of transfer learning with a unified text-to-text transformer. *CoRR*, abs/1910.10683.

Rothe, S., Narayan, S., and Severyn, A. (2019). Leveraging pre-trained checkpoints for sequence generation tasks. *CoRR*, abs/1907.12461.

Scialom, T., Dray, P.-A., Lamprier, S., Piwowarski, B., and Staiano, J. (2020). Mlsum: The multilingual summarization corpus. *arXiv preprint arXiv:2004.14900*.

Tiedemann, J. and Thottingal, S. (2020). OPUS-MT – building open translation services for the world. In *Proceedings of the 22nd Annual Conference of the European Association for Machine Translation*, pages 479–480, Lisboa, Portugal, November. European Association for Machine Translation.

Vinyals, O., Fortunato, M., and Jaitly, N. (2015). Pointer networks. In C. Cortes, et al., editors, *Advances in Neural Information Processing Systems*, volume 28. Curran Associates, Inc.

Xue, L., Constant, N., Roberts, A., Kale, M., Al-Rfou, R., Siddhant, A., Barua, A., and Raffel, C. (2020). mt5: A massively multilingual pre-trained text-to-text transformer. *CoRR*, abs/2010.11934.

Yan, Y., Qi, W., Gong, Y., Liu, D., Duan, N., Chen, J., Zhang, R., and Zhou, M. (2020). Prophetnet: Predicting future n-gram for sequence-to-sequence pre-training. *CoRR*, abs/2001.04063.

Yang, Z., Dai, Z., Yang, Y., Carbonell, J. G., Salakhutdinov, R., and Le, Q. V. (2019). Xlnet: Generalized autoregressive pretraining for language understanding. *CoRR*, abs/1906.08237.

Zhang, J., Zhao, Y., Saleh, M., and Liu, P. J. (2019). PEGASUS: pre-training with extracted gap-sentences for abstractive summarization. *CoRR*, abs/1912.08777.

Zmandar, N., El-Haj, M., Rayson, P., Abura'Ed, A., Litvak, M., Giannakopoulos, G., Pittaras, N., Carbajo-Coronado, B., and Moreno-Sandoval, A. (2022). The financial narrative summarisation shared task (fns 2022). In *Proceedings of the 4th Financial Narrative Processing Workshop*, Marseille, France, 24June. The 13th Language Resources and Evaluation Conference, LREC 2022.

Proceedings of the 4th Financial Narrative Processing Workshop @ LREC 2022, pages 65–72
Marseille, 24 June 2022

DiMSum: Distributed and Multilingual Summarization of Financial Narratives

Neelesh K Shukla, Amit Vaid, Raghu C Katikeri, Sangeeth Keeriyadath, Msp Raja
State Street Corporation
Bengaluru, India
{nshukla, avaid, rkatikeri, skeeriyadath, smaddila1}@statestreet.com

Abstract

This paper was submitted for Financial Narrative Summarization (FNS) task in FNP-2022 workshop. The objective of the task was to generate not more than 1000 words summaries for the annual financial reports written in English, Spanish and Greek languages. The central idea of this paper is to demonstrate automatic ways of identifying key narrative sections and their contributions towards generating summaries of financial reports. We have observed a few limitations in the previous works: First, the complete report was being considered for summary generation instead of key narrative sections. Second, many of the works followed manual or heuristic-based techniques to identify narrative sections. Third, sentences from key narrative sections were abruptly dropped to limit the summary to the desired length. To overcome these shortcomings, we introduced a novel approach to automatically learn key narrative sections and their weighted contributions to the reports. Since the summaries may come from various parts of the reports, the summary generation process was distributed amongst the key narrative sections based on the weights identified, later combined to have an overall summary. We also showcased that our approach is adaptive to various report formats and languages.

Keywords: distributed, financial, narrative, summarization, multilingual

1. Introduction

With increased liberalization across the globe and the sprawling of organizations competing in multiple and varied overlapping sectors, a holistic comparison, and contrast of annual financial reports are in greater demand. Experts are looking for a concise and precise summary of an organization's financial health and future direction to gauge their investment and strategic positions. With the increasing volume of available financial information, the study of NLP methods that automatically summarize the content has grown rapidly into a major research area. A series of Financial Narrative Processing workshops (El-Haj et al., 2022; El-Haj et al., 2021; El-Haj et al., 2020) focused on this area and have invited researchers to participate. The Financial Narrative Summarization (FNS-2022) task (Zmandar et al., 2022) at aims to demonstrate the value and challenges of applying automatic text summarization to financial reports written in different languages: English, Spanish and Greek. Financial reports are a bit more challenging than news articles, because companies usually produce glossy brochures with a much looser structure, they are large, contain financial statements and vast information which deemed repetitive. Instead of summarizing the complete report, the task requires locating key narrative sections found in the annual reports and generate a single structured summary for them in not more than 1000 words. "Narrative sections" or "front-end" sections usually contain textual information and reviews by the firm's management and board of directors. Sections containing financial statements in terms of tables and numbers are usually referred to as "back-end" sections and are not supposed to be part of the narrative summaries. The task dataset has been extracted from annual reports published in PDF file format. These extracted reports were very noisy, making the task even more challenging.

Previous participating systems used a variety of approaches but have one of these limitations. Generating summaries from the complete report instead of identifying narrative sections to summarize or relying on language summarizers to automatically identify the salient sentences and areas without using the contexts of narrative sections. (Litvak and Vanetik, 2021; Krimberg et al., 2021), using heuristics or manual investigations to identify the narrative sections (Orzhenovskii, 2021; Gokhan et al., 2021; Li et al., 2020). A very important aspect of summarization is to produce a short and clear summary with the limits of words or sentences. But while generating a final summary of K words, most of the approaches didn't pay much attention and have lost some part of the novelty in this process, either by taking top K words (Litvak and Vanetik, 2021; Orzhenovskii, 2021) or by dropping sections completely (Ait Azzi and Kang, 2020) or treating all sections equally (Litvak et al., 2020).

We approached the problem by focusing on two sub problems: 1) Automatically identify the key narrative sections (in English reports) or narrative areas (in Spanish/Greek reports), from where the summary needs to be generated, 2) Quantify the contributions of these key narrative sections or areas towards summary in terms of number of words to be generated. To the best of our knowledge, this is the first time, that the distribution of words has been explored. These can now be fed to a summarizer to generate summaries from individual narrative sections in a distributed manner to be combined later for an overall K-words summary.

2. Dataset

FNS-2022 dataset contains annual reports produced by UK , Spanish and Greek firms listed on stock exchange market of each of those countries. English dataset was randomly split into into training (75%), testing and validation (25%). This is a bit different for Greek and Spanish as we have a smaller dataset, the split for each language is training (60%), testing and validation (40%). Experts have considered few relevant sections from the annual reports to generate respective gold standard summaries. On average there are at least 3 gold-standard summaries for each English annual report and 2 gold-standard summaries for Spanish and Greek reports. Table 1 2 and 3 details the split of dataset for all the three languages. We further analyzed these datasets and have these findings:

- Texts extracted form the PDF reports had lot of noise: special characters, unexpected spaces, sentence broken into multiple lines and varied character casing of section headers. While this was mostly the case for English and Greek, the Spanish reports had a much cleaner text.
- Gold summaries for the English training dataset were extracted directly from the reports and had a good overlap while very less overlap was found in Spanish and Greek datasets.
- Almost all of the English training dataset (99.996%) reports were structured with the table of contents (TOCs) and the respective headers provided for each section in the body of the report. This arrangement helped us understand the narrative sections of the report and use them for modeling purposes.
- The Spanish and Greek reports did not have any reliable TOCs or section headers.

Type	Training	Validation	Testing
Report Full Text	3000	363	500
Gold Summaries	9873	1250	1673

Table 1: English Dataset

Type	Training	Validation	Testing
Report Full Text	162	50	50
Gold Summaries	324	100	100

Table 2: Spanish Dataset

Type	Training	Validation	Testing
Report Full Text	162	50	50
Gold Summaries	324	100	100

Table 3: Greek Dataset

3. Approach

A fundamental problem to solve in summarization is to identify the relevant aspects like sections, paragraphs or sentences and produce them in short and clear format with limits on the number of words or sentences. Our approach was focused on addressing these problems considering the financial context presented in these reports by A: Identifying key narrative sections or areas and their respective weights (Section 3.1), and B: Quantifying the contribution of key narrative sections or areas in 'number of words' to be extracted based on the weights (Section 3.2). Later, we pass identified key narrative sections and respective number of words to a summarizer for extracting distributed summaries, later to be combined for an overall summary. We explored various summarizers and tecnhiques to generate and combine summaries as described in Section 3.3

3.1. Identifying Key Narrative Sections or Areas with Weights

This section describes our approach of identifying key areas in the reports and their respective weights on datasets based on the formats as detailed in subsequent sub-sections.

3.1.1. Key Narrative Sections and Weights in English Reports

In the English dataset, the presence of TOCs in the reports and section names in the respective gold summaries, we defined narrative section identification as a classification problem, where section can be narrative ('true') or non-narrative ('false').

Building Annotated Dataset: To train a section classification model, we built an annotated dataset (Figure 1). For each section in a report a row was created with attributes like section name, section page number, section body length i.e. the number of words. A section was labeled as 'true', if the title was narrative (a title has been considered narrative if it was present in any one of the respective gold summaries) and 'false' otherwise. We applied automatic lookup of section names in the respective gold summaries. This process was repeated for each report in the training dataset.

Further the section title names and page numbers were extracted by parsing the TOCs present in the reports. For parsing TOC, we utilized the methods by (Zheng et al., 2020). Their TOC parsing approach captures the section names along with the respective start page numbers. Having those page numbers helped us extract the complete sections from the report by extracting the pages from start page number of current section till one page before the next section's start page number.

Label Correction: After annotation, we identified that for many of the sections, the labels were overlapping, marking them both narrative and non-narrative (Table 4). For each unique title, label was corrected to the majority label if the percentage of majority label was above 70% (based on our empirical studies and which also holds true for most frequent sections (Table 4)). Final dataset had total 67893 sections with around 20% of sections labeled as narrative or 'true'.

Section Title	#Positive	#Negative
board of directors	367 (22%)	**1342 (78%)**
chairmans statement	**1729 (72%)**	668 (28%)
chief executives review	**811 (70%)**	345 (30%)
consolidated balance sheet	152 (13%)	**1012 (87%)**
consolidated cash flow statement	132 (13%)	**872 (87%)**
highlights	**713 (75%)**	240 (25%)

Table 4: Label Distribution in Annotated Dataset Before Label Correction

Model Training: Before training the model, the text was processed (removed extra spaces, special characters and punctuation, converted to lower case, performed lemmatization and stemming). Stratified sampling was applied to handle imbalance in the labels while splitting. We experimented with many models and found L2 regularized Logistic Regression to the best performing one with 5-fold cross validation accuracy of 93% with weighted average F1 (.92). F1 scores for 'true' and 'false' classes were 0.78 and 0.96 respectively.

Key Narrative Sections and Weights: Approach for identifying key narrative sections and their weights is shown in Figure 2. Given an English report, TOC was parsed to extract section features: section name, page number, length. With these features, classification model was used to categorize the section as narrative ('true') or non-narrative ('false'). Weight of a section can be defined as probability of it being narrative, assigned by the model.

$$W_i : Pr(narrative = true)$$

3.1.2. Key Narrative Areas and Weights in Spanish/Greek Reports

Upon investigating the Spanish reports, we didn't find the concept of TOC and sections like in English reports. Though we found TOCs in Greek reports but TOC parsing methods used for English reports were not applicable on the Greek reports. Instead of reinventing the wheel again, we focused on identifying a cluster of sentences defined as 'Key Narrative Areas' by adopting our work on the English dataset to other languages based on the following assumptions:

Assumption 1: Language Independence of Narratives: The key narratives should be independent of language given all are financial reports. i.e. if 'Chairman's Statement' is a key narrative in English reports, so 'Declaración del Presidente' should be in Spanish.

Assumption 2: Structure Independence: If narratives are not defined as sections, the presence of narrative keywords or key phrases in a sentence indicates it being part of some narrative.

Assumption 3: Neighbourhoods Assumption: If a sentence is part of some narrative, most likely its N neighbouring sentences are also part of the same narrative, defining a set of sentences or paragraph as key narrative area

Given these assumptions, we came up with an approach as depicted in Figure 3 and detailed below:

- Extract top M key narrative section titles from English dataset according to their weights as defined in Section 3.1.1.
- Translate key narrative sections to Spanish and Greek. We used Google Translator API[1] for the same.
- Process and tokenize the translated narrative titles into weighted 'Narrative Keywords' [2]. Weight of a narrative keyword can be defined as:

  $$Wt(w) = \sum Wt(Ns) : w \epsilon Ns$$

  where Wt(Ns): Weight of narrative section title Ns.

- Tokenize the report into sentences, process them and compute the weights of sentences based on presence of these narrative keywords as defined below:

  $$Wt(S) = \sum Wt(w) : w \epsilon S$$

  where Wt(w): Weight of narrative keyword w.

[1] https://pypi.org/project/deep-translator/

[2] We used nltk (https://www.nltk.org/) to process the text and tokenize.

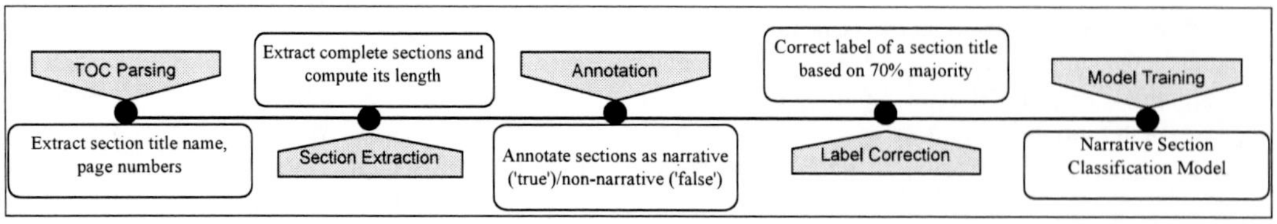

Figure 1: Pipeline for Building Annotated Dataset and Training

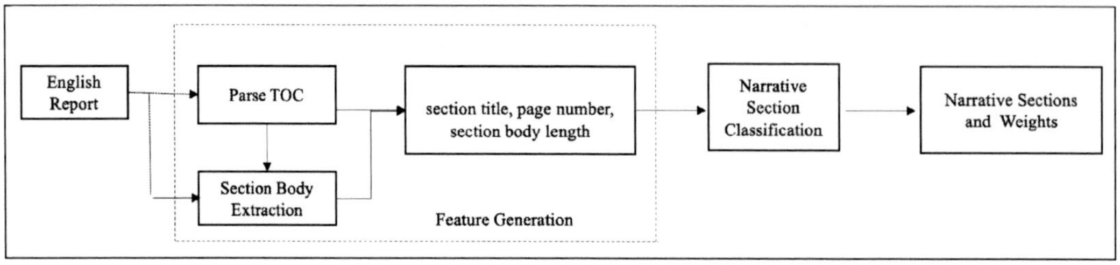

Figure 2: Identifying Key Narrative Sections and Weights in English Reports

- Select top Q sentences (by weight) and its position in original report. These sentences can be assumed as centroid or seed sentences around which key narrative areas can be built.
- For a sentence Si at position 'i', key narrative area can be defined as set of sentences from position 'i-N to i+N' as applicable. The weight of this key narrative area can be defined as sum of weights of all sentences in the identified key narrative area.

Key Narrative Area:

$$[S(i-N), .., Si...., S(i+N)]$$

Weight of Narrative Area:

$$\sum Wt(Sj) : Sj\epsilon[S(i-N), .., Si...., S(i+N)]$$

We maintained both raw and processed sentences and summaries were extracted from raw sentences based on position indexes.

Parameters M, Q and N can be fine-tuned for individual dataset. We have fine-tuned to M=50, N=20, Q=2 on respective validation dataset of Spanish and Greek languages.

3.2. Quantify the Contribution of Key Narrative Sections or Areas

The goal of summarization system is to generate a brief version of the document that highlights the most salient aspects in a limit on amount of words or sentences as K. In a financial report or in any document, these salient aspects are spread across document with varied subjectivity of being considered for summary. When we looked into gold summaries, we discovered that summaries were coming from various parts of the report. Based on this observation, we decided to distribute K words among key narrative sections by their respective weights. Sometimes sections do not have enough words in their body as required by the weights assigned, failing to generate complete K word summary, decreasing recall or precision or both. To overcome this problem, we have devised an algorithm called 'K-Maximal Word Allocation' which maximally distributes the required K words among section according to their weights and number of available words in the sections (Algorithm 1). Let's take an example as shown in Table 5. Assume, there are three sections 'section a', 'section b' and 'section c' with their respective weights of 0.9, 0.9 and 0.6. The required number of words for the summary is 1000. In iteration 1, these weights are normalized to the 0-1 scale as 0.375, 0.375 and 0.25. By multiplying 1000 to these weights we can get the number of words required from these sections as 375, 375 and 250. Assume that available numbers of words in respective sections are 75, 500 and 300. With this 'section a' can't generate required 375 words, falling short of 300 words. At the same time other sections 'section b' and 'section c' have extra words 125 (500-275), 50 (300-250) respectively. In iteration 2, we will consider remaining 300 words to be generated for summary, and distribute them in 'section b' and 'section c' according to their new normalized weights. Considering only 'section b' and 'section c', there new normalized weight will be 0.5 and 0.5. These iterations will continue till expected K=1000 have been allocated or number of words in all sections have been exhausted.

3.3. Distributed Summary Generation

In previous Sections 3.1 and 3.2, we have identified set of pairs (narrative_section, num_words_to_be_generated). Given these inputs, any type and combination of summarizers can be

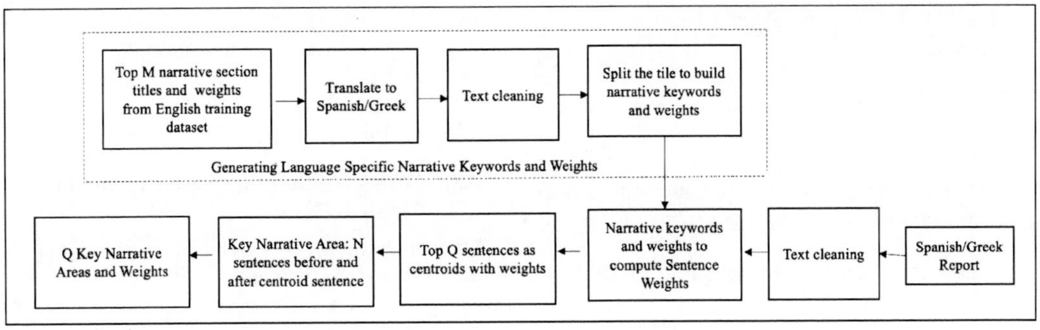

Figure 3: Identifying Key Narrative Areas and Weights in Spanish/Greek Reports

iter.	section	weight (norm weight)	required #words for summary	#words in section	remaining #words required for summary	remaining #words in section
1	section a	0.90 (0.375)	375	75	300	0
1	section b	0.90 (0.375)	375	500	0	125
1	section c	0.60 (0.25)	250	300	0	50

Iteration 1: Required: 1000, Allocated: 700, Remaining Required: 300, Available in Sections: 175

iter.	section	weight (norm weight)	required #words for summary	#words in section	remaining #words required for summary	remaining #words in section
2	section b	0.90 (0.60)	180	125	55	0
2	section c	0.60 (0.40)	120	50	70	0

Iteration 2: Required: 1000, Allocated: 875, Remaining Required: 125, Available in Sections: 0

Table 5: Example of Maximal Word Allocation for 1000-words Summary

used to generate summary as depicted in Figure 4. Each pair is passed to a summarizer to generate a sub summary later to be combined for an overall summary. Various combination approaches can be followed. To have a similar flow as the report, we structured the narrative summaries in order of their respective section's positions in the original report.

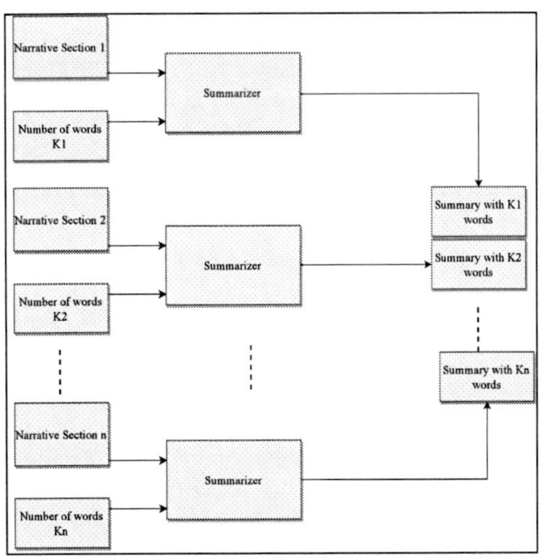

Figure 4: Distributed Summary Generation

4. Experiments and Results

We used ROUGE (Lin, 2004) metrics, ROUGE-1 and ROUGE-2 and evaluated methods on the validation dataset using python package [3]. Since there were multiple golden summaries, for each report, we computed the ROUGE scores with each corresponding summary and took an average.

4.1. Comparison of Summarizers

As described in Section 3.3, any summarizer can be used in the distributed summary generation process,

[3]https://pypi.org/project/rouge-score/

Algorithm 1 K-Maximal Word Allocation

Inputs:

$S_w \leftarrow list\_of\_section\_weights$

$W \leftarrow list\_of\_number\_of\_words\_in\_each\_section$

$K \leftarrow required\_number\_of\_words\_in\_final\_summary$

$K_{Alloc} \leftarrow list\_of\_allocated\_number\_of\_words\_to\_each\_section\_till\_previous\_iterations$

procedure ALLOCATE_MAXIMAL_WORDS

  if $K = 0$ or $sum\_of(S_w) = 0$ **then**

    return K_{Alloc}

  end if

  $S_w\_normalized = S_w / sum\_of(S_w)$

  $W_{Req} = K \times S_w\_normalized$

  if $W_{Req} \leq W$ **then**

    return $K_{Alloc} + W_{Req}$

  else

    return $K_{Alloc} + W$

  end if

  for $i = 0$ to $length\_of(S_w)$ **do**

    if $W_{Req}[i] >= W[i]$ **then**

      $K_{Alloc}[i] = K_{Alloc}[i] + W[i]$

      $K = K - W[i]$

      $W[i] = 0$

    else

      $K_{Alloc}[i] = K_{Alloc}[i] + W_{Req}[i]$

      $K = K - W_{Req}[i]$

      $W[i] = W[i] - W_{Req}[i]$

    end if

  end for

  $allocate\_maximal\_words(S_w, W, K, K_{Alloc})$

end procedure

we compared three extractive summarizers: 1) Top-k summarizer, which extracts the first k words from given text, 2) Google BERT (Devlin et al., 2018) based Extractive Summarizer[4] by (Miller, 2019) and 3) Facebook BART (Lewis et al., 2020) based extractive summarizer provided by Hugging Face [5]. Table 6 shows the results on the English dataset where Top-k summarizer outperformed other summarizers. We used the Top-k extractor for further experiments.

4.2. K-Maximal Allocation and Distributed Summary Generation

We built systems using our novel approaches, K-Maximal Word Allocation and Distributed Summary Generation (Sections 3.2, 3.3) on English, Spanish and Greek datasets as *SSC_AI_RG_English*, *SSC_AI_RG_Spanish* and *SSC_AI_RG_Greek* respectively. We used one of the official FNS-2021[6] baselines, TextRank (Mihalcea and Tarau, 2004) [7]. As shown in Table 9 our system performed extremely well on English dataset and decently better on Spanish (Table 7) and Greek datasets (Table 8) compared to the baseline. This system was submitted as *SSC-AI-RG-3*.

4.3. Alternate Summary Generation on English Dataset

Since complete sections were extracted for gold summaries, we also experimented with alternate summary generation for English dataset. Once the key narrative sections were identified with weights as described in 3.1.1, instead of applying our novel approaches, we extracted complete sections and combined them in, i) ascending order of page number or position in the report (System *SSC_AI_RG_Alt1_English*) and, ii) descending order of weights learned (System *SSC_AI_RG_Alt2_English*). Top-1000 words were extracted to generate summary. These two systems were combined with the Spanish and Greek systems described in Section 4.2, and were submitted as *SSC-AI-RG-1* and *SSC-AI-RG-2* respectively.

SSC_AI_RG_Alt1_English, was the best performing one (Table 9). It was due to the nature of the dataset where the majority of the summaries were in Top 10% (Zheng et al., 2020). It can also be observed that our novel summarization approach, *SSC_AI_RG_English* worked pretty well without considering this dataset specific characteristic, showcasing the generic nature of it.

4.4. Official Results

The official results are shown in Table 10. Teams were ranked according to ROUGE-2 F1 score on test dataset. With overall score combined across languages, our two systems *SSC-AI-RG-1 and SSC-AI-RG-3* were in Top-3. Our systems performed best on the Greek dataset and second best on the Spanish one. This demonstrates the effectiveness of our approach in multilingual setup.

5. Related Works

(Ait Azzi and Kang, 2020) also defined the problem of narrative section identification as a binary classification system. We would like to highlight a few differences: 1) Our system additionally considers position and length of the section along with its title. 2) Our label correction strategy considers a label change to the majority label only when the proportion exceeds 70%. 3) Compared to their approach of extracting top 1000 words from one section as a summary, we added novelty of generating distributed summary using 'K-Maximal Word Allocation' algorithm as described in Sections 3.2 3.3. Our system achieved better classification accuracy 93% compared to their 70%.

[4]https://pypi.org/project/bert-extractive-summarizer

[5]https://huggingface.co/facebook/bart-large-cnn

[6]www.lancaster.ac.uk/staff/elhaj/docs/fns2021_results.pdf

[7]https://pypi.org/project/summa/

Summarizer	R1P	R1R	R1F	R2P	R2R	R2F
BART	0.544	0.444	0.417	0.304	0.244	0.232
BERT	0.56	0.40	0.42	0.32	0.20	0.22
Top-k	0.523	0.596	**0.508**	0.347	0.418	**0.345**

Table 6: Comparision of Summarizers for Generating Distributed Summary on English Validation Dataset

Dataset	R1P	R1R	R1F	R2P	R2R	R2F
SSC_AI_RG_Spanish	0.357	0.566	**0.41**	0.122	0.192	**0.139**
TextRank (Baseline)	0.34	0.543	0.393	0.104	0.166	0.12

Table 7: Result on Spanish Validation Dataset

Dataset	R1P	R1R	R1F	R2P	R2R	R2F
SSC_AI_RG_Greek	0.349	0.429	0.385	0.155	0.194	**0.172**
TextRank (Baseline)	0.532	0.255	0.396	0.259	0.112	0.156

Table 8: Result on Greek Validation Dataset

System	R1P	R1R	R1F	R2P	R2R	R2F
SSC_AI_RG_English	0.523	0.596	**0.508**	0.347	0.418	**0.345**
SSC_AI_RG_Alt1_English	0.551	0.643	**0.546**	0.415	0.512	**0.425**
SSC_AI_RG_Alt2_English	0.499	0.541	0.478	0.297	0.313	0.281
TextRank (Baseline)	0.321	0.339	0.284	0.084	0.087	0.071

Table 9: Results of Different Systems on English Validation Dataset

Team	English	Spanish	Greek	Overall Score
LSIR-1	0.365	**0.157**	0.141	0.257
SSC-AI-RG-1	0.327	**0.146**	**0.185**	0.24625
SSC-AI-RG-3	0.319	**0.146**	**0.185**	0.24225
IIC	0.366	0.125	0.095	0.238
SSC-AI-RG-2	0.3	**0.146**	**0.185**	0.23275
Team-Tredence-2	0.322	0.131	0.138	0.22825
Team-Tredence-1	0.317	0.131	0.138	0.22575
LIPI	0.374	0.07	0.046	0.216
Team-Tredence-3	0.322	0.131	0.072	0.21175
LSIR-3	0.275	0.138	0.13	0.2045
MACQUARIE-1	0.303	0	0	0.1515
MACQUARIE-3	0.302	0	0	0.151
MACQUARIE-2	0.301	0	0	0.1505
AO-LANCS	0.143	0.134	0.131	0.13775

Table 10: Official FNS-2022 Results on Test Dataset. Ranked According to ROUGE-2 F1 Score. Overall Score: English (50%), Spanish (25%) and Greek (25%)

(Zheng et al., 2020) also built the classification system. They extracted the first 5 sections, and labeled one section as positive with maximum overlap with gold summaries and others as negative. Whereas we consider all the sections and mark the sections positive if they are present in any of the gold summaries otherwise negative. They took into account the complete section (title+body) for classification whereas we used the titles.

6. Conclusion and Future Work

We explored the aspect of finding narrative sections, quantifying their contributions as weights and words to be extracted based on these weights. We introduced a concept of 'Maximal Word Allocation in Summarization' which can be used across problems and domains not limited to financial reports. We also introduced a generic approach that can be adapted to different languages and report formats. In this work, we focused on the inputs and outputs of summarizers. In future work, we would like to explore, we would like to explore more sophisticated approaches for summarization using the foundations that we layed using K-Maximally Allocated Words and Distributed Summary Generations. These concepts are generic enough to be used in any domain with any summarizer. Our current approach is also dependent upon the TOC in English Reports. Alternate approaches need to be explored to reduce this dependency.

7. Bibliographical References

Ait Azzi, A. and Kang, J. (2020). Extractive summarization system for annual reports. In *Proceedings of the 1st Joint Workshop on Financial Narrative Processing and MultiLing Financial Summarisation*, pages 143–147, Barcelona, Spain (Online), December. COLING.

Devlin, J., Chang, M.-W., Lee, K., and Toutanova, K. (2018). Bert: Pre-training of deep bidirectional transformers for language understanding. cite arxiv:1810.04805Comment: 13 pages.

Dr Mahmoud El-Haj, et al., editors. (2020). *Proceedings of the 1st Joint Workshop on Financial Narrative Processing and MultiLing Financial Summarisation*, Barcelona, Spain (Online), December. COLING.

Mahmoud El-Haj, et al., editors. (2021). *Proceedings of the 3rd Financial Narrative Processing Workshop*, Lancaster, United Kingdom, 15-16 September. Association for Computational Linguistics.

Mahmoud El-Haj, et al., editors. (2022). *Proceedings of the 4th Financial Narrative Processing Workshop*, Marseille, France, 24 June. The 13th Language Resources and Evaluation Conference, LREC 2022.

Gokhan, T., Smith, P., and Lee, M. (2021). Extractive financial narrative summarisation using Sentence-BERT based clustering. In *Proceedings of the 3rd Financial Narrative Processing Workshop*, pages 94–98, Lancaster, United Kingdom, 15-16 September. Association for Computational Linguistics.

Krimberg, S., Vanetik, N., and Litvak, M. (2021). Summarization of financial documents with TF-IDF weighting of multi-word terms. In *Proceedings of the 3rd Financial Narrative Processing Workshop*, pages 75–80, Lancaster, United Kingdom, 15-16 September. Association for Computational Linguistics.

Lewis, M., Liu, Y., Goyal, N., Ghazvininejad, M., Mohamed, A., Levy, O., Stoyanov, V., and Zettlemoyer, L. (2020). BART: Denoising sequence-to-sequence pre-training for natural language generation, translation, and comprehension. In *Proceedings of the 58th Annual Meeting of the Association for Computational Linguistics*, pages 7871–7880, Online, July. Association for Computational Linguistics.

Li, L., Jiang, Y., and Liu, Y. (2020). Extractive financial narrative summarisation based on DPPs. In *Proceedings of the 1st Joint Workshop on Financial Narrative Processing and MultiLing Financial Summarisation*, pages 100–104, Barcelona, Spain (Online), December. COLING.

Lin, C.-Y. (2004). ROUGE: A package for automatic evaluation of summaries. In *Text Summarization Branches Out*, pages 74–81, Barcelona, Spain, July. Association for Computational Linguistics.

Litvak, M. and Vanetik, N. (2021). Summarization of financial reports with AMUSE. In *Proceedings of the 3rd Financial Narrative Processing Workshop*, pages 31–36, Lancaster, United Kingdom, 15-16 September. Association for Computational Linguistics.

Litvak, M., Vanetik, N., and Puchinsky, Z. (2020). Hierarchical summarization of financial reports with RUNNER. In *Proceedings of the 1st Joint Workshop on Financial Narrative Processing and MultiLing Financial Summarisation*, pages 213–225, Barcelona, Spain (Online), December. COLING.

Mihalcea, R. and Tarau, P. (2004). TextRank: Bringing order into text. In *Proceedings of the 2004 Conference on Empirical Methods in Natural Language Processing*, pages 404–411, Barcelona, Spain, July. Association for Computational Linguistics.

Miller, D. (2019). Leveraging bert for extractive text summarization on lectures.

Orzhenovskii, M. (2021). T5-LONG-EXTRACT at FNS-2021 shared task. In *Proceedings of the 3rd Financial Narrative Processing Workshop*, pages 67–69, Lancaster, United Kingdom, 15-16 September. Association for Computational Linguistics.

Zheng, S., Lu, A., and Cardie, C. (2020). SUMSUM@FNS-2020 shared task. In *Proceedings of the 1st Joint Workshop on Financial Narrative Processing and MultiLing Financial Summarisation*, pages 148–152, Barcelona, Spain (Online), December. COLING.

Zmandar, N., El-Haj, M., Rayson, P., Abura'Ed, A., Litvak, M., Giannakopoulos, G., Pittaras, N., Carbajo-Coronado, B., and Moreno-Sandoval, A. (2022). The financial narrative summarisation shared task (fns 2022). In *Proceedings of the 4th Financial Narrative Processing Workshop*, Marseille, France, 24June. The 13th Language Resources and Evaluation Conference, LREC 2022.

Proceedings of the 4th Financial Narrative Processing Workshop @ LREC 2022, pages 73–78
Marseille, 24 June 2022

Transformer-based Models for Long Document Summarisation in Financial Domain

Urvashi Khanna, Samira Ghodratnama, Diego Mollá, Amin Beheshti
Macquarie University
Sydney, New South Wales, Australia
{urvashi.khanna, samira.ghodratnama, diego.molla-aliod, amin.beheshti}@mq.edu.au

Abstract

Summarisation of long financial documents is a challenging task due to the lack of large-scale datasets and the need for domain knowledge experts to create human-written summaries. Traditional summarisation approaches that generate a summary based on the content cannot produce summaries comparable to human-written ones and thus are rarely used in practice. In this work, we use the Longformer-Encoder-Decoder (LED) model to handle long financial reports. We describe our experiments and participating systems in the financial narrative summarisation shared task. Multi-stage fine-tuning helps the model generalise better on niche domains and avoids the problem of catastrophic forgetting. We further investigate the effect of the staged fine-tuning approach on the FNS dataset. Our systems achieved promising results in terms of ROUGE scores on the validation dataset.

Keywords: Document summarisation, Financial documents, Longformer, LED, Sequential fine-tuning

1. Introduction

Large amounts of unstructured data generated electronically in different organisations makes decision-making and gaining insights challenging, especially in the financial domain. Financial reports are critical to a company's financial performance and provide a snapshot of its financial situation. Financial statements not only help executives and investors understand the company's financial position, assets, and liabilities, but also provide a sense of financial transparency. Investors and stakeholders use these reports to make informed investment decisions, and to either vote in favour of or against corporate actions. Annual reports of various organisations from around the world typically include income statements, cash flow, statements from the chief executive officer, highlights, reviews of operating, investing, and financing activities, auditor's reports, risk disclosures, press releases, and so on (El-Haj et al., 2020b).

Annual reports in the financial sector are typically over 180 pages long (Leidner, 2020). This overload of textual data that investors and stakeholders must read is a time-consuming and exhausting process. Furthermore, in order to maximise profits, it is critical to make financial decisions in the shortest amount of time possible. As a result, automatic summarisation makes use of technology to simplify the process of concisely summarising long financial documents.

Despite recent advancements in automatic summarisation approaches, summarising long financial documents remains difficult due to the lack of large-scale datasets. Furthermore, the requirement for domain knowledge experts to create human-written summaries complicates the situation. As a result, traditional summarisation approaches that generate a summary based on the content cannot produce summaries comparable to human-written summaries and are thus rarely used in practice.

The use of unsupervised pretraining for natural language tasks is being driven by the availability of huge amounts of raw text on the web, as well as ever-increasing computational processing capacity. Fine-tuning a Pre-trained Language Model (PLM) on the target dataset is the norm these days. These PLMs are already pretrained on a massive amount of data and achieve state-of-the-art results on most of the Natural Language Understanding (NLU) tasks (Devlin et al., 2019; Lan et al., 2019; Liu et al., 2019). Longformer-Encoder-Decoder (LED) (Beltagy et al., 2020), a variant of longformer, scales efficiently on sequence-to-sequence tasks for long input sequences of up to 16k tokens. LED has performed exceedingly well on long-summarisation datasets like arXiv and PubMed (Cohan et al., 2018).

Language models are usually pretrained on general language like news articles and Wikipedia data, and then adapted to domain-specific downstream tasks. However, domain-specific tasks face the issue of scarcity of good quality manually labelled data. Thus, an intermediate stage of fine-tuning on a larger related dataset before fine-tuning on the target dataset has been a widely used approach in different domains like financial, biomedical, and scientific articles (Lee et al., 2019; Yoon et al., 2019; Phang et al., 2020; Khanna and Mollá, 2021). This addition of an intermediate stage helps the model generalise better on niche domains and also avoids the problem of catastrophic forgetting. In this paper, we describe the experimental setup, and approach of our participating systems at the Financial

Narrative Summarisation (FNS) shared task[1]. Both our systems use LED as pretrained language model considering the size of the financial documents. We formulate the task as one of extractive summarisation and also investigate the effect of multi-stage fine-tuning via our submissions at the FNS shared task. All of our systems outperformed the current publicly available validation results of other state-of-the-art systems.

The rest of the paper is organized as follows: in Section 2, we provide an overview of the related work and literature. Section 3 reviews the FNS dataset in detail, pre-processing and post-processing techniques, and the evaluation metrics used in this work. Section 4 discusses the methodology behind the proposed systems. In Section 5, we present evaluation results before concluding the paper with remarks for future directions in Section 6.

2. Related Work

Summarisation of documents can either be extractive or abstractive. Extractive summarisation selects a subset of sentences from the text to create a summary; on the other hand, abstractive summarisation reorganises the text's language and, if necessary, adds new words or phrases to the summary. In past FNS workshops, both extractive (Gokhan et al., 2021; Orzhenovskii, 2021) and abstractive (Singh, 2020) approaches were applied.

Unsupervised approaches have been used previously for the extractive summarisation of documents. TextRank (Mihalcea and Tarau, 2004) and LexRank (Erkan and Radev, 2004) are graph-based ranking models used for text processing. MUSE (MUltilingual Sentence Extractor), which is a language-independent approach for summarising extractive documents, uses linear optimisation of various sentence ranking measures using a generic algorithm (Litvak et al., 2010).

Participants in past years of the FNS workshop series used a variety of machine learning techniques for automatic summarisation of financial documents. Baldeon Suarez et al. (2020) used a combination of machine learning and statistical methods to calculate the importance of sentences based on features such as keywords, position, similarity, and topics. Litvak et al. (2020) combined topic modelling and discourse structure based on heuristic assumptions to create a new method for hierarchical summarisation of reports. Krimberg et al. (2021) used the Term Frequency-Inverse Document Frequency (TF-IDF) weighing method to identify the top 1000 most important words in a document and extract them as the summary.

Litvak et al. (2010) used the MUSE tool to filter large financial summaries, then combined different techniques like BERT and node embeddings, a similarity graph, and finally a neural LSTM model to train for sentence classification (Litvak and Vanetik, 2021). The participants also explored a combination of knowledge graph and deep learning approaches (Arora and Radhakrishnan, 2020; Vhatkar et al., 2020).

Language models like BERT (Devlin et al., 2019) and T5 (Raffel et al., 2020) are also used by participants in the FNS shared task (La Quatra and Cagliero, 2020; Orzhenovskii, 2021). Zmandar et al. (2021b) proposed a method that uses a combination of pointer network (Vinyals et al., 2015) and T5. They first use pointer network to extract the important sentences from the documents and then paraphrase the extracted sentences using a T5 model. To bridge the two models, they also use policy-based reinforcement learning. Sentence-BERT based clustering has also been effectively used by Gokhan et al. (2021).

3. FNS Data

The FNS 2022 shared task is organised annually to illustrate the challenges and potential of using automatic text summarisation for financial text documents in Spanish, English and Greek languages. These financial text documents can be anything ranging from financial company disclosures, budgeting, company's future prospects, etc. The FNS dataset contains the text extracted from United Kingdom (UK), Spanish and Greek companies' financial reports that are published annually in PDF format (El-Haj et al., 2020a).

Participants are asked to provide concise single summaries extracted from important sections from the financial annual reports of UK companies. The system generated summaries should reflect on the analysis and appraisal of the businesses' financial pattern over the last year, as supplied by annual reports. The FNS golden reference summaries are not written by human experts; instead, the experts who have created the financial reports inform which sections in the annual reports are considered a summary of the entire annual report, and those sections are used as gold standard summaries.

A typical financial report includes both numerical and narrative sections. Numerical sections refer to tables about tax returns, budgeting, expenditure and financial statements. The narrative sections comprise annual or quarterly highlights of the company, their future outlook, statements from the board of directors and management, etc. In this shared task, the participants are required to extract information from key narrative sections and produce a concise summary for each annual report such that the length of the summary should not exceed 1000 words (Zmandar et al., 2021a).

Dataset	Reports	Summaries
Training	3000	9873
Validation	363	1250
Testing	500	N/A

Table 1: Statistics of FNS 2022 dataset for Training, Validation and Test.

[1] http://wp.lancs.ac.uk/cfie/fns2022/

Table 1 shows the number of reports in the training, validation and test data provided by the FNS organisers. In the training and validation data provided, there are around 3 to 7 golden summaries for each report.

Recall-Oriented Understudy for Gisting Evaluation (ROUGE) (Lin, 2004) is the measure we utilise to evaluate our systems. Text summarisation tasks are frequently evaluated using ROUGE metrics. ROUGE is a collection of metrics that compare system-generated summaries to a set of ideal or reference summaries automatically. There are several distinct ROUGE measures depending on the amount of granularity of texts between the system and reference summaries. Among all of them, we use ROUGE-N, ROUGE-SU, and ROUGE-L as these metrics are used by FNS organisers. The ROUGE-N measure calculates the overlap between the system-generated summary to be assessed and the reference summaries in terms of unigram, bigram, trigram, and higher-order n-grams. ROUGE-L measures the longest matching sequence of words, while ROUGE-SU measures the co-occurrence statistics based on skip-bigram plus unigrams. The overlap of word pairs with a maximum of two gaps between them is measured by skip-bigram (Ganesan, 2015).

4. Systems Overview

In this section, we describe the approaches used in our two systems and the experimental setup that we explored when addressing the shared task of FNS 2022.

4.1. Longformer-Encoder-Decoder (LED)

BERT-style transformer models typically limit the sequence length to 512 tokens as they scale quadratically due to their self-attention mechanism (Devlin et al., 2019; Liu et al., 2019). To overcome this memory and computational constraint for long sequences, Beltagy et al. (2020) introduced Longformer, a transformer architecture that utilises a self-attention pattern which scales linearly with the sequence length, allowing it to process long documents. Longformer has made it easier to process long documents for natural language tasks like question answering, long document classification, and co-reference resolution.

The original Transformer architecture (Vaswani et al., 2017) uses an encoder-decoder pipeline for generative sequence-to-sequence tasks like translation and text summarisation. Encoder-Deccoder architectures like BART (Lewis et al., 2020) and T5 (Raffel et al., 2020) have achieved good results on sequence-to-sequence tasks but are not able to scale to longer sequences. Longformer-Encoder-Decoder (LED), a Longformer variant (Beltagy et al., 2020), has both encoder and decoder transformer stacks and utilises their efficient local+global attention pattern that can handle the long text sequence-to-sequence tasks efficiently (Sutskever et al., 2014).

We decided to use LED as the pretrained model for all our experiments considering the average report length in the FNS dataset is around 80 pages. We have mainly focused on only English language summarisation and formulated the task as an extractive summarisation task.

In the FNS training and validation datasets, each report has 3 to 7 golden reference summaries. We examined the reports and the golden summaries, and discovered that at least one golden summary was extracted from the report as a continuous sequence of text or section. In addition, the majority of the reference summaries were located at the beginning of the report. To train our systems, we applied the same approach as Orzhenovskii (2021) and chose the summary that had at least one continuous block of text in the report and also the most intersection with other summaries as our golden summary.

Our system takes the first 8192 tokens from the report as input and the first 1024 tokens from the selected golden summary as the target output. The system generates 1024 tokens as output predictions. The ROUGE F1 metrics was very low when we used the 1025 generated tokens as predicted summary because the summary length was less than 1000 words. As a result, we identify the sequence of text in the input report that matches this generated text and choose 1000 words as the output summary.

Hyper-parameters	Values
source length	8192
target length	1024
epochs	3,5
learning rate	5e-5
batch size	1
beam size	2,4

Table 2: Training hyper-parameters.

In our experiments, the pretrained language model was "led-large-16384," along with its tokenizer, all of which are freely available from the Huggingface Transformers Library (Wolf et al., 2020). The hyper-parameters for both fine-tuning steps were set to the default values used by the Longformer developers, unless stated otherwise. The systems were trained on the training dataset to fine-tune the hyper-parameters and later validated on the FNS validation dataset. The hyper-parameters used are listed in Table 2. Due to computational limitations, we were only able to experiment with a batch size of 1. Note that in Table 3, "macquarie1" and "macquarie2" are variations of longformers with different hyper-parameters.

4.2. Sequential Fine-tuning

In our second approach for the system "macquarie3", we follow a sequential fine-tuning approach by first fine-tuning on a large dataset and then on the target FNS dataset. This intermediate stage of fine-tuning is ideal in this case due to the small size of the FNS

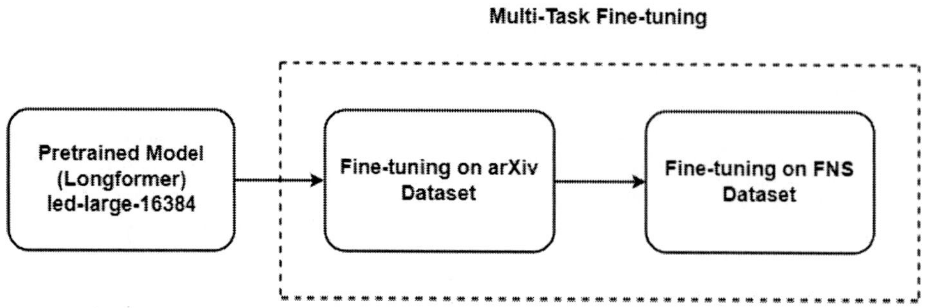

Figure 1: Diagram depicting our system's fine-tuning strategy.

System Name	R-1 / F	R-2 / F	R-L / F	R-SU4 / F
UoBNLP	0.480	0.250	0.400	0.290
TFIDF-SUM-3	0.433	0.209	0.374	0.250
MUSE	0.243	0.040	0.238	0.079
macquarie1	0.436	0.294	0.426	0.345
macquarie2	0.442	**0.302**	**0.434**	**0.353**
macquarie3	**0.443**	0.302	0.432	0.352

Table 3: Results of our systems on the FNS validation dataset. Our top scoring model is highlighted in bold. The rouge F-measure scores at unigram, bigram, longest common sub-sequence, and skip-gram based metrics are represented by the columns R-1/F, R-2/F, R-L/F, and R-SU4/L, respectively. UoBNLP (Gokhan et al., 2021), TFIDF-SUM-3 (Krimberg et al., 2021) are the validation results from past years and MUSE (Litvak et al., 2010) is the top baseline model. The highest score among our submissions is in bold.

dataset. We choose the arXiv summarisation dataset (Cohan et al., 2018), as there is no other large scale financial summarisation dataset that was readily available. We first fine-tune the "led-large-16384" model on the arXiv dataset and then on the target FNS dataset. We used the same hyper-parameters listed in Table 2. This approach is illustrated in Figure 1.

5. Results and Discussion

System Name	R-2 / F
Top Ranked System	0.374
macquarie1	0.303
macquarie2	0.301
macquarie3	0.302

Table 4: Results of our three submissions along with the top ranked system (LIPI) from the official FNS 2022 shared task results.

Table 3 contains the results of our validation experiments. Note that "macquarie1" and "macquarie2" are fine-tuned with the traditional approach and "macquarie3" is fine-tuned using the staged fine-tuning approach discussed in Section 4.2. "UoBNLP" is Sentence-BERT based system that applies clustering algorithm to generate dynamic summaries (Gokhan et al., 2021). "TFIDF-SUM-3" uses TF-IDF features to extract the important sentences to form summaries.

We used the ROUGE Java package[2] evaluation metrics as our main metrics for the evaluation of our models (Ganesan, 2015). FNS organisers also use ROUGE 2 as their main metric for ranking the teams' submissions on the leaderboard. ROUGE-2 F1 score on the test dataset is used for ranking the teams.

Based on the validation results, we observe that our systems performed better than the current state-of-the-art systems in all the ROUGE metrics except one (R-1/F). We also observed that there was no significant improvement in the performance of the system using the sequential fine-tuning approach. Table4 lists the results of our submissions in the FNS 2022 shared task. We observe that our results are similar to our validation results. However, other participants' systems performed better than ours in the FNS 2022 shared task [3].

On analysis of the predicted summaries, we found that LED is good at identifying the beginning part of the narrative section, however, the challenge still remains to identify the end span for a long length documents like financial reports. LED can handle up to 16K input tokens but not 16K decoder output tokens. The idea

[2]https://github.com/kavgan/ROUGE-2.0.

[3]http://wp.lancs.ac.uk/cfie/fns2022/

behind LED was to be able to process very long inputs (articles to summarise) with the assumption that the decoder outputs did not have to be very long (summaries). This is also the reason for the model not showing any significant improvement when using the sequential fine-tuning approach.

6. Conclusion and Future Work

Our participation in the FNS 2022 was primarily focused on English language summarisation. We submitted three LED-based systems and also investigated the effect of sequential fine-tuning with the FNS dataset as our use case. Our systems performed better than the current state-of-the-art systems on the validation dataset. However, from our experiments we also found that staged fine-tuning had no impact on the performance of the system.

In future work, to locate the end span of the summary, the input sequence can be truncated into smaller chunks and fed into the language models. Later, each extracted summary could be concatenated to get the final summary. To capture the inter-sentence relationships better, graph-based neural networks can also be explored.

7. Bibliographical References

Arora, P. and Radhakrishnan, P. (2020). AMEX AI-labs: An investigative study on extractive summarization of financial documents. In *Proceedings of the 1st Joint Workshop on Financial Narrative Processing and MultiLing Financial Summarisation*, pages 137–142, Barcelona, Spain (Online), December. COLING.

Baldeon Suarez, J., Martínez, P., and Martínez, J. L. (2020). Combining financial word embeddings and knowledge-based features for financial text summarization UC3M-MC system at FNS-2020. In *Proceedings of the 1st Joint Workshop on Financial Narrative Processing and MultiLing Financial Summarisation*, pages 112–117, Barcelona, Spain (Online), December. COLING.

Beltagy, I., Peters, M. E., and Cohan, A. (2020). Longformer: The long-document transformer. *arXiv preprint arXiv:2004.05150*.

Cohan, A., Dernoncourt, F., Kim, D. S., Bui, T., Kim, S., Chang, W., and Goharian, N. (2018). A discourse-aware attention model for abstractive summarization of long documents. In *Proceedings of the 2018 Conference of the North American Chapter of the Association for Computational Linguistics: Human Language Technologies, Volume 2 (Short Papers)*, pages 615–621, New Orleans, Louisiana, June. Association for Computational Linguistics.

Devlin, J., Chang, M.-W., Lee, K., and Toutanova, K. (2019). BERT: Pre-training of deep bidirectional transformers for language understanding. In *Proceedings of the 2019 Conference of the North American Chapter of the Association for Computational Linguistics: Human Language Technologies, Volume 1 (Long and Short Papers)*, pages 4171–4186, Minneapolis, Minnesota, June. Association for Computational Linguistics.

El-Haj, M., AbuRa'ed, A., Litvak, M., Pittaras, N., and Giannakopoulos, G. (2020a). The financial narrative summarisation shared task (FNS 2020). In *Proceedings of the 1st Joint Workshop on Financial Narrative Processing and MultiLing Financial Summarisation*, pages 1–12, Barcelona, Spain (Online), December. COLING.

El-Haj, M., Litvak, M., Pittaras, N., Giannakopoulos, G., et al. (2020b). The financial narrative summarisation shared task (fns 2020). In *Proceedings of the 1st Joint Workshop on Financial Narrative Processing and MultiLing Financial Summarisation*, pages 1–12.

Erkan, G. and Radev, D. R. (2004). Lexrank: Graph-based lexical centrality as salience in text summarization. *Journal of artificial intelligence research*, 22:457–479.

Ganesan, K. (2015). Rouge 2.0: Updated and improved measures for evaluation of summarization tasks.

Gokhan, T., Smith, P., and Lee, M. (2021). Extractive financial narrative summarisation using sentencebert based clustering. In *Proceedings of the 3rd Financial Narrative Processing Workshop*, pages 94–98.

Khanna, U. and Mollá, D. (2021). Transformer-based language models for factoid question answering at bioasq9b. In *CLEF 2021 Working Notes*, CEUR Workshop Proceedings, pages 247–257. CEUR.

Krimberg, S., Vanetik, N., and Litvak, M. (2021). Summarization of financial documents with TF-IDF weighting of multi-word terms. In *Proceedings of the 3rd Financial Narrative Processing Workshop*, pages 75–80, Lancaster, United Kingdom, 15-16 September. Association for Computational Linguistics.

La Quatra, M. and Cagliero, L. (2020). End-to-end training for financial report summarization. In *Proceedings of the 1st Joint Workshop on Financial Narrative Processing and MultiLing Financial Summarisation*, pages 118–123, Barcelona, Spain (Online), December. COLING.

Lan, Z., Chen, M., Goodman, S., Gimpel, K., Sharma, P., and Soricut, R. (2019). Albert: A lite bert for self-supervised learning of language representations. *arXiv preprint arXiv:1909.11942*.

Lee, J., Yoon, W., Kim, S., Kim, D., Kim, S., So, C. H., and Kang, J. (2019). Biobert: pre-trained biomedical language representation model for biomedical text mining. *arXiv preprint arXiv:1901.08746*.

Leidner, J. L. (2020). Summarization in the financial and regulatory domain. In *Trends and Applications of Text Summarization Techniques*, pages 187–215. IGI Global.

Lewis, M., Liu, Y., Goyal, N., Ghazvininejad, M., Mohamed, A., Levy, O., Stoyanov, V., and Zettlemoyer,

L. (2020). Bart: Denoising sequence-to-sequence pre-training for natural language generation, translation, and comprehension. In *Proceedings of the 58th Annual Meeting of the Association for Computational Linguistics*, pages 7871–7880.

Lin, C.-Y. (2004). ROUGE: A package for automatic evaluation of summaries. In *Text Summarization Branches Out*, pages 74–81, Barcelona, Spain, July. Association for Computational Linguistics.

Litvak, M. and Vanetik, N. (2021). Summarization of financial reports with AMUSE. In *Proceedings of the 3rd Financial Narrative Processing Workshop*, pages 31–36, Lancaster, United Kingdom, 15-16 September. Association for Computational Linguistics.

Litvak, M., Last, M., and Friedman, M. (2010). A new approach to improving multilingual summarization using a genetic algorithm. In *Proceedings of the 48th annual meeting of the association for computational linguistics*, pages 927–936.

Litvak, M., Vanetik, N., and Puchinsky, Z. (2020). SCE-SUMMARY at the FNS 2020 shared task. In *Proceedings of the 1st Joint Workshop on Financial Narrative Processing and MultiLing Financial Summarisation*, pages 124–129, Barcelona, Spain (Online), December. COLING.

Liu, Y., Ott, M., Goyal, N., Du, J., Joshi, M., Chen, D., Levy, O., Lewis, M., Zettlemoyer, L., and Stoyanov, V. (2019). Roberta: A robustly optimized bert pretraining approach. *arXiv preprint arXiv:1907.11692*.

Mihalcea, R. and Tarau, P. (2004). Textrank: Bringing order into text. In *Proceedings of the 2004 conference on empirical methods in natural language processing*, pages 404–411.

Orzhenovskii, M. (2021). T5-LONG-EXTRACT at FNS-2021 shared task. In *Proceedings of the 3rd Financial Narrative Processing Workshop*, pages 67–69, Lancaster, United Kingdom, 15-16 September. Association for Computational Linguistics.

Phang, J., Calixto, I., Htut, P. M., Pruksachatkun, Y., Liu, H., Vania, C., Kann, K., and Bowman, S. R. (2020). English intermediate-task training improves zero-shot cross-lingual transfer too. In *Proceedings of the 1st Conference of the Asia-Pacific Chapter of the Association for Computational Linguistics and the 10th International Joint Conference on Natural Language Processing*, pages 557–575, Suzhou, China, December. Association for Computational Linguistics.

Raffel, C., Shazeer, N., Roberts, A., Lee, K., Narang, S., Matena, M., Zhou, Y., Li, W., and Liu, P. J. (2020). Exploring the limits of transfer learning with a unified text-to-text transformer. *Journal of Machine Learning Research*, 21:1–67.

Singh, A. (2020). PoinT-5: Pointer network and T-5 based financial narrative summarisation. In *Proceedings of the 1st Joint Workshop on Financial Narrative Processing and MultiLing Financial Summarisation*, pages 105–111, Barcelona, Spain (Online), December. COLING.

Sutskever, I., Vinyals, O., and Le, Q. V. (2014). Sequence to sequence learning with neural networks. *Advances in neural information processing systems*, 27.

Vaswani, A., Shazeer, N., Parmar, N., Uszkoreit, J., Jones, L., Gomez, A. N., Kaiser, Ł., and Polosukhin, I. (2017). Attention is all you need. In *Advances in neural information processing systems*, pages 5998–6008.

Vhatkar, A., Bhattacharyya, P., and Arya, K. (2020). Knowledge graph and deep neural network for extractive text summarization by utilizing triples. In *Proceedings of the 1st Joint Workshop on Financial Narrative Processing and MultiLing Financial Summarisation*, pages 130–136, Barcelona, Spain (Online), December. COLING.

Vinyals, O., Fortunato, M., and Jaitly, N. (2015). Pointer networks. *Advances in neural information processing systems*, 28.

Wolf, T., Debut, L., Sanh, V., Chaumond, J., Delangue, C., Moi, A., Cistac, P., Rault, T., Louf, R., Funtowicz, M., Davison, J., Shleifer, S., von Platen, P., Ma, C., Jernite, Y., Plu, J., Xu, C., Scao, T. L., Gugger, S., Drame, M., Lhoest, Q., and Rush, A. M. (2020). Transformers: State-of-the-art natural language processing. In *Proceedings of the 2020 Conference on Empirical Methods in Natural Language Processing: System Demonstrations*, pages 38–45, Online, October. Association for Computational Linguistics.

Yoon, W., Lee, J., Kim, D., Jeong, M., and Kang, J. (2019). Pre-trained language model for biomedical question answering. *arXiv preprint arXiv:1909.08229*.

Zmandar, N., El-Haj, M., Rayson, P., Abura'Ed, A., Litvak, M., Giannakopoulos, G., and Pittaras, N. (2021a). The financial narrative summarisation shared task FNS 2021. In *Proceedings of the 3rd Financial Narrative Processing Workshop*, pages 120–125, Lancaster, United Kingdom, 15-16 September. Association for Computational Linguistics.

Zmandar, N., Singh, A., El-Haj, M., and Rayson, P. (2021b). Joint abstractive and extractive method for long financial document summarization. In *Proceedings of the 3rd Financial Narrative Processing Workshop*, pages 99–105, Lancaster, United Kingdom, 15-16 September. Association for Computational Linguistics.

Proceedings of the 4th Financial Narrative Processing Workshop @ LREC 2022, pages 79–82
Marseille, 24 June 2022

Financial narrative Summarisation Using a Hybrid TF-IDF and Clustering summariser: AO-Lancs System at FNS 2022

Andrew Ogden and Mahmoud El-Haj
UCREL NLP Group, Lancaster University
{a.g.ogden1,m.el-haj}@lancaster.ac.uk

Abstract

This paper describes the HTAC system submitted to the Financial Narrative Summarization Shared Task (FNS-2022). A methodology implementing Financial narrative Processing (FNP) to summarise financial annual reports, named Hybrid TF-IDF and Clustering (HTAC). This involves a hybrid approach combining TF-IDF sentence ranking as an NLP tool with a state-of-the-art Clustering Machine learning model to produce short 1000-word summaries of long financial annual reports. These Annual Reports are a legal responsibility of public companies and are in excess of 50,000 words. The model extracts the crucial information from these documents, discarding the extraneous content, leaving only the crucial information in a shorter, non-redundant summary. Producing summaries that are more effective than summaries produced by two pre-existing generic summarisers.

Keywords: FNS, Summarization, English, Spanish, Greek, NLP

1. Introduction

Each financial year companies release an annual report, these reports serve to describe their current financial state as well as their financial state throughout the previous year. These reports vary in length and composition but are often dozens of pages in length and contain numerous different sections such as statements from the company's Chief Executive Officer (CEO), Chief Financial Officer (CFO) and President, as well as many others. The reports also contain the financial statements from the past year such as Balance sheets, income statements and cash flow statements[1]. These documents must be summarized effectively allowing readers to ignore any superfluous information, making the process of parsing the reports much faster. To effectively summarise lengthy and complex documents such as financial annual reports, as much information as possible must be collated to determine the sentence rankings, providing them as much weight as possible. To this point, hybrid summarizers can be implemented, which take the information produced by several Natural Language Processing (NLP) and machine learning techniques and combine them to produce new sentence rankings, using all of the available information. This paper covers a hybrid TF-IDF and Clustering summarizer combining the base NLP technique of TF-IDF with the results of a K-Means Clustering model, using state of the art Word2Vec Embeddings, intending to improve upon the individual results of each.

2. Background

NLP summarisation has been a well-researched topic for the past decade as researchers have recognised the benefits of automatically generating summaries of large blocks of text. The purpose of automatic text summarisation is to produce a condensed, non-redundant summary text from either a single or multiple input texts (Nenkova and McKeown, 2011). The field of automatic test summarisation branched into two distinct approaches; Extractive summarisation in which sentences from the initial document compose the summary (Gupta and Lehal, 2010) and Abstractive summarisation where the summary text is entirely generated by the summariser but based on the contents of the input document (Moratanch and Chitrakala, 2016). The summariser in this project utilises extractive techniques. Extractive summarisation uses a variety of statistical methods to score parts of the original document (i.e., sentences and phrases) based on their perceived importance. This incorporates a number of different feature extraction/engineering methods and evaluations. The methods used in this Hybrid summariser are TF-IDF sentence Ranking (Luhn, 1958) and a Clustering Machine Learning Model (Radev et al., 2004; Liu and Lindroos, 2006; El-Haj et al., 2011). TF-IDF sentence ranking is a statistical technique utilising word frequencies to score the importance of certain words, it is a seminal concept in automatic text summarisation (Nenkova and McKeown, 2011). Clustering, specifically K-Means clustering is a machine learning model that clusters numerical data points around a set of iteratively generated centroids (Kanungo et al., 2002), which can be used after the input text has been converted to numerical vectors. To conclude, research into the greater area of this paper, namely NLP summarisation has been taking place for over half a century, with the seminal piece of research taking place in 1958 (Luhn, 1958). Since the publication of Luhns paper, research into NPL summarisation has come a long way with the discipline splitting up into Abstractive and Ex-

[1]Corporate Finance Institute(CFI) 2022 `https://corporatefinanceinstitute.com/resources/knowledge/finance/annual-report/`

tractive approaches and the use of machine learning to enhance results. However, despite the many new techniques published since that time, the core of Luhn's research using statistical analysis of words and word counts remains important and widely used.

3. Methodology

This paper describes the HTAC system submitted to the Financial Narrative Summarization Shared Task (FNS-2022) (Zmandar et al., 2022). The shared task has been running since 2020 (El-Haj et al., 2020b; Zmandar et al., 2021) as part of the Financial Narrative Processing (FNP) workshop series (El-Haj et al., 2022; El-Haj et al., 2021; El-Haj et al., 2020a; El-Haj et al., 2019; El-Haj et al., 2018).

The Summariser uses an extractive hybrid approach, using a statistical method to combine the TF-IDF scores of each sentence with the Euclidean distance to the centre point of its cluster. These new scores determine the final sentence rankings, the highest-scoring sentences are added to the final summary until the summary reaches the 1000 word limit. The summariser was developed using a highly modular approach, this allows each part to be changed and run separately. Overall, this meant that each part of the process could be changed, and so long as the output format remained consistent, all other parts would continue to function effectively with the new data. Consequently, a lot of time was saved as both summarisers took a significant time to run and now only needed to be re-run when they were altered. With this modularity, it became possible to test different changes to individual parts of the hybrid summariser easily, allowing for different weights when combining the data. The 4 main components are the TF-IDF and Clustering results generators, the range normaliser, and the combination summariser.

3.1. TF-IDF

TF-IDF sentence ranking provides a good base for initial summaries, being a core pillar of NLP. TF-IDF is a statistical technique using word counts to ascribe importance to certain words based on their perceived relevance to the document as whole. Thus sentences scores can be calculated when the scores for each word in the sentence are summed. The training documents in the dataset were used to create a large dictionary of word counts, which was concatenated to the top 20000 entries, removing very low-frequency words and improving computation time later on. This dictionary can then be used to create the TF-IDF word scores. The training data was used instead of a per-document basis as this allows the words of the input document to be compared against a larger cross-section of financial annual reports, not just within the context of its own content. This provided more weight to each of the frequencies and thus TF-IDF scores as they are representative of a greater dataset. For each input document, all words were added to the word dictionary, ensuring every word in the document is present in the dictionary. This dictionary is then used to create a TF-IDF score dictionary contain every discrete word in the input document, and its TF-IDF score. These scores are then added up for each word in a sentence, creating a new dictionary with every sentence and its TF-IDF score. This dictionary is then saved and later accessed by the hybrid summariser.

3.2. Clustering

This component utilises Machine learning to cluster each sentence around a set of cluster points, this then allows us to calculate the Euclidean distance between each point and the centroid of the nearest cluster. The clusters can be interpreted as a group of semantically identical sentences, that carry similar information. Thus sentences with the lowest distance, are more likely to be important as they are closer to a central concept or notion of the input document, which in the abstract is what the clusters represent. This component produces results that are more difficult to utilise in simple sentence ranking. While the TF-IDF scores provide a simple and easy to sort metric, the Euclidean distance between points can be harder to utilise, as the output of the clustering model is the coordinates of the sentences and cluster centroids in an abstract space. This means that for each point we must determine the distance between its location and the centroid of each cluster to find the distance to the nearest cluster and then record it. The summarisation in this version was implemented using K-Means clustering via SciKit Learn (Pedregosa et al., 2011), a machine learning technique that aims to cluster data points around a set of iteratively generated points. Clustering requires the input data to be in a numerical form. To do this the text of each report was converted into mathematical vector representation using Word2Vec from Gensim (Rehurek and Sojka, 2010). Word2Vec was chosen as it is a state of the art and effective way of converting text into a numerical vector representation, thus preferable to older techniques, such as bag-of-words. Word2Vec uses a low-level neural network, implementing both skip-grams and continuous-bag-of-words to return the word embeddings for the input text, producing results that are more accurate and information-dense than older models i.e., bag-of-words (Rehurek and Sojka, 2010). The Word2Vec model was created and then trained on the entire training dataset. This trained model was then loaded into the summariser and for each input document, its vocabulary was updated with every word in the input report. The model then undergoes further training with the input text. The word vectors were then extracted, combined into the appropriate sentence vectors, and passed to the K-Means Clustering model (Pedregosa et al., 2011), using 9 clusters. The number for clusters used was selected using an iterative methodology, the summariser was ran with every cluster number between 4 and 11, the resulting data showd that 9 was the optimal number. The data points were then extracted from the completed model and the Euclidean distance between each point and the centroid of its cluster was calculated. This information was then used to create a dictionary of sentences and their Euclidean distances, which was then saved allowing the combination hybrid summariser to access later.

3.3. Range Normaliser

To combine the results of the two summarisers, they were first normalised ensuring that there are in the same range. The original data points were mapped to the range of 0-100, this was chosen as it is a simple range that is both easy to visualise and to alter, allowing the weightings to be change into several commonly used increments. To normalise the sentence scores produced by each summariser, it takes the original values and replaces them with the corresponding value in the new range (0-100), this is done using the following equation. $N_{val} = \frac{(O_{val} - O_{min})N_{max}}{O_{max}} + N_{min}$ The same process is then applied to the results of the Clustering summariser and then each new value is taken from 100, to reflect that the lower the clustering score, the higher the sentence should be ranked. Once completed, the new datasets will now have the same data as the original, only represented in the new range. The new datasets will be saved and later accessed by the hybrid summariser for it to use accordingly.

3.4. Hybrid TF-IDF and Clustering (HTAC)

To combine the sentence scores, the weightings, 40/60 in favour of clustering were used, this was determined by testing each combination of weightings between 10/90 and 90/10 in 9 evenly spaced increments, and comparing results. For each summary, the two sentence scores are combined and added to a new data frame once the appropriate weights have been applied. The new data frame containing the combined sentence scores is then sorted, from highest to lowest. This data frame will then be iterated through, starting with the highest scored sentence. Each sentence, after passing several quality checks discussed below, will be added to two lists -

- The first, contains the sentences for the final summary.
- The second, contains the sentences index in the original document.

Once no more sentences will fit in the list without exceeding the word limit, the two new lists will be used to create a new data frame where the first column contains the sentences, and the second contains their corresponding index in the original report. This data frame will then be sorted by the indexes, resulting in the sentences being in their original order as found in the input report. The sorted sentences will then be joined to create a String containing the final summary.

3.5. Quality checks

Before a sentence is added to the final summary, several checks are applied to make sure that it is not redundant.

- The first and simplest is a length check, ensuring that only sentences over 10 characters are added. This removes any issues with the tokenization process which often produces some single word sentences and while these may have a high score due to their low length, they tend to have a low value in a summary as they have little of their original context remaining.
- The second check is to ensure that a very similar sentence has not already been added. This check involves comparing each new sentence to all sentences in the current summary using their Rouge-1 score. Sentences which score 0.7 or above indicates that they are 70 per cent alike, and so the sentence is not added, allowing different, more unique sentence can take its place.

Rouge Variant	English	Spanish	Greek
Rouge-1/F	0.381	0.402	0.336
Rouge-L/F	0.297	0.165	0.250
Rouge-SU4/F	0.200	0.192	0.178
Rouge-2/F	0.141	0.123	0.129

Table 1: Results on Official Validation

Table 1 shows the average Rouge score produced for each language dataset, using several Rouge variants. The Rouge-2 / F scores are similar across the 3 languages, with the English set expectedly producing the best results, being a far larger dataset.

Rouge Variant	English	Spanish	Greek
Rouge-1/F	0.317	0.448	0.334
Rouge-L/F	0.257	0.164	0.252
Rouge-SU4/F	0.185	0.211	0.182
Rouge-2/F	0.143	0.134	0.131

Table 2: Results on Official Testing Set

Table 2 shows the results of the FNS 2022 Task for this System, generated using the testing datasets. The results from the Validation and training data sets were similar, with a small increase in each of the Rouge-2 / F scores across the 3 languages in the Testing results. Once again, The English language set has the highest scoring results.

4. Conclusion

To conclude, the extractive HTAC (Hybrid TF-IDF And Clustering) system discussed in this paper constitutes an effective method of summarising financial annual reports, combining the sentence scores produced by multiple individual methodologies into final sentence rankings using statistical techniques. The results were consistent across both the validation and training datasets as well as all 3 languages. This is a positive result, with a higher level of consistency across the 3 languages than most other participants in the FNS 2022 shared task. Future work could be undertaken to determine why the system presented in this paper maintained such high levels of consistency across the 3 languages. As this could be combined with learning from the other systems that outperformed on the English dataset, whilst suffering quality drops in within the Greek and Spanish datasets. This could allow the strengths of each system to create improvements, consistently across multiple languages.

5. Bibliographical References

El-Haj, M., Kruschwitz, U., and Fox, C. (2011). Exploring clustering for multi-document arabic summarisation. In *Asia Information Retrieval Symposium*, pages 550–561. Springer.

El-Haj, M., Rayson, P., and Moore, A. (2018). The first financial narrative processing workshop (fnp 2018). In *Proceedings of the LREC 2018 Workshop*.

Mahmoud El-Haj, et al., editors. (2019). *Proceedings of the Second Financial Narrative Processing Workshop (FNP 2019)*, Turku, Finland, September. Linköping University Electronic Press.

Dr Mahmoud El-Haj, et al., editors. (2020a). *Proceedings of the 1st Joint Workshop on Financial Narrative Processing and MultiLing Financial Summarisation*, Barcelona, Spain (Online), December. COLING.

El-Haj, M., AbuRa'ed, A., Litvak, M., Pittaras, N., and Giannakopoulos, G. (2020b). The financial narrative summarisation shared task (FNS 2020). In *Proceedings of the 1st Joint Workshop on Financial Narrative Processing and MultiLing Financial Summarisation*, pages 1–12, Barcelona, Spain (Online), December. COLING.

Mahmoud El-Haj, et al., editors. (2021). *Proceedings of the 3rd Financial Narrative Processing Workshop*, Lancaster, United Kingdom, 15-16 September. Association for Computational Linguistics.

Mahmoud El-Haj, et al., editors. (2022). *Proceedings of the 4th Financial Narrative Processing Workshop*, Marseille, France, 24 June. The 13th Language Resources and Evaluation Conference, LREC 2022.

Gupta, V. and Lehal, G. S. (2010). A survey of text summarization extractive techniques. *Journal of emerging technologies in web intelligence*, 2(3):258–268.

Kanungo, T., Mount, D. M., Netanyahu, N. S., Piatko, C. D., Silverman, R., and Wu, A. Y. (2002). An efficient k-means clustering algorithm: Analysis and implementation. *IEEE transactions on pattern analysis and machine intelligence*, 24(7):881–892.

Liu, S. and Lindroos, J. (2006). Experiences from automatic summarization of imf staff reports. *Practical Data Mining: Applications, Experiences and Challenges*, page 43.

Luhn, H. P. (1958). The automatic creation of literature abstracts. *IBM Journal of research and development*, 2(2):159–165.

Moratanch, N. and Chitrakala, S. (2016). A survey on abstractive text summarization. In *2016 International Conference on Circuit, power and computing technologies (ICCPCT)*, pages 1–7. IEEE.

Nenkova, A. and McKeown, K. (2011). *Automatic summarization*. Now Publishers Inc.

Pedregosa, F., Varoquaux, G., Gramfort, A., Michel, V., Thirion, B., Grisel, O., Blondel, M., Prettenhofer, P., Weiss, R., Dubourg, V., et al. (2011). Scikit-learn: Machine learning in python. *the Journal of machine Learning research*, 12:2825–2830.

Radev, D. R., Jing, H., Styś, M., and Tam, D. (2004). Centroid-based summarization of multiple documents. *Information Processing & Management*, 40(6):919–938.

Rehurek, R. and Sojka, P. (2010). Software framework for topic modelling with large corpora. In *In Proceedings of the LREC 2010 workshop on new challenges for NLP frameworks*. Citeseer.

Zmandar, N., El-Haj, M., Rayson, P., Abura'Ed, A., Litvak, M., Giannakopoulos, G., and Pittaras, N. (2021). The financial narrative summarisation shared task FNS 2021. In *Proceedings of the 3rd Financial Narrative Processing Workshop*, pages 120–125, Lancaster, United Kingdom, 15-16 September. Association for Computational Linguistics.

Zmandar, N., El-Haj, M., Rayson, P., Abura'Ed, A., Litvak, M., Giannakopoulos, G., Pittaras, N., Carbajo-Coronado, B., and Moreno-Sandoval, A. (2022). The financial narrative summarisation shared task (fns 2022). In *Proceedings of the 4th Financial Narrative Processing Workshop*, Marseille, France, 24June. The 13th Language Resources and Evaluation Conference, LREC 2022.

Proceedings of the 4th Financial Narrative Processing Workshop @ LREC 2022, pages 83–88
Marseille, 24 June 2022

The Financial Document Structure Extraction Shared Task (FinTOC 2022)

Abderrahim Ait Azzi[1], Sandra Bellato[1], Blanca Carbajo Coronado[2], Mahmoud El-Haj[3], Ismail El Maarouf[1], Mei Gan[1], Ana Gisbert[2], Juyeon Kang[1], Antonio Moreno Sandoval[2]

Fortia Financial Solutions[1], Paris, France
Universidad Autónoma de Madrid[2], Madrid, Spain
Lancaster University[1], Lancaster, UK
{abderrahim.aitazzi, sandra.bellato, mei.gan, ismail.elmaarouf, juyeon.kang}@fortia.fr[1]
{blanca.carbajo, ana.gisbert, antonio.msandoval}@uam.es[2]
m.el-haj@lancaster.ac.uk[3]

Abstract

This paper describes the FinTOC-2022 Shared Task on the structure extraction from financial documents, its participants results and their findings. This shared task was organized as part of The 4th Financial Narrative Processing Workshop (FNP 2022), held jointly at The 13th Edition of the Language Resources and Evaluation Conference (LREC 2022), Marseille, France (El-Haj et al., 2022). This shared task aimed to stimulate research in systems for extracting table-of-contents (TOC) from investment documents (such as financial prospectuses) by detecting the document titles and organizing them hierarchically into a TOC. For the forth edition of this shared task, three subtasks were presented to the participants: one with English documents, one with French documents and the other one with Spanish documents. This year, we proposed a different and revised dataset for English and French compared to the previous editions of FinTOC and a new dataset for Spanish documents was added. The task attracted 6 submissions for each language from 4 teams, and the most successful methods make use of textual, structural and visual features extracted from the documents and propose classification models for detecting titles and TOCs for all of the subtasks.

Keywords: Financial Data Annotation, Document Structure Extraction, Table-Of-Contents Extraction, Machine Learning

1. Introduction

A vast amount of financial documents are created and published constantly in machine-readable formats (generally PDF file format), with only minimal structure information. Firms use such documents to report their activities, financial situation or potential investment plans to shareholders, investors and the financial markets, basically corporate annual reports containing detailed financial and operational information.

In some countries as in the US or in France, regulators such as EDGAR SEC or AMF require firms to follow a certain template when reporting their financial results to ensure standardization and consistency across firms' disclosures. In other European countries, on the other hand, the management usually has more discretion on what, where and how to report resulting in lack of standardization between financial documents published within the same market.

Existing work on book and document table of contents (TOC) recognition has been almost all on small size, application-dependent, and domain-specific datasets. However, TOC of documents from different domains differ significantly in their visual layout and style, making TOC recognition a challenging problem for a large scale collection of heterogeneous documents and books. Compared to regular books (mostly provided in a full text format with limited structural information such as pages and paragraphs), Financial documents, containing textual and non textual content, have a more sophisticated structure including, parts, sections, subsections, sub-sub-sections.

In this shared task, we focus on analyzing two types of financial documents: 1) Fund Prospectuses, official PDF documents in which investment funds precisely describe their characteristics and investment modalities, and 2) financial annual reports, publicly available PDF documents on which firms publish a year-end summary of their operations and financial conditions. In the case of the fund prospectuses, although the content they must include is often regulated, their format is not standardized and displays a great deal of variability ranging from plain text format, towards more graphical and tabular presentation of data and information. The layout information becomes more heterogeneous from a company to another in the case of the annual reports as there is no regulations on their document structure. While the majority of annual reports often contain a simplified table of contents (TOC), the majority of prospectuses are published without a TOC, which is usually needed to help readers to navigate within the document by following a simple outline of headers and page numbers, and assist legal teams in checking if all the contents required are fully included in both cases. Thus, automatic analyses of those documents to extract their structure is becoming more and more vital to many firms across the world.

Thanks to the contribution of the Autonomous University of Madrid (UAM, Spain) (Moreno-Sandoval et al., 2020), the fourth edition of the FinTOC shared task proposes the same welcomes a new track for Spanish documents in addition to English and French, and it will score systems on both Title detection and TOC generation performance as has been the practice from previous editions.

In this paper, we report the results and findings of the FinTOC-2022 shared task[1]. The Shared Task was organized as part of The 4th Financial Narrative Processing Workshop (FNP 2022)[2], to be held at The 13th Edition of the Language Resources and Evaluation Conference (LREC 2022)[3].

The shared task attracted 6 system submissions from 4 teams for each language and for the Title Detection and TOC extraction tasks. In general, the systems which make use of textual, structural and visual features, and exploit observed features during classification models training for the Title Detection and TOC extraction, perform better.

2. Previous Work on Document structure extraction

Previous work can be divided into two approaches for the TOC extraction. The first approach parses the hierarchical structure of sections and subsections from the TOC pages embedded in the document. This area of research was mostly motivated by the INEX ((Dresevic et al., 2009)) and ICDAR competitions ((Doucet et al., 2013), (Beckers et al., 2010); (Nguyen et al., 2017)) which aim at extracting the TOC of old and lenghtly OCR-ised books. The documents we target in this shared task are very different: they contain graphical elements, and the text is not displayed to respect a linear reading direction but is optimized to condense information and catch the eye of the reader. Apart from these competitions, we find the methods proposed by El-Haj et al. ((El-Haj et al., 2014),(El-Haj et al., 2019)), also based on the parsing of the TOC page.

In the second category of approaches, we find algorithms that detect the titles of the document using learning methods based on layout and text features. The set of titles is then hierarchically ordered according to a predefined rule-based function ((Doucet et al., 2013); (Liu et al., 2011); (Mysore Gopinath et al., 2018)). Lately, we find systems that address the hierarchical ordering of the titles as a sequence labelling task, using neural networks models such as Recurrent Neural Networks and LSTM networks ((Bentabet et al., 2019)). We also see that the large dataset like PubLayNet (Zhong et al., 2019) which contains various annotated elements in a page such as text, list, figure etc. is created based on over 1 million PDF articles and published allowing to lead interesting experiments on the document layout analysis.

3. Task Description

As part of the FNP 2022 Workshop, we present a shared task on Financial Document Structure Extraction. Participants to this shared task were given three sets of financial prospectuses and annual reports with a wide variety of document structure and length. Their systems had to automatically process the documents to extract their document structure, or TOC. In fact, the three sets were specific to three different subtasks:

TOC extraction from French documents The set of French documents is rather homogeneous in terms of structure, due to the existence of a common template. However, the words and phrasing can differ from one prospectus to another. Also, French prospectuses never include a TOC page that could be parsed.

TOC extraction from English documents English prospectuses are characterized by a wide variety of structures as there is no template to constrain their format. Contrary to the French documents, there is always a TOC page but the latter is usually highly incomplete as only the higher level section titles are displayed.

TOC extraction from Spanish documents This year we have introduced the set of documents in Spanish. The reports were chosen for their availability to annotate the titles in the pdf. However, they varied in size and structure, with little uniformity in structure. In this sense, the Spanish reports resemble the English ones. They tend to have TOC and many levels of nesting in the titles (up to 7). In addition, half of the reports do not follow a coherent structure in the section numbering.

3.1. Shared Task Data

In this section, we describe the datasets prepared for the shared task.

Dataset FinToc 2022 proposes enriched datasets for English and French and a new dataset for Spanish financial documents. As the previous editions, we carefully selected documents for each language with a large variety of structures and layouts, see the Figure 1 for a comparative layouts of the documents in different language.

The table 1 shows the statistics of the elaborated datasets for this edition. The average number of titles are 134 for French, 225 for English and 150 for Spanish and the maximum depth of the tiles are 9 for English and French datasets and 7 for Spanish.

The English and French datasets are composed of the financial prospectuses of different companies, published between 2010 and 2021. The Spanish dataset is taken from the FinT-esp corpus (Moreno-Sandoval et al., 2020) and consists of 90 documents with a distribution similar to the French and English datasets for

[1] http://wp.lancs.ac.uk/cfie/fintoc2022/

[2] http://wp.lancs.ac.uk/cfie/fnp2022/

[3] https://lrec2022.lrec-conf.org/en/

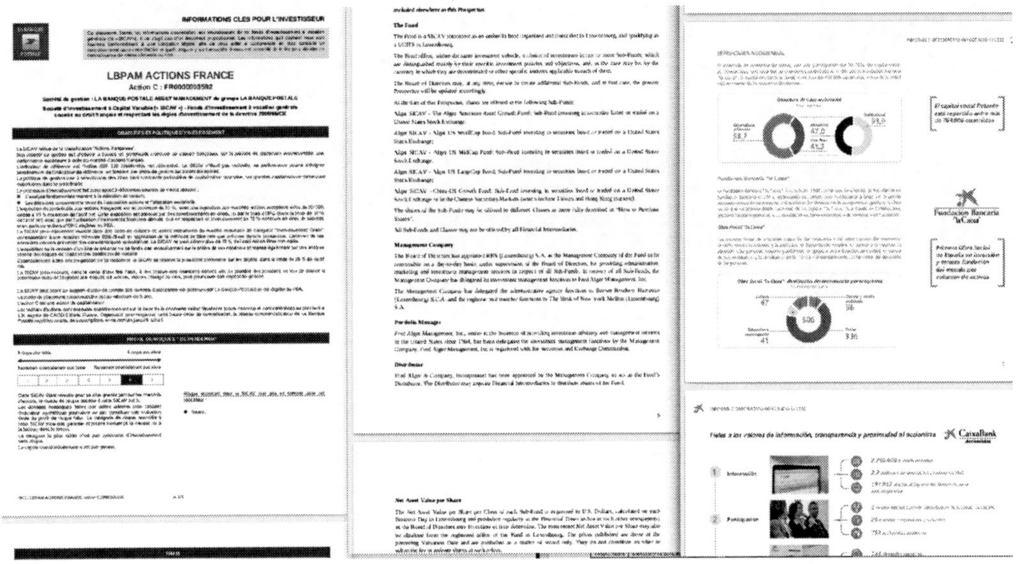

Figure 1: Pages randomly selected from the datasets in French, English and Spanish

	French	English	Spanish
training set	81	79	80
test set	10	10	10
average number of pages	24	90	158

Table 1: Statistics on Dataset

development, validation and test. The dates of the annual reports range from 2014 to 2018. The source is in PDF format, with a total number of pages between 40 and 400. In plain text, the files have an average of 36,285 words. The total number of tags noted in the 90 reports is 10,842, with an average of 148 tags per document.

All the annotated datasets are proposed in simple JSON files containing a list of entries, where each entry has the following information: textual content, id, level, page number (See the example of a JSON in the Figure 2).

Data Annotation Datasets were annotated by the way that the annotators first locate the position of the titles inside each PDF document, then link the title to the entry level in the TOC and give a depth level to each title ranging from 1 to 10. For each of the datasets, three annotators including one as reviewer collaborated to avoid the possible problems like inconsistencies and resolve the possible conflicts during the data annotation.

3.2. Evaluation metrics

FinTOC 2022 uses the evaluation metric as in the previous edition (Maarouf et al., 2021) since the proposed tasks tackle the same problem on different datasets: *Inex F1 score* and *Inex level accuracy*.

We propose two different metrics for each subtask. We use the F1 score for the title detection, meaning that we consider as correct entries the predicted entries which match the titles of groudtruth entries according to the standard Levenshtein distance.

For the TOC extraction, we adapt the metrics proposed by the Structure Extraction Competition (SEC) held at ICDAR 2013 (Doucet et al., 2013) by replacing the customized Levenshtein distance specifically designed for SEC by a standard Levenshtein distance whose edit cost is 1 in all cases, and removing the constraint on first and last 5 characters. The final ranking is based on the harmonic mean between *Inex F1 score* and *Inex level accuracy*. The *Inex F1 score* considers as correct entries in the predicted TOC those which match the title of an entry in the TOC groundtruth and have the same page number as this entry. The *Inex level accuracy* evaluates the hierarchy of the predicted TOC. If we denote by E_{ok} an entry in the predicted TOC with a correct page number, and by E'_{ok} an entry in the predicted TOC with a correct page number and a correct hierarchical level, then the *Inex level accuracy* is:

$$\frac{\sum E'_{ok}}{\sum E_{ok}}$$

For both tasks, the threshold on the Levenshtein score was set to 0.85.

4. Participants and Systems

A total of 24 teams registered this year to FinTOC Shared Task from different academic and private institutions. 4 teams submitted the systems results all for

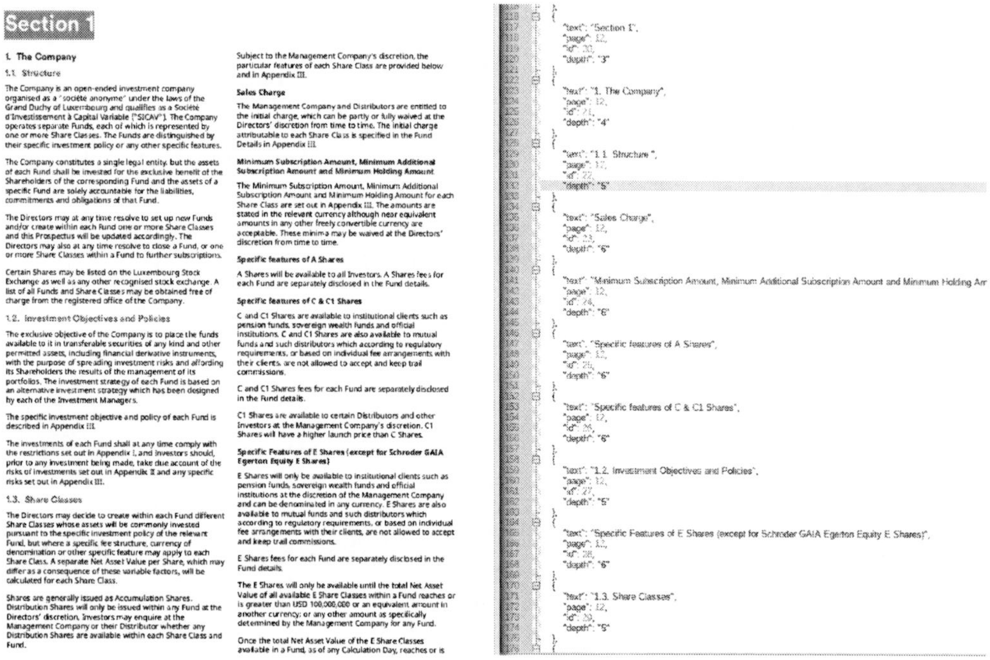

Figure 2: Example of a labeled document in a JSON format with its original PDF document.

three subtasks and 3 teams submitted a system description paper on their method and results as shown in the table 2.

Team	Affiliation
CILAB	KIT, Gumi, Korea
GREYC	CNRS, France
ISPRAS	ISP RAS, Moscow, Russia
swapUNIBA	University of Bari, Italy

Table 2: Participants and affiliations

GREYC ((Giguet and Lucas, 2022)) submitted the results of 2 standard runs on each of the datasets for Title Detection and TOC structure extraction. They propose an end-to-end pipeline which processes documents to first extract textual and visual information of the documents such as token, line, text block, text background, framed content, underline, table grid, bounding boxes of figures and of graphical bullets. Then, using those extracted features, the pipeline performs the document delimitation from the bundle of the datasets, detects header and footer areas from the individual document and applies the Page Layout Analysis which recognizes and labels content areas like texts, tables, figures, lists, headers and footers. They use predefined heuristics to detect a TOC from each document and link the TOC entries to its matching text lines and corresponding page number in the document where the detected line is considered as title.

ISP RAS ((Kozlov et al., 2021)) submitted also the results of 2 standard runs on each of the datasets for the Title Detection and the TOC extraction. They design a full pipeline including two main stages of classification using a decision tree-based algorithm, XGBoost classifier to classify a line as title or not and for each detected title, to find its depth. The PDF documents are preprocessed by PDFMiner and they trained a binary classifier for the first stage and a multiclass classifier for the second, based on the extracted textual, visual and structural features such as color, font style, indentation, list, line depth, letters, words and line statistics, etc. The first run for each language is the result of the classifiers which were trained on the dataset of a specific language, separately, and the second runs are the results of the classifiers trained on all of the datasets.

swapUNIBA ((Cassotti et al., 2022)) submitted the results of 1 standard run on each of the datasets for the Title detection and the TOC extraction. They design a system of Document Image Analysis by exploiting layout features like title, table, list and texts along with an object detector, Faster R-CNN. A pretrained Faster R-CNN model on the PubLayNet dataset was finetuned on the datasets of the shared task for the titles detection, which was preprocessed by pdfplumber. Then level classification module performs the inference of hierarchical level of each title using a multiclass Random Forest classifier trained on the given datasets. At this level, they consider in input the features of a single TOC entry detected by the Title detection module like first five and last two characters of the text title, font name and size, bounding boxes normalized by the document width and height, etc.

5. Results and Discussion

The scores, based on the metrics described in the Section 3.2, are calculated for each document and then averaged over the documents for each language to produce two performance figures per team submission: one for Title Detection, and another for TOC Extraction. The title detection ranking is based on F1-score, while the TOC extraction ranking is based on the harmonic mean between *Inex F1 score* and *Inex level accuracy*.
Table 3 compares the results of both tasks in terms of the *F1 score* and *Inex level accuracy* on French data. We have two different winning systems for each subtask: ISP RAS1 for the Title Detection and ISP RAS2 for the TOC Extraction. The binary classifier trained only on the French data performs better for the Title detection, while the classifier trained on all the datasets performs better for the TOC extraction.

Team	Title Detection	TOC Extraction
CILAB	0.304	12,90
GREYC1	0.669	7,24
GREYC2	0.671	6,95
ISP RAS1	**0.778**	38,93
ISP RAS2	0.758	**41,58**
swapUNIBA	0.695	34,08

Table 3: Results obtained by the participants for the subtask on French data

Table 4 compares the results of both tasks on English data. Similarly to the results on French data, we also have two different winning systems: ISP RAS1 for the first task and ISP RAS2 for the second, showing that a multilingual dataset can be helpful for improving the overall results.

Team	Title Detection	TOC Extraction
CILAB	0.738	36,99
GREYC1	0.790	0,20
GREYC2	0.793	0,20
ISP RAS1	**0.900**	62,16
ISP RAS2	0.876	**63,17**
swapUNIBA	0.838	51,24

Table 4: Results obtained by the participants for the subtask on English data

Table 5 compares the results of both tasks on Spanish data. We have one winning system for both tasks: swapUNIBA. The best system achieved the F1 score of 0.569% for the title detection and 43,01 for the TOC extraction, indicating that the task needs to be more investigated to solve the problem. But knowing that the Spanish dataset is composed of the annual reports which contain more complex layouts comparing to the fund prospectus documents used in English and French datasets, the produced scores by the systems remain encouraging.

Team	Title Detection	TOC Extraction
CILAB	0.077	8,63
GREYC1	0.196	5,10
GREYC2	0.206	5,22
ISP RAS1	0.554	40,80
ISP RAS2	0.558	40
swapUNIBA	**0.569**	**43,01**

Table 5: Results obtained by the participants for the subtask on Spanish data

Teams submitting multiple systems were able to slightly improve their score within their own submissions, but we did not find that the individual submissions were statistically significantly different. And interestingly, we observe a trade-off from the results of the winning systems on English and French data according to the way that they exploit the datasets as a single dataset or a multilingual dataset (see (Kozlov et al., 2021) for more details.). Since the TOC extraction task depends on the results of the Title detection, the system with a high performance on the Title detection step achieves a high accuracy on the TOC extraction. For English data, the scores for both tasks were significantly improved comparing to those of the previous edition (Maarouf et al., 2021)[4]. Otherwise, both tasks on French and Spanish data are still far from solved.

6. Conclusions

This paper describes the fourth edition of the FinTOC shared task on extraction of the document structure from financial documents. The 6 system submissions from 4 teams for each of the languages, English, French and Spanish, showed that they all exploit textual and visual features extracted from the PDF documents using different text preprocessing tools. Interestingly, the best systems for the Title detection and the TOC extraction on English and French data achieved a good accuracy for the Title detection with a classifier trained on a single dataset while they perform better for the TOC extraction with a classifier trained on a multilingual dataset. More investigation on the error analysis will allow to clarify those impacts. For the Spanish data, the Object Detection approach using a pretrained deep neural model on the large dataset, PubLayNet,

[4]The scores published in the shared task description paper of FinTOC 2021 were miscalculated for the submissions Christopher Bourez1 and 2. The harmonic means are relatively 43,10 and 39 for the TOC extraction on English data and 46,20 and 39 on French data.

performs slightly better than a decision tree-based algorithm. It can be explained by the fact that the datasets used for English and French, and the dataset used for Spanish are quite different in terms of its type (fund prospectuses vs. annual reports), consequently, their structures and layouts are different and the annual reports contain much more visual elements like figures, graphs, tables, bulleted lists, etc. Introducing Spanish fund prospectuses in the shared task data and/or enriching the English and French datasets by adding annual reports would be interesting for the next edition of FinTOC.

7. Acknowledgements

We would like to thank our dedicated annotators who contributed to the building of the corpora used in this Shared Task over the years: Anais Koptient, Aouataf Djillani, Lidia Duarte, Bianca Chong, Marion Cargill, Sandra Bellato, Mei Gan, Anaïs Lhuissier for English and French data, Ana Gisbert, Blanca Carbajo, Ana García, Andrea Castillo, Victoria Matínez, Kateryna Sushkova and Antonio Moreno for Spanish data, and authors of this paper.

8. Bibliographical References

Beckers, T., Bellot, P., Demartini, G., Denoyer, L., De Vries, C. M., Doucet, A., Fachry, K. N., Fuhr, N., Gallinari, P., Geva, S., et al. (2010). Report on inex 2009. In *ACM SIGIR Forum*, volume 44:1, pages 38–57. ACM New York, NY, USA.

Bentabet, N.-I., Juge, R., and Ferradans, S. (2019). Table-of-contents generation on contemporary documents. *arXiv preprint arXiv:1911.08836*.

Cassotti, P., Musto, C., de Gemmis, M., Lekkas, G., and Semeraro, G. (2022). swapuniba@fintoc2022: Fine-tuning pre-trained document image analysis model for title detection on the financial domain. In *Proceedings of Language Resources and Evaluation (LREC'22)*, Marseille, France, June. European Language Resources Association (ELRA).

Doucet, A., Kazai, G., Colutto, S., and Mühlberger, G. (2013). Icdar 2013 competition on book structure extraction. In *2013 12th International Conference on Document Analysis and Recognition*, pages 1438–1443. IEEE.

Dresevic, B., Uzelac, A., Radakovic, B., and Todic, N. (2009). Book layout analysis: Toc structure extraction engine. In Shlomo Geva, et al., editors, *Advances in Focused Retrieval*, pages 164–171, Berlin, Heidelberg. Springer Berlin Heidelberg.

El-Haj, M., Rayson, P., Young, S., and Walker, M. (2014). Detecting document structure in a very large corpus of UK financial reports. In *Proceedings of the Ninth International Conference on Language Resources and Evaluation (LREC'14)*, pages 1335–1338, Reykjavik, Iceland, May. European Language Resources Association (ELRA).

El-Haj, M., Alves, P., Rayson, P., Walker, M., and Young, S. (2019). Retrieving, classifying and analysing narrative commentary in unstructured (glossy) annual reports published as pdf files. *Research Methods & Methodology in Accounting eJournal*.

Mahmoud El-Haj, et al., editors. (2022). *Proceedings of the 4th Financial Narrative Processing Workshop*, Marseille, France, 24 June. The 13th Language Resources and Evaluation Conference, LREC 2022.

Giguet, E. and Lucas, N. (2022). Greyc@fintoc-2022: Handling document layout and structure in native pdf bundle of documents. In *Proceedings of Language Resources and Evaluation (LREC'22)*, Marseille, France, June. European Language Resources Association (ELRA).

Kozlov, I., Belyaeva, O., Bogatenkova, A., and Perminov, A. (2021). Ispras@ fintoc-2021 shared task: Two-stage toc generation model. In *Proceedings of the 3rd Financial Narrative Processing Workshop*, pages 81–85.

Liu, C., Chen, J., Zhang, X., Liu, J., and Huang, Y. (2011). Toc structure extraction from ocr-ed books. In *INEX*.

Maarouf, I. E., Kang, J., Azzi, A. A., Bellato, S., Gan, M., and El-Haj, M. (2021). The financial document structure extraction shared task (FinTOC2021). In *Proceedings of the 3rd Financial Narrative Processing Workshop*, pages 111–119, Lancaster, United Kingdom, 15-16 September. Association for Computational Linguistics.

Moreno-Sandoval, A., Gisbert, A., and Montoro, H. (2020). Fint-esp: a corpus of financial reports in spanish. In Fuster, et al., editors, *Multiperspectives in analysis and corpus design*, pages 89–102, Granada. Comares.

Mysore Gopinath, A. A., Wilson, S., and Sadeh, N. (2018). Supervised and unsupervised methods for robust separation of section titles and prose text in web documents. In *Proceedings of the 2018 Conference on Empirical Methods in Natural Language Processing*, pages 850–855, Brussels, Belgium, October-November. Association for Computational Linguistics.

Nguyen, T.-T.-H., Doucet, A., and Coustaty, M. (2017). Enhancing table of contents extraction by system aggregation. In *2017 14th IAPR International Conference on Document Analysis and Recognition (ICDAR)*, volume 01, pages 242–247.

Zhong, X., Tang, J., and Yepes, A. J. (2019). Publaynet: largest dataset ever for document layout analysis. In *2019 International Conference on Document Analysis and Recognition (ICDAR)*, pages 1015–1022. IEEE, Sep.

Proceedings of the 4th Financial Narrative Processing Workshop @ LREC 2022, pages 89–94
Marseille, 24 June 2022

ISPRAS@FinTOC-2022 Shared Task: Two-stage TOC Generation Model

Anastasiia Bogatenkova, Oksana Belyaeva, Andrew Perminov, Ilya Kozlov
Ivannikov Institute for System Programming of the RAS
25, Alexander Solzhenitsyn Str., Moscow, 109004, Russia
{nastyboget, belyaeva, perminov, kozlov-ilya}@ispras.ru

Abstract

This work is connected with participation in FinTOC-2022 Shared Task: "Financial Document Structure Extraction". The competition contains two subtasks: title detection and TOC generation. We describe an approach for solving these tasks and propose the pipeline, consisting of extraction of document lines and existing TOC, feature matrix forming and classification. Classification model consists of two classifiers: the first binary classifier separates title lines from non-title, the second one determines the title level. In the title detection task, we got 0.900, 0.778 and 0.558 F1 measure, in the TOC generation task we got 63.1, 41.5 and 40.79 the harmonic mean of Inex F1 score and Inex level accuracy for English, French and Spanish documents respectively. With these results, our approach took first place among English and French submissions and second place among Spanish submissions. As a team, we took first place in the competition in English and French categories and second place in the competition in Spanish.

Keywords: document structure, TOC generation, machine learning

1. Introduction

Currently, electronic documents have become widespread. A large number of documents are presented in a PDF format, but only a few of them contain an automatic table of contents (TOC). However, there may be the need for a quick search of information and it may be a problem for large documents. One example is financial documents, which can be over 100 pages long. Financial documents contain a lot of important information and can have different appearances and structures. The task of automatically extracting the table of contents from financial documents seems to be relevant and its solution is not obvious.

FinTOC-2022 offers to solve the problem of extracting structure from financial documents in three languages: English, French and Spanish. The results of solving two subtasks are evaluated:

- **Title detection (TD)** - selection from all lines of the document only those that should be included in the table of contents;
- **Table of contents (TOC) generation** - identification nesting depths of selected titles.

The competition is held for the fourth time. Similar tasks were solved at FinTOC-2019 (Juge et al., 2019), FinTOC-2020 (Bentabet et al., 2020), FinTOC-2021 (El Maarouf et al., 2021); in 2020, documents in French were added, and the dataset was supplemented with Spanish documents in 2022.

In FinTOC-2019, the best solution (Tian and Peng, 2019) for title detection is based on the LSTM with augmentation and attention. The best solution (Giguet and Lejeune, 2019) for the TOC generation task relies on the decision tree classifier DT 10 and TOC page detection.

In FinTOC-2020, the best solution (Hercig and Kral, 2020) for title detection (French) was obtained with the maximum entropy classifier. For title detection in English documents (Premi et al., 2020) LSTM, CharCNN, and a fully connected network with some handcrafted features were used. The best approach for TOC generation (Kosmajac et al., 2020) consisted in extracting linguistic and structural information and using the Random Forest classifier.

In FinTOC-2021, for both title detection and TOC generation task, both English and French languages, the best solution (Bourez, 2021) consisted of statistical features extraction on style properties and using XGBoost classifier to predict the needed information.

We also participated in FinTOC-2021 (Kozlov et al., 2021) and took second place in all subtasks. Our decision also relies on XGBoost classifier, that is used separately for solving title detection and TOC item depth prediction subtasks.

In this paper, we describe enhancements of our previous solution to the shared task. As in (Kozlov et al., 2021), we make a list of features for each document line and use two classifiers for the consequent solution of both title detection and TOC generation tasks. We tried to train the classifiers on all data in three languages, as well as on each language separately. In addition, the selection of parameters of the classifiers for each of the subtasks was carried out.

The paper is organized as follows. We describe the given dataset for the competitions and compare it with the previous one in Section 2. We present our approach and its improvement in Section 3. Results and a discussion are given in Section 4 and 5 respectively. Section 6 contains a conclusion about our work.

		English	French	English	French	Spanish
train	Number of documents	49	47	79	81	80
	Mean number of pages	64	30	77	27	119
	Number of TOC	43	4	69	6	74
	Mean number of titles	181	142	225	134	150
	Max title depth	9	6	9	9	7
test	Number of documents	10	10	10	10	10
	Mean number of pages	66	26	102	20	198
	Number of TOC	9	0	8	2	9
		2021		*2022*		

Table 1: Training and test datasets' statistics for 2021 and 2022

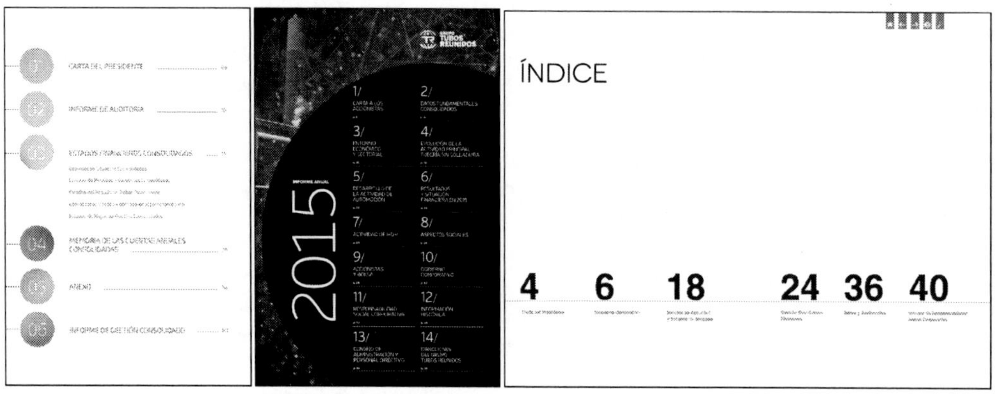

Figure 1: Examples of TOCs in Spanish documents

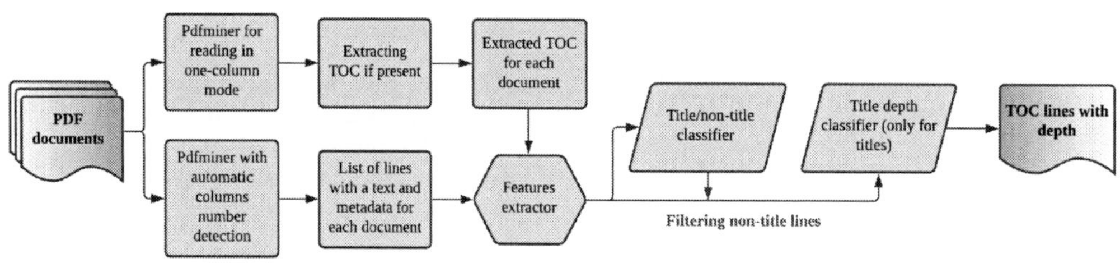

Figure 2: Full pipeline description

2. Datasets

The training data of the FinTOC-2022 shared task consists of 71 English, 81 French and 80 Spanish financial PDF documents with a textual layer. The documents are very heterogeneous, all groups contain documents with and without TOC.

The main information about the datasets of 2021 and 2022 is in the Table 1. Disregarding Spanish documents, the number of documents almost doubled in comparison with the previous year. The dataset contains one-column, two-column, and even three-column documents. At the same time, a different number of columns may occur within one document. Moreover, documents are different in their appearance (e. g. the appearance of titles or existing TOC) and logical structure. We should especially mention Spanish documents, which are extremely difficult to parse due to the variety of layouts. Almost all the Spanish documents have a table of contents, still, these TOCs greatly differ from one to another (Figure 1).

There is a set of annotations for each document in the training set. Annotations include only titles with the text and the depth for each title. The number of titles and maximum title depth are different for each document. The number of titles varies from 20 to 1036, from 12 to 527, from 0 to 468 for documents in English, French and Spanish, respectively. Maximum title depth is from 1 to 9 for English and French documents, while it equals from 1 to 7 for Spanish documents. Thus, samples of very different documents are presented at

Features group	Description	Type
Visual	Colour (red, green, blue) and colour dispersion	float
	Font style (bold, italic)	bool
	Indentation, spacing between lines, font size (normalized)	float
Letter, words, and line statistics	The percentage of letters, capital letters, numbers, brackets in a line	float
	The number of words in a line	int
	Normalized page number, line number, and line length	float
TOC	Indicator, if non-empty TOC was extracted for the given document	bool
	Indicator, if the given line is the part of TOC (the page of this line is the page where TOC is located)	bool
	Indicator, if the line is a header included in TOC (the page of this line is mentioned in TOC)	bool
Textual	Indicators, if the line matches regular expressions for different lists like 1), a), I., 1., i), –, etc.	bool
	Indicator, if the line ends with a dot, colon, semicolon, comma	bool
Window bound features	If the line is a list item, the number of predecessors and predecessors with the same indentation in the window of sizes 10, 25, 100 (normalized by the length of the window)	float
	The number of lines with the same indentation in the window of sizes 10, 25, 100 (normalized by the length of the window)	float
Lines depth	The level of numbering for list with dots (like 1.1.1), relative font size and indentation	int
Contextual	The aforesaid features for 3 previous and 3 next lines	float, int, bool

Table 2: Features description

the competition.
The test dataset is similar to the training dataset. It contains 10 documents for each language.

3. Proposed approach

As in the previous year (Kozlov et al., 2021), we propose the 2-stage method for solving the both tasks TD and TOC generation (Figure 2). Each stage includes classification using the XGBoost classifier.

1. The binary classifier classifies each line as title or non-title.

2. For each filtered title from the first stage, its depth is found using the second multiclass classifier.

The main steps of our algorithm are described below.

3.1. Text and metadata extraction.

We extracted text, bold and italic font, colours, etc. of the text with help of PDFMiner (Yusuke Shinyama, 2019), which has different layout reading modes. To read the entire document we have chosen the universal layout mode for multi-column documents with parameters *LAParams(line_margin=1.5, line_overlap=0.5, boxes_flow=0.5, word_margin=0.1, detect_vertical=False)*. Thus the list of lines with text and metadata is extracted from the input documents. To obtain lines with labels we matched the provided labelled titles and the extracted lines using a Levenshtein distance with 0.8 threshold.

As preprocessing, we remove footers and headers from a document using the method (Lin, 2003). It helps to improve the quality of the binary classifier and the TOC extraction module. Moreover, we delete empty lines because they aren't useful for our target result.

3.2. Existing TOC extraction.

As additional information, we separately extract a table of content (TOC) for each document. We look for the keywords of the TOC heading in the document (for example, "Table of contents", "CONTENT") as the beginning of TOC. Then, we detect the TOC's body using regular expressions.

Most tables of contents in the given documents are one-column regardless of the number of columns in the whole document. The TOC extraction module requires PDFMiner to be run in the single column mode because the TOC text may be read automatically as a multi-column. In this case, PDFMiner should be run with the parameters *LAParams(line_margin=3.0, line_overlap=0.1, boxes_flow=0.5, word_margin=1.5, char_margin=100.0, detect_vertical=False)*.

3.3. Features extraction.

The list of extracted lines and extracted TOCs (if present) are processed to obtain a vector of features for each extracted line. We formed a vector from 197 features, some of which are grouped and described in the Table 2.

Option name	Binary classifier			Depth classifier		
	En	Fr	Sp	En	Fr	Sp
learning_rate	0.25	0.1	0.25	0.07	0.4	0.25
max_depth	5	5	4	4	5	3
n_estimators	400	800	600	800	800	600
colsample_bynode	0.8	0.5	0.5	1	1	0.5
colsample_bytree	0.5	0.8	0.5	1	0.5	1
tree_method	*hist*	*approx*	*approx*	*hist*	*exact*	*hist*

Table 3: The resulting classifiers parameters

Model type	TD			TOC		
	En	Fr	Sp	En	Fr	Sp
ISP RAS1	0.79	0.74	0.57	55.8	45.4	42.9
ISP RAS2	0.81	0.73	0.58	57.7	43.4	41.8

Table 4: The mean results from cross-validation on the training dataset

3.4. Classification

For both tasks, we experimented with the XGBoost classifier. During training, we fed the classifiers with different data:

1. **ISP RAS1** – for each language, classifiers were trained only on the documents of that language. Namely, classifiers for English documents were trained only on English documents, etc.

2. **ISP RAS2** – for each language, classifiers were trained on the documents of all available languages.

While training separate classifiers for each language, we selected the best classifiers' options. We tried the grid of possible parameters combinations and found options that gave the highest score. The resulting options are enlisted in the Table 3.
Due to the lack of time, during training classifiers on documents of all languages, we also used the parameters shown in the Table 3.
We use 3-fold cross-validation for evaluate the results of each model. The mean results for both experiments (ISP RAS1 and ISP RAS2) are given in the Table 4. The evaluation script is provided by the organizers.

4. Results

The competition results on test dataset are presented in the table 5 (Title Detection), and tables 6, 7, 8 (TOC generation). In addition, the best three results of the previous year were added. Our approach ranks first among submitted solutions in 2022 for English and French documents, and second for Spanish documents.

Team run	F1 (EN)	F1 (FR)	F1 (SP)
Christopher B.1	0.822	0.817	–
Christopher B.2	0.830	0.818	–
ISP RAS (2021)	0.813	0.787	–
CILAB	0.738	0.304	0.077
GREYC1	0.790	0.669	0.196
GREYC2	0.793	0.671	0.206
ISP RAS1	**0.900**	**0.778**	0.554
ISP RAS2	0.876	0.758	0.558
swapUNIBA	0.838	0.695	**0.569**

Table 5: Title Detection Competition results

5. Discussion

The two-stage model demonstrates high scores for both tasks. But the model has disadvantages. Primarily, the model misclassifies questionable titles, the ground truth of which are interpreted differently for different documents. For example, one document has a line with some features (color, font size, style, etc.) as a title, but the equivalent line in another document is not a title. Also, we don't combine adjacent titles together as in the ground truth of the data sets.
As well, a two-stage model accuracy in the title detection task is limited by the binary classifier. If the model filters out the title lines in the first step, it will not be able to determine their depths in the second one. Therefore, the accuracy of the two-stage model will not exceed the accuracy of the binary classifier.
As a development of the work, we propose to consider more advanced and complicated models, e. g. the LSTM model. This model can give greater accuracy through the use of long-term memory. Thus, we will be able to remember the previous predictions made up to this point in the document.

6. Conclusion

We proposed the approach for automatic title detection and TOC generation for PDF financial documents with a textual layer. We extracted lines with metadata using Pdfminer and found existing TOCs using the regular expressions. Empty lines, headers and footers were removed from consideration. Extracted lines were transformed to the feature matrix with the vector of predefined features for each line. Then we used a two-stage model for title detection and TOC generation. First, we filter titles from all document lines using the XGBoost binary classifier. Then, we find the depths of the filtered lines using the second XGBoost classifier. Optimal parameters for the classifiers were found to improve the

Team run	Inex08-P	Inex08-R	Inex08-F1	Inex08-Title acc	Inex08-Level acc	harm mean
Christopher Bourez1 (2021)	53.3	52	52.5	59	36.5	52.5
Christopher Bourez2 (2021)	55.4	52.6	53.6	60.3	30.6	53.6
ISP RAS (2021)	51.1	45.3	47.6	55.6	31.5	37.9
CILAB	56.2	57.4	56.5	70.7	27.5	36.99
GREYC1	44.0	42.1	42.5	51.3	0.1	0.19
GREYC2	44.6	42.3	42.8	51.7	0.1	0.19
ISP RAS1	**76.3**	**67.2**	**71.3**	**77.5**	55.1	62.16
ISP RAS2	75.2	63.8	68.8	76.8	**58.4**	**63.17**
swapUNIBA	61.4	66.4	63.6	71.4	42.9	51.23

Table 6: TOC Generation Competition on English documents

Team run	Inex08-P	Inex08-R	Inex08-F1	Inex08-Title acc	Inex08-Level acc	harm mean
Christopher Bourez1 (2021)	60.9	54.2	57.3	63.6	39	57.3
Christopher Bourez2 (2021)	60.8	54.3	57.3	63.5	38.7	57.3
ISP RAS (2021)	52.6	38.8	44.5	53.6	39.9	42.1
CILAB	34.9	6.7	11.2	35.5	15.2	12.89
GREYC1	25.8	20.9	22.8	29.1	4.3	7.23
GREYC2	26.0	20.9	22.9	29.3	4.1	6.95
ISP RAS1	52.7	**39.2**	**44.5**	53.7	34.6	38.93
ISP RAS2	**53.2**	38.1	43.9	**54.3**	**39.5**	**41.58**
swapUNIBA	40.0	37.0	38.3	43.8	30.7	34.08

Table 7: TOC Generation Competition on French documents

Team run	Inex08-P	Inex08-R	Inex08-F1	Inex08-Title acc	Inex08-Level acc	harm mean
CILAB	14.8	3.8	4.9	23.8	36.2	8.63
GREYC1	11.4	15.8	6.5	36.0	4.2	5.10
GREYC2	11.7	15.9	6.9	36.1	4.2	5.22
ISP RAS1	**51.6**	35.4	39.4	68.5	42.3	40.79
ISP RAS2	**51.6**	36.9	39.9	**69.1**	40.1	39.99
swapUNIBA	31.8	**59.0**	**40**	65.5	**46.5**	**43.00**

Table 8: TOC Generation Competition on Spanish documents

results, and we used different techniques to train classifiers. The described approach can be used for documents in any language. As a result, our team has taken first place in all categories for English and French documents, and second place for Spanish documents.

7. Bibliographical References

Bentabet, N.-I., Juge, R., El Maarouf, I., Mouilleron, V., Valsamou-Stanislawski, D., and El-Haj, M. (2020). The Financial Document Structure Extraction Shared Task (FinToc 2020). In *The 1st Joint Workshop on Financial Narrative Processing and MultiLing Financial Summarisation (FNP-FNS 2020)*, Barcelona, Spain.

Bourez, C. (2021). Fintoc 2021-document structure understanding. In *Proceedings of the 3rd Financial Narrative Processing Workshop*, pages 89–93.

El Maarouf, I., Kang, J., Aitazzi, A., Bellato, S., Gan, M., and El-Haj, M. (2021). The Financial Document Structure Extraction Shared Task (FinToc 2021). In *The Third Financial Narrative Processing Workshop (FNP 2021)*, Lancaster, UK.

Giguet, E. and Lejeune, G. (2019). Daniel@ fintoc-2019 shared task: toc extraction and title detection. In *Proceedings of the Second Financial Narrative Processing Workshop (FNP 2019)*, pages 63–68.

Hercig, T. and Kral, P. (2020). UWB@FinTOC-2020 shared task: Financial document title detection. In *Proceedings of the 1st Joint Workshop on Financial Narrative Processing and MultiLing Financial Summarisation*, pages 158–162, Barcelona, Spain (Online), December. COLING.

Juge, R., Bentabet, I., and Ferradans, S. (2019). The fintoc-2019 shared task: Financial document structure extraction. In *Proceedings of the Second Financial Narrative Processing Workshop (FNP 2019)*, pages 51–57.

Kosmajac, D., Taylor, S., and Saeidi, M. (2020).

DNLP@FinTOC'20: Table of contents detection in financial documents. In *Proceedings of the 1st Joint Workshop on Financial Narrative Processing and MultiLing Financial Summarisation*, pages 169–173, Barcelona, Spain (Online), December. COLING.

Kozlov, I., Belyaeva, O., Bogatenkova, A., and Perminov, A. (2021). Ispras@ fintoc-2021 shared task: Two-stage toc generation model. In *Proceedings of the 3rd Financial Narrative Processing Workshop*, pages 81–85.

Lin, X. (2003). Header and footer extraction by page association. In *Document Recognition and Retrieval X*, volume 5010, pages 164–171. International Society for Optics and Photonics.

Premi, D., Badugu, A., and Sharad Bhatt, H. (2020). AMEX-AI-LABS: Investigating transfer learning for title detection in table of contents generation. In *Proceedings of the 1st Joint Workshop on Financial Narrative Processing and MultiLing Financial Summarisation*, pages 153–157, Barcelona, Spain (Online), December. COLING.

Tian, K. and Peng, Z. J. (2019). Finance document extraction using data augmentation and attention. In *Proceedings of the Second Financial Narrative Processing Workshop (FNP 2019)*, pages 1–4.

Yusuke Shinyama, P. G. . P. M. (2019). Pdfminer.six documentation.

Proceedings of the 4th Financial Narrative Processing Workshop @ LREC 2022, pages 95–99
Marseille, 24 June 2022

swapUNIBA@FinTOC2022: Fine-tuning pre-trained Document Image Analysis model for Title Detection on the Financial Domain

Pierluigi Cassotti*, Cataldo Musto*, Marco de Gemmis*, Georgios Lekkas†, and *Giovanni Semeraro
*University of Bari
Italy
{name}.{surname}@uniba.it

†Objectway SpA
Italy
{name}.{surname}@objectway.com

Abstract

In this paper, we introduce the results of our submitted system to the FinTOC 2022 task. We address the task using a two-stage process: first, we detect titles using Document Image Analysis, then we train a supervised model for the hierarchical level prediction. We perform Document Image Analysis using a pre-trained Faster R-CNN on the PublyaNet dataset. We fine-tuned the model on the FinTOC 2022 training set. We extract orthographic and layout features from detected titles and use them to train a Random Forest model to predict the title level. The proposed system ranked #1 on both Title Detection and the Table of Content extraction tasks for Spanish. The system ranked #3 on both the two subtasks for English and French.

Keywords: keyword1, keyword2, keyword3

1. Introduction

Financial prospectuses contain relevant information about financial funds. These documents are typically released as PDF documents, which can feature very different layouts. Often these documents miss the Table Of Content (TOC) which can help the reader to focus on relevant content. Most of the existing datasets for Table Of Content extraction are domain-specific. The FinTOC task aims to fill the gap, proposing a TOC task specifically for financial documents.

In this work, we address the FinTOC task using a Document Image Analysis approach, exploiting the graphical layout for the Title Detection task. Page Layout Analysis is a long-studied task in the field of Computer Vision. We focus on approaches that exploit Convolutional Neural Networks (CNN) for Object Detection. R-CNN (Girshick et al., 2014) is an object detector that involves three stages: Regions Proposal, Feature Extraction and Classification. The Region Proposal is implemented using the Selective Search (van de Sande et al., 2011) algorithm and aims to find the Regions of Interest (ROI). R-CNN use a Convolutional Neural Network to extract the features from each ROI. The extracted features are used in a Support Vector Machine (SVM) classifier to predict the object class. Fast R-CNN (Girshick, 2015) improves R-CNN, avoiding the feature extraction for each ROI. Fast R-CNN computes a feature map using CNN on the image and extracts ROI from the feature map. Both R-CNN and Fast R-CNN use Selective Search as algorithms for the ROI extraction. The Selective Search algorithm can results inexpensive in terms of computation time. Faster R-CNN (Ren et al., 2015) is a neural network for object detection which jointly train the three object detection stages, implementing the Region Proposal Network (RPN). The RPN is a Convolutional Neural Network that tunes the Region Proposals according to the specific object detection task. While these models offer high performance and efficiency, they require large datasets to be trained. The PubLayNet (Zhong et al., 2019) is an automatically annotated dataset consisting of more than 360,000 pages of scientific articles. Each page is annotated with typical layout elements: title, table, list and text. In particular, it contains more than two million title instances. Since the layout structure of financial documents can diverge in a significant way from those of scientific articles we finetuned a pre-trained model on the PubLayNet dataset for the FinTOC 2022 task. In Section 2 we report the related works. In Section 4 we introduce the proposed TOC extraction pipeline including the Title Detection module and the module for the Level classification. Finally, in Section 5 we report the results on the FinTOC 2022 task.

2. Related Work

(Bourez, 2021) ranked first on the FinTOC 2021 task (Maarouf et al., 2021) on the subtasks of Title Detection and TOC extraction for both English and French. (Bourez, 2021) relies on the commercial software ABBYY[1] for the blocks and tables extraction, then the XGBoost classifier (Chen and Guestrin, 2016) is

[1] `https://www.abbyy.com/`

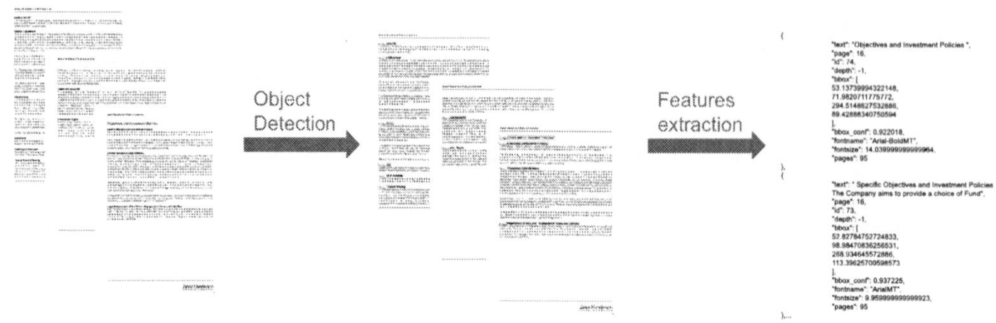

Figure 1: An overview of the pipeline.

trained on style features such as font color, name, size and weight and the involved text.

(Hercig and Kral, 2020) focuses on the Title Detection task for the FinTOC 2020 task (Bentabet et al., 2020). (Hercig and Kral, 2020) perform an ablation analysis on the features using the leave-one-out cross-validation. From the results emerged that character bigrams, orthographical features and font type represents relevant features. On the contrary, the Title Detection task seems to take no advantages from binary features such as is_bold, is_italic, is_all_caps. A prior work on Title Detection using Document Image Analysis is represented by (Gupta et al., 2021). (Gupta et al., 2021) fine-tune a pre-trained Faster R-CNN on the PubLayNet and filter the detected titles using a Gradient Boosting Classifier. The system proposed by (Gupta et al., 2021) achieves the highest precision with respect all the other systems submitted in the FinTOC 2021 task.

3. Task

The FinTOC 2022 task is the fourth edition of the shared task on Table of Contents extraction from financial documents. FinTOC 2022 extends the FinTOC 2021 task (Maarouf et al., 2021) including spanish documents. In particular, the training data consist of a set of pdf documents for each language, namely English, French and Spanish. For each document, the table of contents is provided. The table of contents includes the text of the title and the related page on which the title appears and the depth of the title. The FinTOC 2020 shared task involves two subtasks. The former is the Title Detection (TD) task, which is a binary task expecting the positive label for text blocks representing a title and a negative label for non-title text blocks. The latter is the Table Of Content (TOC) task, which requires extracting the hierarchical structure of the headers.

4. TOC extraction pipeline

In this section, we introduce the TOC extraction pipeline (Figure 1). It consists of two modules: the Title Detection module and Level classification module. The Title Detection module aims to detect titles in the pdf documents. On the other side, the Level classification module extracts the features from the detected titles and predicts for each title the respective hierarchical level.

4.1. Title Detection

To model the Title Detection task as a Document Image Analysis task, we extract the bounding boxes associated with each title. We use the Python library pdfplumber [2] for the processing of the pdf documents. We search the text occurrences of titles reported in the training set on the specific page. It is important to state here that the same text of the title can occur multiple times on the same page. Consequently the training set we build can be affected by noise due to title text ambiguities.

Once we find an exact match with the text of the title we extract the related bounding box. For each character belonging to the extracted text pdfplumber provides the char coordinates $(c_{x_0}, c_{y_0}, c_{x_1}, c_{y_1})$ which represent respectively the distance of the left side of character from the left side of the page, the distance of the top of character from the top of the page, the distance of right side of character from the left side of the page, and the distance of the bottom of the character from the top of the page. We extract the bounding box (x_0, y_0, x_1, y_1) coordinates of the overall title text as follows:

- x_0 is computed as the minimum distance from the left page border $\min_{\forall c \in T} c_{x_0}$
- y_0 is computed as the minimum distance from the top page border $\min_{\forall c \in T} c_{y_0}$

[2] https://github.com/jsvine/pdfplumber

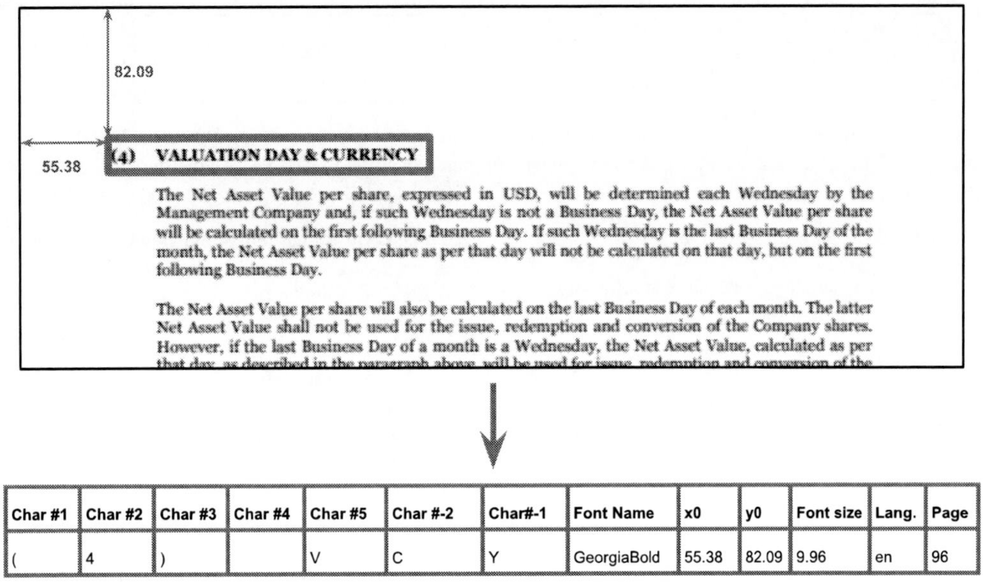

Figure 2: Extracted features.

- x_1 is computed as the maximum distance from the left page border $\max_{\forall c \in T} c_{x_1}$
- y_1 is computed as the maximum distance from the top page border $\max_{\forall c \in T} c_{y_1}$

The extracted bounding boxes are arranged in the COCO format (Lin et al., 2014) for the Object Detection task. Each pdf document d is converted into images $i_1, i_2, ..., i_N$, where N is the number of pages. We train the pretrained model Faster R-CNN included in the Model Zoo [3] of the LayoutParser library (Shen et al., 2021). Specifically, the model uses the Feature Pyramid Networks (FPN) (Lin et al., 2017) as backbone model. We finetuned the model for 80,000 iterations using Detectron [4].

Once the titles of a specific page are extracted, we filter those for which the bounding box has a confidence level greater than 0.5 and we sort them. First, we check for titles that appear in the second column (for double-column documents). A title that has the x_0 coordinate greater than the page width is considered to belong to the second column. Then, we sort titles belonging to the first column in decreasing order sorted by the y_0 coordinate. If there are titles in the second column they are sorted in decreasing order by the y_0 coordinate and appended to the titles in the first column.

Lang.	Precision	Recall	F1
FR	0.728	0.672	0.695
EN	0.802	0.885	0.838
SP	0.462	0.827	0.569

Table 1: Results on TD subtask.

4.2. Level classification

The level classification module attempt to predict the hierarchical level of the title. The hierarchical level of a title is strongly dependent on the overall TOC structure, i.e. the level of a single TOC entry depends on the previous and next titles features. (Bentabet et al., 2019) model the level classification task as a sequence labelling task representing the document hierarchy as a sequence. For simplicity, we propose an element-wise approach that takes into account only the features of a single TOC entry. For the level classification, we train a multi-class Random Forest classifier (Breiman, 2001) that takes in input the features of a single TOC entry extracted by the module of Title Detection and predict the title hierarchical level. The classes correspond to the hierarchical level that goes from 1 to 10 for the FinTOC 2022 task. We use the default hyper-parameters provided by the Scikit-learn library[5], i.e. 100 estimators, and the gini function to measure the quality of the split. The input features (Figure 2) of the Random Forest classifier are:

- First five Characters: one-hot encoding of the first

[3] https://layout-parser.readthedocs.io/en/latest/notes/modelzoo.html

[4] https://github.com/facebookresearch/Detectron

[5] https://scikit-learn.org/stable/modules/generated/sklearn.ensemble.RandomForestClassifier.html

Lang.	Inex08-P	Inex08-R	Inex08-F1	Inex08-Title acc.	Inex08-Level acc.	harmonic mean
FR	40.0	37.0	38,3	43.8	30,7	34,08
EN	61.4	66.4	63,6	71.4	42,9	51,24
SP	31.8	59.0	40	65.5	46,5	43,01

Table 2: Results on TOC subtask. Namely Precision, Recall and F1 measure of Inex08 score, Inex08-Title accuracy, Inex08-Level accuracy and the harmonic mean computed over the Inex08 F1 and the Inex08-Level accuracy.

five characters of the text title

- Last two Characters: one-hot encoding of the last two characters of the text title
- Bounding box x_0 normalized by the document width
- Bounding box y_0 normalized by the document height
- Page number normalized by the number of pages of the document
- Language, one-hot encoding of language class: English, French and Spanish
- Font name, pre-processed by removing punctuation and foundry names (i.e., LT, MT, FF, EF) by the font name.
- Font size

We use the same special ID for padding the character sequences and for out-of-dictionary characters. Financial documents can be grouped based on several different aspects. In particular, the language can be discriminative since in some countries the financial documents have to follow specific templates (e.g., EDGAR SEC [6] or AMF[7]). Previous works show that documents belonging to the same class often share the same specific page layout pattern (Esposito et al., 1990). For this reason, we argue that the use of the document class can represent a relevant feature in the TOC task.

5. Results

Results on the Title Detection and Table of Content tasks are reported in Table 4.1 and Table 4.1, respectively. The Title Detection task is evaluated using the F-measure computed on the predicted titles that match the ground truth titles. The TOC task instead evaluates the systems against the harmonic mean computed over the Inex08 F1 score and the Inex08-Level accuracy. In particular, for the Inex08 F1 score the predicted TOC entries are considered correct if match the ground truth TOC entries and have the same page number. The Inex08-Level accuracy evaluates the number of predicted titles with the correct page number and the correct hierarchical level.

[6]https://www.sec.gov/edgar.shtml

[7]https://www.amf-france.org/

We perform a qualitative analysis on the three document classes, i.e. English, French and Spanish documents. The English fund documents are simple and of regulatory nature. The French fund documents are also regulatory but more oriented to investors with graphical elements and colour. The Spanish documents are annual reports with a strong emphasis on creative communication with a large variety in form, colour, text flow and photographs, which makes them less predictable. Our system ranked #1 on the Spanish TD subtask with an F1 score of 0.569 and the TOC subtask with a harmonic mean of 43.01. The system performs better for the Title Detection task in English achieving an F1 score of 0.838. On the other side, for the level classification, the system performs better in Spanish, achieving 46.5 of Inex08-Level accuracy.

6. Conclusion

In this work, we presented our system submitted to the FinTOC 2022 task. Our system ranked #1 on the Spanish subtask and #3 on the English and French subtasks, achieving high recall performance. The Title Detection module is language independent and can be extended to a wider scope of documents written in other languages than English, Spanish and French.

In future developments, we plan to fine-tune hyperparameters, such as the level of confidence of the Title Detection model to improve the system performance.

7. Acknowledgements

This research has been partially funded by Objectway SpA under the “intelligent Business Platform for Wealth & Asset Management - iBWAM” project. The authors would like to thank Dr. Sciancalepore and Dr. Marvulli for supporting the preliminary development of the Title Detection pipeline.

8. References

Bentabet, N., Juge, R., and Ferradans, S. (2019). Table-of-Contents Generation on Contemporary Documents. In *2019 International Conference on Document Analysis and Recognition, ICDAR 2019, Sydney, Australia, September 20-25, 2019*, pages 100–107. IEEE.

Bentabet, N.-I., Juge, R., El Maarouf, I., Mouilleron, V., Valsamou-Stanislawski, D., and El-Haj, M. (2020). The financial document structure extraction shared task (FinToc 2020). In *Proceedings of the 1st Joint Workshop on Financial Narrative Processing and MultiLing Financial Summarisation*, pages 13–22, Barcelona, Spain (Online), December. COLING.

Bourez, C. (2021). FINTOC 2021 - Document Structure Understanding. In *Proceedings of the 3rd Financial Narrative Processing Workshop*, pages 89–93, Lancaster, United Kingdom, 15-16 September. Association for Computational Linguistics.

Breiman, L. (2001). Random forests. *Machine learning*, 45(1):5–32.

Chen, T. and Guestrin, C. (2016). XGBoost: A Scalable Tree Boosting System. In Balaji Krishnapuram, et al., editors, *Proceedings of the 22nd ACM SIGKDD International Conference on Knowledge Discovery and Data Mining, San Francisco, CA, USA, August 13-17, 2016*, pages 785–794. ACM.

Esposito, F., Malerba, D., Semeraro, G., Annese, E., and Scafuro, G. (1990). An experimental page layout recognition system for office document automatic classification: an integrated approach for inductive generalization. In *Proceedings 10th International Conference on Pattern Recognition*, volume 1, pages 557–562.

Girshick, R. B., Donahue, J., Darrell, T., and Malik, J. (2014). Rich Feature Hierarchies for Accurate Object Detection and Semantic Segmentation. In *2014 IEEE Conference on Computer Vision and Pattern Recognition, CVPR 2014, Columbus, OH, USA, June 23-28, 2014*, pages 580–587. IEEE Computer Society.

Girshick, R. B. (2015). Fast R-CNN. In *2015 IEEE International Conference on Computer Vision, ICCV 2015, Santiago, Chile, December 7-13, 2015*, pages 1440–1448. IEEE Computer Society.

Gupta, A., Akl, H. A., and de Mazancourt, H. (2021). Not All Titles are Created Equal: Financial Document Structure Extraction Shared Task. In *Proceedings of the 3rd Financial Narrative Processing Workshop*, pages 86–88, Lancaster, United Kingdom, 15-16 September. Association for Computational Linguistics.

Hercig, T. and Kral, P. (2020). UWB@FinTOC-2020 Shared Task: Financial Document Title Detection. In *Proceedings of the 1st Joint Workshop on Financial Narrative Processing and MultiLing Financial Summarisation*, pages 158–162, Barcelona, Spain (Online), December. COLING.

Lin, T.-Y., Maire, M., Belongie, S., Hays, J., Perona, P., Ramanan, D., Dollár, P., and Zitnick, C. L. (2014). Microsoft coco: Common objects in context. In *European conference on computer vision*, pages 740–755. Springer.

Lin, T., Dollár, P., Girshick, R. B., He, K., Hariharan, B., and Belongie, S. J. (2017). Feature Pyramid Networks for Object Detection. In *2017 IEEE Conference on Computer Vision and Pattern Recognition, CVPR 2017, Honolulu, HI, USA, July 21-26, 2017*, pages 936–944. IEEE Computer Society.

Maarouf, I. E., Kang, J., Azzi, A. A., Bellato, S., Gan, M., and El-Haj, M. (2021). The Financial Document Structure Extraction Shared Task (FinTOC2021). In *Proceedings of the 3rd Financial Narrative Processing Workshop*, pages 111–119, Lancaster, United Kingdom, 15-16 September. Association for Computational Linguistics.

Ren, S., He, K., Girshick, R. B., and Sun, J. (2015). Faster R-CNN: Towards Real-Time Object Detection with Region Proposal Networks. In Corinna Cortes, et al., editors, *Advances in Neural Information Processing Systems 28: Annual Conference on Neural Information Processing Systems 2015, December 7-12, 2015, Montreal, Quebec, Canada*, pages 91–99.

Shen, Z., Zhang, R., Dell, M., Lee, B. C. G., Carlson, J., and Li, W. (2021). LayoutParser: A Unified Toolkit for Deep Learning Based Document Image Analysis. *arXiv preprint arXiv:2103.15348*.

van de Sande, K. E. A., Uijlings, J. R. R., Gevers, T., and Smeulders, A. W. M. (2011). Segmentation as selective search for object recognition. In Dimitris N. Metaxas, et al., editors, *IEEE International Conference on Computer Vision, ICCV 2011, Barcelona, Spain, November 6-13, 2011*, pages 1879–1886. IEEE Computer Society.

Zhong, X., Tang, J., and Jimeno-Yepes, A. (2019). PubLayNet: Largest Dataset Ever for Document Layout Analysis. In *2019 International Conference on Document Analysis and Recognition, ICDAR 2019, Sydney, Australia, September 20-25, 2019*, pages 1015–1022. IEEE.

Proceedings of the 4th Financial Narrative Processing Workshop @ LREC 2022, pages 100–104
Marseille, 24 June 2022

GREYC@FinTOC-2022: Handling Document Layout and Structure in Native PDF Bundle of Documents

Emmanuel Giguet, Nadine Lucas
Normandie Univ, UNICAEN, ENSICAEN, CNRS, GREYC
14000 Caen, France
emmanuel.giguet@cnrs.fr, nadine.lucas@unicaen.fr

Abstract

In this paper, we present our contribution to the FinTOC-2022 Shared Task "Financial Document Structure Extraction". We participated in the three tracks dedicated to English, French and Spanish document processing. Our main contribution consists in considering financial prospectus as a bundle of documents, i.e., a set of merged documents, each with their own layout and structure. Therefore, Document Layout and Structure Analysis (DLSA) first starts with the boundary detection of each document using general layout features. Then, the process applies inside each single document, taking advantage of the local properties. DLSA is achieved considering simultaneously text content, vectorial shapes and images embedded in the native PDF document. For the Title Detection task in English and French, we observed a significant improvement of the F-measures for Title Detection compared with those obtained during our previous participation.

Keywords: Document Structure Extraction, Document Layout Analysis

1. Introduction

FinTOC-2022 comes as part of a series of shared tasks dedicated to financial document processing. It follows previous editions of FinTOC relating to Financial Document Structure Extraction, in particular FinTOC-2021 organized by (El Maarouf et al., 2021).

In the FinTOC competitions, two tasks are proposed by the organizers: *Title Detection* and *Table of Content Structure Extraction*, aiming at identifying and organizing the headers of the document according to its hierarchical structure. In this edition, three languages are considered: English, French and Spanish.

Table of Content (ToC) extraction can be considered in two complementary ways: (i) extracting a logical structure that has been explicitly marked in a ToC and map it to the titles present in the document, and (ii) creating a ToC from scratch when no such section is present in the document. In the latter case, the process consists in detecting the titles and computing their level in the hierarchy of titles.

Keeping to the tradition of our earlier work, we choose to enrich an end-to-end pipeline aiming at fully structuring documents from the native PDF files. Our intention is to build a language independent solution and a domain independent system. Our motivation is to better understand abstract structuring processes where *contrast* and *positioning* are key features. Therefore, titles and tables of content should be derivative outputs of our system.

In this work, we choose to pay attention to the global structure of the documents, and to highlight how the global structure might help to improve the analysis of local inner structures. Therefore, for the first time, we consider financial prospectus as a *bundle of documents*, i.e., a set of merged documents, each with their own layout and structure. And that's what they are.

In our approach, Document Layout and Structure Analysis (DLSA) first starts with the boundary determination of each document of the bundle using general layout features. Then, the process applies inside each individual document, taking advantage of its local properties. Our preliminary work shows that computing background properties on the whole document, or inside a sliding window, is a non-sense and may lead to analytical errors when processing bundle documents. *Background style* and more broadly any deduction related to the document should be computed within the document space.

The paper is organized as follows. In section 2. we briefly present the datasets. In section 3. we present financial prospectuses as document bundles and we analyse the document structure and layout of each part. In Section 4., we describe our structuring approach. In Section 5. we present a discussion about our results, and we draw some perspectives for future work.

2. Datasets

The training set and test set of the shared tasks are composed of financial documents written in French, English and Spanish. The documents are distributed as native PDF documents. The French and English sets contain financial prospectuses. The Spanish set contain financial information reports.

lang.	train set	test set
English	79	10
French	81	10
Spanish	80	10

Table 1: Document count in datasets

lang.	train set min	max	avg.	test set min	max	avg.
en	3	405	77	66	136	102
fr	2	155	26	12	28	20
sp	15	318	118	92	444	198

Table 2: Page count in datasets

3. Document Structure and Layout of Prospectus Document Bundles

The document layout and the document structure of the financial prospectuses are interesting to observe. Most of them are indeed bundles of documents: each individual document of the bundle has its own structure, its own layout, including headers, footers, and even sometimes page numbering counters. The bundles may result of a simple merge of PDF documents.

Concerning the bundle structure, three main parts should be considered: (1) the Key Investor Information Document (KIID), (2) the prospectus, (3) the regulatory terms.

3.1. The Key Investor Information Document

The first part of the bundle is a two-page factual document which provides key information to the investor. It is also called Key Investor Information Document (KIID). Its structure is guided and supervised by authorities. In some bundles, the first part is made of a series of concatenated KIIDs.

The KIID tends to look like a commercial document – although it is not one – with an attractive presentation, a coherent color palette for text attributes, text backgrounds, logos, short and understandable texts and figures. The mandatory structure and the synthetic nature of the document lead to high text density with small font sizes, small text interline, small vertical spaces between document objects.

3.2. The prospectus

The second part of the bundle, also called prospectus, is a detailed written presentation combining descriptions, written texts, and tables. The text structure is more free but there are similarities from one document to another. Inconsistencies in the numbering of list items or titles can be observed, as stated by (Bourez, 2021).

The prospectus has a more straightforward presentation that can be observed in technical reports. The text structure is rich and quite complex with multi-level headings, combined to embedded lists of several types: numbered list, bulleted list, checkbox list, description list, tabular list. The tables may also be complex with multiple page-spanning layout.

3.3. The regulatory terms

The third part is a regulatory section which is organized in titles and articles. The text has a formal legal style. The regulatory terms has a traditional sober and rigorous layout, with often centered titles, and independent page numbering counters for titles and articles.

Most of the prospectuses are published without a table of content (ToC), which means you can not rely on a ToC detection and parsing module to achieve the tasks. Some prospectuses may include a cover page or may be complemented by appendices. All these characteristics make the challenge all the more interesting.

4. Method

The experiment is conducted on native PDF documents. In line with the work presented in FinSBD-2 task by (Giguet and Lejeune, 2021a) and FinTOC-2021 (Giguet and Lejeune, 2021b), we choose to implement an end-to-end pipeline from the PDF file itself to a fully structured document. This approach allows to control the entire process. Titles and Table of Contents that we generate for the shared tasks are derivative outputs of the system.

4.1. Document Preprocessing

The document content is extracted using the `pdf2xml` command (Déjean, 2007). Three useful types of content are extracted from the document: text, vectorial shapes, and images.

Text Preprocessing

`Pdf2xml` introduces the concepts of token, line and block, as three computational text units. We choose to only rely on the "token" unit. In practice, most output tokens correspond to words or numbers but they can also correspond to a concatenation of several interpretable units or to a breakdown of an interpretable unit, depending on character spacing. We choose to redefine our own "line" unit in order to better control the coherence of our hierarchy of graphical units. We abandon the concept of "block" whose empirical foundations are too weak.

Vectorial Shapes Preprocessing

Using `pdf2xml` allows to rely on vectorial information during document analysis. Text background, framed content, underline text, table grid are crucial information that contributes to sense making. They simplify the reader's task, and contribute in a positive way to automatic document analysis.

Most vectorial shapes are basic closed path, mostly rectangles. Graphical lines or graphical points do not exist: lines as well as points are rectangles interpreted by the cognitive skills of the reader as lines or points. In order to use vectorial information in document analysis, a preprocessing stage builds composite vectorial shapes and interprets them as background colors or borders. This preprocessing component returns shapes that are used by our system to detect framed content, table grids, and text background. It improves the detection of titles which are presented as framed text and it avoids considering table headers as titles.

Images Preprocessing

`Pdf2xml` extracts images from the pdf. They may be used in different context such as logos in the title page, figures in the document body. An other interesting feature lies in the fact that certain character symbols are serialized as images, in particular specific item bullets such as arrows or checkboxes. They are indistinguishable from a standard symbol character by the human eye.

We choose to handle images as traditional symbol characters, so that they can be exploited by the structuration process, in particular by the list identification module. Identical images are grouped, and a virtual token containing a fake character glyph is created. The bounding box attributes are associated to the token and a fake font name is set. These virtual tokens are inserted at the right location by the line builder module thanks to the character x-y coordinates. This technique significantly improves the detection of list items and, as a consequence, the recognition of the global document structure.

4.2. Document Layout and Structure Analysis

Document Delimitation in the Bundle

As stated above, the delimitation of individual documents inside a bundle is the main contribution of our work for this edition. This problem has been examined in specific studies (Taghva and Cartright, 2009). In previous work we have also faced quite similar problems: the delimitation of parts and chapters in OCRed books (Giguet and Lucas, 2010).

The experimentations we carried out reveal that (1) frequency of hashes of font family concatenated with font size, (2) colors palettes, (3) text content and position in headers and footers, (4) page number sequence and position in headers and footers are interesting features to compute document boundaries.

In this prototype, we rely on (1) text content and position in headers and footers, and (2) page numbers sequence and position in headers and footers to detect a new individual document. Due to time constraint, we did not include information related to font attributes and colors.

The process detects inconsistencies in the sequence of headers and footers in order to split the bundle: appearance of new content, disappearance of content, change of position of the content, break or reset in page number series.

Detecting Header and Footer Areas

Header and footer area boundaries are computed from the repetition of similar tokens located at similar positions at the top and at the bottom of contiguous pages (Déjean and Meunier, 2006). We take into account possible odd and even page layouts.

Header and footer pattern is inferred from a set of a maximum of twenty contiguous pages. While this number is arbitrary, we consider it is enough to consider the pattern reliable in case of odd and even layouts. Once the pattern is inferred, we check if it is still applicable on the following pages. If not, a document limit is detected, a new document is created, and the header and footer pattern induction process is launched.

A special process detects page numbering and computes the shift between the PDF page numbering and the document page numbering. Page numbering is computed from the repetition of tokens containing decimals and located at similar positions at the top or at the bottom of contiguous pages. These tokens are taken into account when computing header and footer boundaries.

Page Layout Analysis

Page Layout Analysis (PLA) aims at recognizing and labeling content areas in a page, e.g., text regions, tables, figures, lists, headers, footers. It is the subject of abundant research and articles (Antonacopoulos et al., 2009).

While PLA is often achieved at page scope and aims at bounding content regions, we have taken a model-driven approach at document scope. We try to directly infer Page Layout Models from the whole document and we then try to instantiate them on pages.

Our Page Layout Model (PLM) is hierarchical and contains 2 positions at top-level: the *margin area* and the *main content area*. The *margin area* contains two particular position, the *header area* located at the top, and the *footer area* located at the bottom. *Aside areas* may contain particular data such as vertically-oriented text. The *main content area* contains *column areas* containing text, figures or tables. *Floating areas* are defined to receive content external to column area, such as large figures, tables or framed texts.

The positions that we try to fill at document scope are header, footer and main columns. First, pages are grouped depending on their size and orientation (i.e., portrait or landscape). Then header area and footer area are detected. Column areas are in the model but due to time constraints, the detection module is not fully implemented in this prototype yet.

Detecting the Table of Contents

The TOC is located in the first pages of the document. It can spread over a limited number of contiguous pages. One formal property is common to all TOCs: the page numbers are right-aligned and form an increasing sequence of integers.

These characteristics are fully exploited in the core of our TOC identification process: we consider the pages of the first third of the document as a search space. Then, we select the first right-aligned sequence of lines ending by an integer and that may spread over contiguous pages.

Linking TOC Entries and Headers

Linking Table of Content Entries to main content is one of the most important process when structuring a document (Déjean and Meunier, 2010). Computing successfully such relations demonstrates the reliability of header detection and permits to set hyperlinks from toc entries to document headers.

Once TOC is detected, each TOC Entry is linked to its corresponding page number in the document. This page number is converted to the PDF page number thanks to the page shift (see section 4.2.). Then header is searched in the related PDF page. When found, the corresponding line is categorized as header.

Table Detection

Table detection to exclude table content from the main text stream. It allows to exclude tables when searching for list items, sentences or titles.

The table detection module analyzes the PDF vectorial shapes. Our algorithm builds table grids from adjacent framed table cells. The framed table cells are built from vectorial shapes that may represent cell borders. The table grid is defined by the graph of adjacent framed table cells.

Unordered List Structure Induction

Unordered lists are also called *bulleted lists* since the list items are supposed to be marked with bullets. Unordered lists may spread over multiple pages.

Unordered list items are searched at page scope. The typographical symbols (glyphs) used to introduce items are not predefined. We infer the symbol by identifying multiple left-aligned lines introduced by the same single-character token. In this way, the algorithm captures various bullet symbols such as squares, white bullets... Alphabetical or decimal characters are rejected as possible bullet style type. Images of character symbols are transparently handled thanks to virtual tokens created during the preprocessing stage.

The aim of the algorithm is to identify PDF lines which corresponds to new bulleted list item (i.e., list item leading lines). The objective is not to bound list items which cover multiple lines. Indeed, the end of list items are computed while computing paragraph structures: a list item ends when the next list item starts (i.e., same bullet symbol, same indentation) or when less indented text objects starts.

Ordered List Structure Induction in PDF Documents

Ordered list items are searched at document scope. We first select numbered lines thanks to a set of regular expressions, and we analyse each numbering prefix as a tuple $\langle P, S, I, C \rangle$ where *P* refers to the numbering pattern (string), *S* refers to the numbering style type (single character), *I* refers to the numbering count written in numbering style type (single character), and *C* refers to the decimal value of the numbering count (integer).

The numbering style types are defined as follows: Decimal (D), Lower-Latin (L), Upper-Latin (M), Lower-Greek (G) Upper-Greek (H), Lower-Roman (R), Upper-Roman (S), Lower-Latin OR Lower-Roman (?), Upper-Latin OR Upper-Roman (!).

To illustrate, the line "A.2.c) My Header" is analysed as $\langle$ A.2.L), L, c, 3 $\rangle$.

Lines are grouped in clusters sharing the same numbering pattern. A disambiguation process assigns an unambiguous style type to ambiguous lines. The underlying strategy is to complement unambiguous yet incomplete series in order to build coherent, ordered series.

Paragraph Structure Induction

The aim of paragraph structure induction is to infer paragraph models that are later used to detect paragraph instances. The underlying idea to automatically infer the settings of paragraph styles.

Paragraphs are complex objects: a canonical paragraph is made of a leading line, multiple body lines and a trailing line. The leading line can have positive or negative indentation. In context, paragraphs may be visually separated from other objects thanks to above spacing and below spacing.

In order to build paragraph models, we first identify reliable paragraph bodies: sequences of three or more lines with same line spacing and compatible left and right coordinates. Then, leading lines and trailing lines are identified considering same line spacing, compatible left and/or right coordinates (to detect left and right alignments), same style. Paragraph lines are categorized as follows: L for leading line, B for body lines, T for trailing line. Header lines are categorized H. Other lines are categorized as ? for undefined.

In order to fill paragraph models, paragraph settings are derived from the reliable paragraphs that are detected. When derived, leading lines of unordered and ordered list items are considered to create list item models.

Once paragraph models and list item models are built, the models are used to detect less reliable paragraphs and list items (i.e., containing less than three body lines). Compatible models are applied and lines are categorized L, B (if exists) or T (if exists). Remaining undefined lines are categorized considering line-spacing.

5. Results and discussion

The document-wise approach we presented was evaluated on both tasks at FinTOC 2022 : *Title Detection* and *Table of Content extraction*. However, due to lack of time, we only produced results for the Title Detection task. Results for the second task are not relevant.

In table 3 and 4 we present the results we obtained respectively for *Title Detection* at FinTOC 2021 and FinTOC 2022.

	Prec	Rec	F1
French	0.842	0.485	0.606
English	0.913	0.338	0.465

Table 3: Results for Title Detection at FinTOC 2021

	Prec	Rec	F1
French	0.766	0.610	0.671
English	0.812	0.794	0.793
Spanish	0.293	0.507	0.206

Table 4: Results for Title Detection at FinTOC 2022

These results are encouraging and show a significant improvment of the F-measure on French and English test sets. These improvements are partly due to the handling of document bundles: it permits a better computation of background style and constrast among styles. The very low precision for the Spanish test set is due to a specific table layout not covered by our table detection system. The improvement of this module should solve the problem.
The rationale of our method is to have an end-to-end pipeline from the PDF file itself to a fully structured document. The approach is systemic: any improvment in a particular module benefits to all other modules, and more broadly to the global system. The advantage of this approach is to solve every problem where it has to be solved. The drawback, for such a challenge, is that we have to model and implement all the document objects recognition modules and their interaction to obtain competitive results.
Today, our system includes an individual document delimitation module to handle bundles of document, a basic page layout analysis module, a header/footer detection system, a basic table detection module, a list detection module and a paragraph induction module. They all seem to contribute in a good way to the document structuration process. They all have to be improved. New components should be developed, in particular, a graph detection module. Still, we believe there is a great interest in representing a fairly unusual but ambitious way to deal with the document structure as a whole.

6. Bibliographical References

Antonacopoulos, A., Bridson, D., Papadopoulos, C., and Pletschacher, S. (2009). A realistic dataset for performance evaluation of document layout analysis. In *Proceedings of the International Conference on Document Analysis and Recognition, ICDAR*, pages 296–300, 01.

Bourez, C. (2021). FINTOC 2021 - document structure understanding. In *Proceedings of the 3rd Financial Narrative Processing Workshop*, pages 89–93, Lancaster, United Kingdom, 15-16 September. Association for Computational Linguistics.

Déjean, H. and Meunier, J.-L. (2006). A system for converting pdf documents into structured xml format. In Horst Bunke et al., editors, *Document Analysis Systems VII*, pages 129–140, Berlin, Heidelberg. Springer Berlin Heidelberg.

Déjean, H. and Meunier, J.-L. (2010). Reflections on the inex structure extraction competition. In *Proceedings of the 9th IAPR International Workshop on Document Analysis Systems*, DAS '10, page 301–308, New York, NY, USA. Association for Computing Machinery.

Déjean, H., (2007). *pdf2xml open source software*. Last access on July 31, 2019.

El Maarouf, I., Kang, J., Aitazzi, A., Bellato, S., Gan, M., and El-Haj, M. (2021). The Financial Document Structure Extraction Shared Task (FinToc 2021). In *The Third Financial Narrative Processing Workshop (FNP 2021)*, Lancaster, UK.

Giguet, E. and Lejeune, G. (2021a). Daniel at the FinSBD-2 task : Extracting Lists and Sentences from PDF Documents: a model-driven end-to-end approach to PDF document analysis. In *Second Workshop on Financial Technology and Natural Language Processing in conjunction with IJCAI-PRICAI 2020*, Proceedings of the Second Workshop on Financial Technology and Natural Language Processing, pages 67–74, Kyoto, Japan, January.

Giguet, E. and Lejeune, G. (2021b). Daniel@FinTOC-2021: Taking advantage of images and vectorial shapes in native PDF document analysis. In *Proceedings of the 3rd Financial Narrative Processing Workshop*, pages 70–74, Lancaster, United Kingdom, 15-16 September. Association for Computational Linguistics.

Giguet, E. and Lucas, N. (2010). The book structure extraction competition with the resurgence software for part and chapter detection at caen university. In *Comparative Evaluation of Focused Retrieval - 9th Workshop of the Initiative for the Evaluation of XML Retrieval (INEX 2010), Revised Selected Papers*, pages 128–139.

Taghva, K. and Cartright, M.-A. (2009). Document boundary determination using structural and lexical analysis. In Kathrin Berkner et al., editors, *Document Recognition and Retrieval XVI*, volume 7247, pages 22 – 26. International Society for Optics and Photonics, SPIE.

Proceedings of the 4th Financial Narrative Processing Workshop @ LREC 2022, pages 105–107
Marseille, 24 June 2022

The Financial Causality Extraction Shared Task (FinCausal 2022)

Dominique Mariko[1], Kim Trottier[2] and Mahmoud El-Haj[3]
[1]Yseop, France [2]HECMontreal, Canada [3]Lancaster University, UK
[1]lab@yseop.com, [2]kim.trottier@hec.ca, [1]m.el-haj@lancaster.ac.uk

Abstract

We present the FinCausal 2020 Shared Task on Causality Detection in Financial Documents and the associated FinCausal dataset, and discuss the participating systems and results. The task focuses on detecting if an object, an event or a chain of events is considered a cause for a prior event. This shared task focuses on determining causality associated with a quantified fact. An event is defined as the arising or emergence of a new object or context in regard to a previous situation. Therefore, the task will emphasise the detection of causality associated with transformation of financial objects embedded in quantified facts. A total number of 7 teams submitted system runs to the FinCausal task and contributed with a system description paper. FinCausal shared task is associated with the 4th Financial Narrative Processing Workshop (FNP 2022) (El-Haj et al., 2022) which is held at the The 13th Language Resources and Evaluation Conference (LREC 2022) in Marseille, France, on June 24, 2022.

1. Introduction

Financial analysis needs factual data, but also explanation on the variability of these data. Data state facts, but provide little to no knowledge regarding how these facts materialised. The Financial Document Causality Detection Task aims to develop an ability to explain, from external sources, the reasons why a transformation occurs in the financial landscape, as a preamble to generating accurate and meaningful financial narrative summaries. Its goal is to evaluate which events or which chain of events can cause a financial object to be modified or an event to occur, regarding a given external context. This context is available in the financial news, but due to the high volatility of such information, mapping an external cause to a given consequence is not trivial.

FinCausal 2022 shared task follows the successful FinCausal shared tasks on 2020 (Mariko et al., 2020) and 2021 (Mariko et al., 2021). In this edition we chose to propose only the data and task details of the Causality Task, formerly named Task 2, which is a causality detection task. The training and evaluation sets have been augmented with extracts of the Management Discussion and Analysis (MD&A) sections from 10k filings found on the EDGAR Company Filings database of the U.S. Securities and Exchange Commission (SEC).

2. Data

The data are extracted from a corpus of 2019 financial news provided by Qwam[1], collected from 14,000 economics and finance websites. The original raw corpus is an ensemble of HTML pages corresponding to daily information retrieval from financial news feed. These news mostly inform on the 2019 financial landscape, but can also contain information related to politics, micro economics or other topics considered relevant for finance information. This edition contains the training data from 2021 (2020 data slightly augmented with 643 examples added in the Practice data set), in addition to the newly created SEC data presented below. For a detailed overview of the corpus creation and 2020 edition systems, see (Mariko et al., 2020). Data are released under the CC0 License.

2.1. 2022 Augmentation

2022 data have been augmented from the 2021 data samples with the following

- 537 data points have been added to the training data
- 934 data points have been added to the blind test data

3. Task

The purpose of this task is to extract, from provided text sections, the chunks identifying the causal sequences and the chunks describing the effects. The trial and practice samples were provided to participants as csv files with headers: Index; Text; Cause; Effect

- Index: ID of the text section. Is a concatenation of [file increment . text section index]
- Text: Text section extracted from a 2019 news article
- Cause: Chunk referencing the cause of an event (event or related object included)
- Effect: Chunk referencing the effect of the event

A data sample for the task is provided in Table 1. Interesting results (up to 95.50 F1 score) had been achieved during the 2020 and 2021 edition, one of the remaining difficulty being the prediction of complex causal chains considered during the annotation process, leading to one text section possibly containing multiple causes or effects.

[1]https://www.qwamci.com/

Index	Text	Cause	Effect
0009.00052.1	Things got worse when the Wall came down. GDP fell 20% between 1988 and 1993. There were suddenly hundreds of thousands of unemployed in a country that, under Communism, had had full employment.	Things got worse when the Wall came down.	GDP fell 20% between 1988 and 1993.
0009.00052.2	Things got worse when the Wall came down. GDP fell 20% between 1988 and 1993. There were suddenly hundreds of thousands of unemployed in a country that, under Communism, had had full employment.	Things got worse when the Wall came down.	There were suddenly hundreds of thousands of unemployed in a country that, under Communism, had had full employment.
23.00006	In case where SGST refund is not applicable, the state is offering a 15% capital subsidy on investments made in Tamil Nadu till end of 2025.	In case where SGST refund is not applicable	the state is offering a 15% capital subsidy on investments made in Tamil Nadu till end of 2025

Table 1: Three examples from FinCausal 2021 Corpus - Practice dataset

4. Participants and Systems

In total, 7 different teams have participated and submitted their system to FinCausal 2022, the teams are presented in Table 2.

SPOCK team addressed the information extraction problem with span-based and sequence tagging neural network models. Specifically, they fine tuned pretrained language models to perform text span classification and sequence labeling tasks. They trained a span-based causality extraction system by fine tuning the BERT-Base model. This model resulted in an F1 score of 89.36 and Exact Match score of 81.67. Their best performing model was an ensemble of sequence tagging models based on the BIO scheme using the RoBERTa-Largemodel, which achieved an F1 score of 94.70 to win the FinCausal 2022 challenge.

DCU-Lorcan employed advanced pre-trained language models (PLMs) to facilitate the causality extraction task as PLMs have been proven to be effective in many NLP tasks including text classification, text generation especially on span extraction/sequence labeling task such as Named-entity Recognition and Question Answering. Building on PLMs, they also propose a heuristically-induced post-processing strategy to refine the system predictions. Their best system (BERT-large + post-process) achieved F-1, Recall, Precision and Exact Match scores of 92.76, 92.77, 92.76 and 68.60 respectively.

LIPI reused the implementation of two the state of the art approaches (Nayak et al., 2022) and (Kao et al., 2020). They trained the CEPN architecture proposed by (Nayak et al., 2022) separately on FinCausal-2020 and FinCausal2021 datasets and evaluated them on the FinCausal2022 data set. Subsequently, they combined the entire labelled dataset available up to 2022 and retrained the same architecture.

iLab introduced graph construction techniques to inject cause-effect graph knowledge for graph embedding. The graph features combining with BERT embedding, then are used to predict the cause effect spans. Their results show that their proposed graph builder method outperforms the other methods with and without external knowledge.

MNLP focused their approach on employing Nested NER using the Text-to-Text Transformer (T5) generative transformer models while applying different combinations of datasets and tagging methods. Their system reports accuracy of 79% in Exact Match comparison and F-measure score of 92% token level measurement.

ExpertNeurons proposed a solution with intelligent pre-processing and post-processing to detect the number of cause and effect in a financial document and extract them. This approach achieved 90% as F1 score(weighted-average) for the official blind evaluation dataset.

ATL presented two independent transformer based deep neural network architectures for the causal sentence classification and cause-effect relation extraction task. They have used the fine-tuned Bidirectional Encoder Representations from Transformers (BERT) language model cascaded with a sequence-labeling architecture.

5. Evaluation

We used CodaLab to allow participants to train and test their systems. Table 3 shows the FinCausal 2022 results run on our blind test set. A baseline was provided on the trial samples for the Causality Task Tasks 2)[2]. Participating systems were ranked on blind Evaluation datasets based on a weighted F1 score, recall, precision for Task 1, plus an additional Exact Match for Task 2. Regarding official ranking, weighted metrics from the scikit-learn package[3] were used for both Tasks, and the

[2] https://github.com/yseop/YseopLab/tree/develop/FNP_2020_FinCausal/baseline

[3] https://scikit-learn.org/stable/modules/model_evaluation.html#multiclass-and-multilabel-classification

Team	Affiliation
SPOCK	Rensselaer Polytechnic Institute and IBM
DCU-Lorcan	Dublin City University
LIPI	Fidelity Investments, Jadavpur University
iLab	National Institute of Advanced Science and Technology, Japan Advanced Institute of Science and Technology, and Tokyo Institute of Technology
MNLP	George Mason University
ExpertNeurons	Oracle
ATL	TCS Research

Table 2: FinCausal 2022 participating teams and their affiliations

official evaluation script is available on Github[4]. Participating teams were allowed to submit up to 100 runs, while only their highest score was withheld to represent them during the evaluation phase[5]. Only the scores validated during the evaluation phase of the competition are displayed below.

Team	F1	R	P	EM
SPOCK	**0.95 (1)**	**0.95 (1)**	**0.95 (1)**	**0.86 (1)**
ilab	0.94 (2)	0.94 (2)	0.94 (2)	0.83 (2)
DCU Lorcan	0.93 (3)	0.93 (3)	0.93 (3)	0.69 (5)
LIPI	0.92 (4)	0.92 (4)	0.93 (4)	0.79 (3)
MNLP	0.92 (5)	0.92 (5)	0.92 (5)	0.79 (3)
Expert Neurons	0.90 (6)	0.90 (6)	0.91 (6)	0.71 (4)
ATL	0.64 (7)	0.65 (7)	0.62 (7)	0.21 (7)

Table 3: FinCausal 2022 Results. R: Recall, P: Precision, F1, F1 Measure, EM: Exact Match.

6. Conclusion

In this paper, we present the framework and the results for the FinCausal Shared Task. In addition , we present the new FinCausal dataset built specifically for this shared task. We plan to run similar shared tasks in the near future, possibly with some augmented data, in association with the FNP workshop.

Acknowledgements

We would like to thank our dedicated annotators who contributed to the building the FinCausal Corpus: Yagmur Ozturk, Estelle Labidurie, Minh Anh Nguyen, Aurélie Nomblot, Lilia Ait Ouarab, Laura Sasso and Léonie Muller, as well as the FNP Committee for their gracious support.

7. Bibliographical References

Mahmoud El-Haj, et al., editors. (2022). *Proceedings of the 4th Financial Narrative Processing Workshop*, Marseille, France, 24 June. The 13th Language Resources and Evaluation Conference, LREC 2022.

Kao, P.-W., Chen, C.-C., Huang, H.-H., and Chen, H.-H. (2020). Ntunlpl at fincausal 2020, task 2: improving causality detection using viterbi decoder. In *Proceedings of the 1st Joint Workshop on Financial Narrative Processing and MultiLing Financial Summarisation*, pages 69–73.

Mariko, D., Abi-Akl, H., Labidurie, E., Durfort, S., De Mazancourt, H., and El-Haj, M. (2020). The financial document causality detection shared task (FinCausal 2020). In *Proceedings of the 1st Joint Workshop on Financial Narrative Processing and MultiLing Financial Summarisation*, pages 23–32, Barcelona, Spain (Online), December. COLING.

Mariko, D., Akl, H. A., Labidurie, E., Durfort, S., de Mazancourt, H., and El-Haj, M. (2021). The financial document causality detection shared task (FinCausal 2021). In *Proceedings of the 3rd Financial Narrative Processing Workshop*, pages 58–60, Lancaster, United Kingdom, 15-16 September. Association for Computational Linguistics.

Nayak, T., Sharma, S., Butala, Y., Dasgupta, K., Goyal, P., and Ganguly, N. (2022). A generative approach for financial causality extraction. *arXiv preprint arXiv:2204.05674.*

[4]https://github.com/yseop/YseopLab/tree/develop/FNP_2020_FinCausal/scoring

[5]https://codalab.lisn.upsaclay.fr/competitions/3802

Proceedings of the 4th Financial Narrative Processing Workshop @ LREC 2022, pages 108–111
Marseille, 24 June 2022

SPOCK at FinCausal 2022: Causal Information Extraction Using Span-Based and Sequence Tagging Models

Anik Saha, Jian Ni, Oktie Hassanzadeh, Alex Gittens, Kavitha Srinivas, Bulent Yener
RPI, IBM Research, IBM Research, RPI, IBM Research, RPI
sahaa@rpi.edu, {nij, hassanzadeh}@us.ibm.com, gittea@rpi.edu, kavitha.srinivas@ibm.com, yener@cs.rpi.edu

Abstract

Causal information extraction is an important task in natural language processing, particularly in finance domain. In this work, we develop several information extraction models using pre-trained transformer-based language models for identifying cause and effect text spans from financial documents. We use FinCausal 2021 and 2022 data sets to train span-based and sequence tagging models. Our ensemble of sequence tagging models based on the RoBERTa-Large pre-trained language model achieves an F1 score of 94.70 with Exact Match score of 85.85 and obtains the 1st place in the FinCausal 2022 competition.

1. Introduction

An important step in extraction of causal information and narratives from text documents is the extraction of cause-effect pairs where causes and effects are text spans in the input sentences. The FinCausal shared task at the Financial Narrative Processing Workshop (FNP) addresses this step (Mariko et al., 2020). The causality information can be stated explicitly using well-known indicators such as *due to*, *caused by*, or *as a result of*. But in many cases, a causal relationship can be inferred based on the sequence of events even in the absence of specific patterns. This is more applicable to the financial domain where financial performance is often reported with the causal relation stated implicitly. Language understanding is an important step in extracting the cause-effect pairs from these financial reports.

In this paper, we address this information extraction problem with span-based and sequence tagging neural network models. Specifically, we fine tune pre-trained language models to perform text span classification and sequence labeling tasks. We trained a span-based (Eberts and Ulges, 2019) causality extraction system by fine tuning the BERT-Base (Devlin et al., 2018) model. This model resulted in an F1 score of 89.36 and Exact Match score of 81.67. Our best performing model was an ensemble of sequence tagging models based on the BIO scheme using the RoBERTa-Large (Liu et al., 2019) model. This model achieved an F1 score of 94.70 to win the FinCausal 2022 challenge.

2. System Description

We describe the two types of models trained for the FinCausal 2022 challenge.

2.1. Span-based Model

This model, based on (Eberts and Ulges, 2019), selects a sequence of tokens from the input text and classifies them to be a cause or an effect.

Preprocessing

We tokenize the text using the *word_tokenize* function from the `NLTK` library. To use BERT-Base model to get the embeddings, we split the tokens with the HuggingFace's *BertTokenizer* function (Wolf et al., 2019).

The FinCausal data set contains examples with multiple cause-effect pairs. These examples have the same input sentence with different cause and effect labels. There is an additional index number to denote these types of examples. Since our model takes the text as input, it is not possible for the model to predict two different labels for the same sentence. So we add a number to the start of these examples so the model has different inputs to work with. We follow the FinCausal 2020's winning system (Kao et al., 2020) to add a number to the start of the input text for multi-causal examples.

Model Description

We adopt the span-based model from (Eberts and Ulges, 2019) to classify spans of words as causes and effects. This model represents a span/sequence of words by max-pooling the output layer embeddings from BERT. The CLS token embedding is used as a context embedding in the span representation. The number of words in the span is embedded with a width embedding matrix to get a span width embedding. Span embedding is the concatenation of the span width embedding, max-pooled span embeddings and the CLS token embedding.

$$\mathbf{e}(s) = f(\mathbf{e}_i, \mathbf{e}_{i+1}, \ldots \mathbf{e}_{i+k}) \circ w_{k+1} \circ c$$

where $\mathbf{e}(s)$ is the span embedding, $\mathbf{e}_i$ the embedding for i-th token and w is the width embedding, c is the CLS token embedding. A candidate span is classified into 3 classes (cause, effect or none) using a softmax classifier.

$$y_s = \text{softmax}(W_s.\mathbf{e}(s) + b_s)$$

There is also a binary relation classifier that is trained to predict the existence of a relationship between a pair of spans. The concatenation of the output embeddings from BERT and the max-pooled embeddings of the tokens in between the spans is used as input to the relation classifier.

This model is trained by selecting negative examples for the cause and effect spans by randomly sampling

1	Ceteris	paribus	,	the	fiscal	deficit	this	fiscal	will	widen	to	around
O	B-E	I-E	I-E	I-E	I-E	I-E	I-E	I-E	I-E	I-E	I-E	I-E
4	%	owing	to	the	stimulus	if	extra	transfers	from	RBI	are	counted
I-E	I-E	O	O	B-C	I-C	O	O	O	O	O	O	O
,	the	deficit	's	size	could	be	3.8	%	.			
O	O	O	O	O	O	O	O	O	O			

2	Ceteris	paribus	,	the	fiscal	deficit	this	fiscal	will	widen	to	around
O	O	O	O	O	O	O	O	O	O	O	O	O
4	%	owing	to	the	stimulus	if	extra	transfers	from	RBI	are	counted
O	O	O	O	O	O	O	B-C	I-C	I-C	I-C	I-C	I-C
,	the	deficit	's	size	could	be	3.8	%	.			
O	B-E	I-E	I-E	I-E	I-E	I-E	I-E	I-E	I-E			

Figure 1: Examples with multiple cause-effect pairs are distinguished by adding a number to the front. The BIO tags are shown under each token.

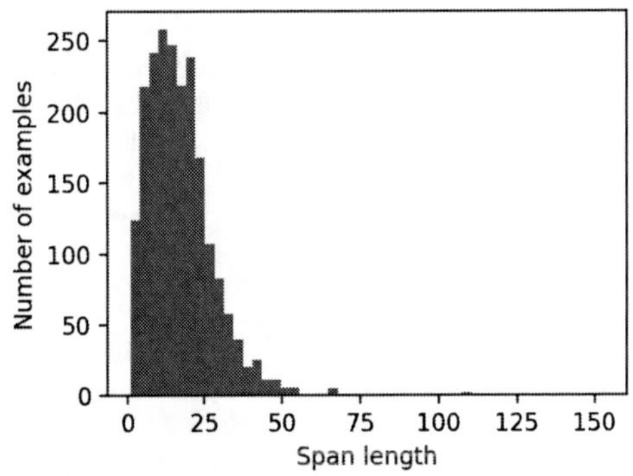

Figure 2: Span length distribution of the practice set

spans from the input text. We sample negative spans up to a maximum span size. During evaluation, a list of candidate spans is generated up to this maximum span length for predicting cause or effect with the span classifier. The cross-entropy loss function is used to train the model.

A challenge in the use of the span-based model is selecting the right span size. The distribution of the length of cause and effect spans in the training data is depicted in Figure 2. Our experiments showed that a span size equal to the 99-percentile span length (maximum span length after discarding the longest 1% spans) in the training data worked well across various data sets.

2.2. Sequence Tagging Models

This is a token classification model that predicts a tag for each token in the sentence using the output embeddings from RoBERTa-Large.

Preprocessing

We use NLTK and HuggingFace tokenizers for the input text. To format this problem as a token classification problem, we use BIO tagging scheme. For an input sequence, each token is assigned one of the following tags: {B-Cause, I-Cause, B-Effect, I-Effect, O}, where "B" stands for "Beginning", "I" for "Inside", and "O" for "Outside". We also add a number at the start of examples with multiple cause-effect pairs. Figure 1 shows such an example with the BIO tags.

Model

We use RoBERTa-Large (Liu et al., 2019) as the input sequence encoder. This is a transformer model with 24 layers and the dimension of each layer embedding is 1024. A linear layer is added on top of the embeddings from the output layer to predict the BIO tags for each token. We fine-tune the model with the practice dataset and use the trial dataset for hyper-parameter tuning. For the final submissions, we submitted:

- Single models that are trained with practice data only.
- An ensemble model of 11 single models that are trained with practice data only via majority voting.
- Single models that are trained with all data.
- An ensemble of 11 single models that are trained with all data via majority voting.

3. Experiments

3.1. Data Set

We use the data sets from FinCausal 2021 in our experiments. The practice set is used as training set and the trial set is used as test set. For submission to the FinCausal 2022 challenge, we combine the practice set, trial set and additional practice set from FinCausal 2022 into a training set.

Model	Trial Set				Blind Test Set			
	F1	R	P	EM	F1	R	P	EM
BIO Tagging Model (Single) - Practice Data	87.92	88.00	87.98	75.63	94.57	94.57	94.62	83.06
BIO Tagging Model (Ensemble) - Practice Data	88.01	88.07	88.23	78.12	94.51	94.51	94.55	84.03
BIO Tagging Model (Single) - All Data	x	x	x	x	94.30	94.30	94.32	84.67
BIO Tagging Model (Ensemble) - All Data	x	x	x	x	**94.70**	**94.70**	**94.71**	**85.85**

Table 1: F1 score, Recall (R), Precision (P) and Exact Match score (EM) of different sequence tagging models on the trial and blind test sets.

Data Set	Size
Practice (FinCausal 2021)	1752
Trial (FinCausal 2021)	641
Practice-addition (FinCausal 2022)	535

Table 2: Data set statistics

3.2. Training

The span-based model was trained on a system with Tesla V100 gpu. We set the maximum span size to 60 as it covers 90% of the training data spans. The model is trained for 40 epochs with a learning rate of $5e-5$. The number of negative samples for the span classifier is 10. We selected the hyperparameters by using the trial set performance as validation score and selecting the model with highest score for exact matching.

4. Results

Span-based Model

The span-based model classifies candidate spans to predict cause and effect spans for a sentence. But it is possible that in some cases the model does not predict any cause or effect for an example. As we know, each example has 1 cause and effect pair in this data set, we modified the model prediction method. For each example we predict 1 span for the cause and effect classes by selecting the span with the maximum probability to be in the respective class. In Table 3, we see that predicting the span with the maximum probability to be a cause or an effect gives a big boost to the Exact Match score.

Model	F1	Rec.	Prec.	EM
SpERT	82.07	81.56	81.33	68.02
SpERT (Max)	83.94	83.57	83.42	74.10

Table 3: Result of the span-based model on the Trial data set

For submitting to the FinCausal challenge, we train this model by combining all data sets (practice, trial and practice-addition). This model gets a F1 score of 89.36 and Exact Match score of 81.67 (3rd rank in the competition in terms of Exact Match).

Sequence Tagging Model

The sequence tagging model based on RoBERTa-Large gets better partial F1 score compared to the span-based model. In the trial set, the single model trained on practice data achieves a F1 score 4% higher than the span-based model. We adopt the ensemble approach to improve the performance of this model. As random seeds play an important role in the optimization of deep networks, we train the same model with different random seeds and combine their prediction. We use majority voting as a simple approach to convert the predictions from different models into a single prediction. The ensemble approach ensures that the model does not have a low score due to a bad optimum resulting from a random seed. We submitted an ensemble of 11 models trained with different random seeds that obtains the best F1 score on the competition (Table 1).

Model	Text
SpERT (Max)	One of the pilot program's unique aspects is to encourage homeowners in six targeted community areas to opt in and put their houses in the land trust in exchange for significantly lower property taxes and access to a $30,000 grant for home repairs and energy upgrades.
BIO Tagging Model (Ensemble)	One of the pilot program's unique aspects is to encourage homeowners in six targeted community areas to opt in and put their houses in the land trust in exchange for significantly lower property taxes and access to a $30,000 grant for home repairs and energy upgrades.
SpERT (Max)	The group said international restaurant sales increased by 12.3 percent, benefiting from the opening of a record 20 restaurants during the year, but this was offset by a 15.9 percent sales decline in Australia and New Zealand.
BIO Tagging Model (Ensemble)	The group said international restaurant sales increased by 12.3 percent, benefiting from the opening of a record 20 restaurants during the year, but this was offset by a 15.9 percent sales decline in Australia and New Zealand.

Figure 3: Sample predictions from the span-based model and the sequence tagging model. ▮ for Cause and ▮ for Effect

Output Analysis

We compare the predictions from the span-based model and the sequence tagging model in Figure 3. The span-based model selects a shorter Cause phrase by focusing on the causal cue phrase 'to' whereas the sequence tagging model selects the clause before 'in exchange for' as the Cause phrase. In the second example, the predictions from the span-based model and the sequence tagging model are reverse, i.e. the span-based model classifies the first span as Cause but the sequence tagging model tags the first span as Effect. We can see that the sequence tagging model is correct here. As the span-based model predicts a span for each class, it can result to this type of error. So the sequence tagging model has a better performance on this task.

5. Conclusion

In this paper, we train different types of deep neural models based on pre-trained language models for the FinCausal 2022 shared task. We find that using an ensemble of sequence tagging models trained with the BIO tagging scheme based on the RoBERTa-large model achieves the best score in the competition.

6. References

Devlin, J., Chang, M.-W., Lee, K., and Toutanova, K. (2018). Bert: Pre-training of deep bidirectional transformers for language understanding. *arXiv preprint arXiv:1810.04805.*

Eberts, M. and Ulges, A. (2019). Span-based joint entity and relation extraction with transformer pre-training. *arXiv preprint arXiv:1909.07755.*

Kao, P.-W., Chen, C.-C., Huang, H.-H., and Chen, H.-H. (2020). NTUNLPL at FinCausal 2020, task 2: Improving causality detection using Viterbi decoder. In *Proceedings of the 1st Joint Workshop on Financial Narrative Processing and MultiLing Financial Summarisation*, pages 69–73, Barcelona, Spain (Online), December. COLING.

Liu, Y., Ott, M., Goyal, N., Du, J., Joshi, M., Chen, D., Levy, O., Lewis, M., Zettlemoyer, L., and Stoyanov, V. (2019). RoBERTa: A robustly optimized BERT pretraining approach. *arXiv preprint arXiv:1907.11692.*

Mariko, D., Labidurie, E., Ozturk, Y., Akl, H. A., and de Mazancourt, H. (2020). Data processing and annotation schemes for FinCausal shared task.

Wolf, T., Debut, L., Sanh, V., Chaumond, J., Delangue, C., Moi, A., Cistac, P., Rault, T., Louf, R., Funtowicz, M., et al. (2019). HuggingFace's transformers: State-of-the-art natural language processing. *arXiv preprint arXiv:1910.03771.*

Proceedings of the 4th Financial Narrative Processing Workshop @ LREC 2022, pages 112–115
Marseille, 24 June 2022

Multilingual Financial Documentation Summarization by Team_Tredence for FNS2022

Manish Pant, Ankush Chopra
Tredence Analytics
Bengaluru (India)
{manish.pant, ankush.chopra}@tredence.com

Abstract

This paper describes multi-lingual long document summarization systems submitted to the Financial Narrative Summarization Shared Task (FNS 2022[1]) by Team-Tredence. We developed task-specific summarization methods for 3 languages – English, Spanish and Greek. The solution is divided into two parts, where a RoBERTa model was finetuned to identify/extract summarizing segments from English documents and T5 based models were used for summarizing Spanish and Greek documents. A purely extractive approach was applied to summarize English documents using data-specific heuristics. An mT5 model was fine-tuned to identify potential narrative sections for Greek and Spanish, followed by finetuning mT5 and T5(Spanish version) for abstractive summarization task. This system also features a novel approach for generating summarization training dataset using long document segmentation and the semantic similarity across segments. We also introduce an N-gram variability score to select sub-segments for generating more diverse and informative summaries from long documents.

Keywords : Long Document Summarization, Abstractive Summarization, Extractive Summarization

1. Introduction

Huge corpus of financial documents is published around the world in various languages. These documents hold enormous information that can be very useful for the finance analysts and market stakeholders if it could be streamlined, structured, or summarized into a concise piece of text. Automating this task using NLP techniques can substantially reduce the gap between supply of unstructured text data and the availability of consumable piece of text information.

The objective of Financial Narrative Summarization (FNS 2022) (Zmandar et al., 2022) was to implement a system for automating text summarization of financial text written in **English, Spanish** and **Greek**. The task dataset was extracted from annual reports of the firms listed on UK, Spanish and Greek stock exchanges, published in the pdf format. The details of work submitted by various teams is collated by (Mahmoud et al., 2022).

The expected outcome was to provide structured single summaries, based on real-world, publicly available financial annual reports by extracting information from different key sections and generate summaries that reflects the analysis and assessment of the financial trend of the business over the past year, as provided by annual reports. The summary length should not exceed **1000 words.**

Gold summaries for English language reports were found to be extractive in nature with around 99.9% summaries as continuous word subsequences of reports. There were one or more gold summaries provided for each report. This task was framed to be purely extractive, where we classified smaller segments of the reports as summary segments and heuristically selected top-n segments as system generated summary.

Gold summaries for Greek and Spanish language reports were identified to be abstractive in nature. We implemented a text classifier to mark line/segment of reports as narrative sections. The classified segments were clustered into semantically related segments of reports. These cluster of report segments were summarized as system generated summaries using transformers-based models (Vaswani et al., 2017). Next, we'll describe the dataset provided by the organizers followed by the systems we developed. We'll then briefly talk about the experiments, results and highlight our learning in the conclusion section.

2. Dataset

The dataset includes annual reports produced by UK, Spanish and Greek firms listed on the Stock Exchange for each of those markets.

The texts can be up to 80 pages long which makes it challenging to analyze them manually. The English summaries were extractive in nature and were created by taking multiple contiguous sentences from the original reports. Spanish and Greek summaries were abstractive in nature and were coming from the Chairman's letter or equivalent section.

Data Type	Train	Val	Test	Total
Report text	3000	363	500	3863
Gold summaries	9873	1250	1673	12796

Table 1: FNS 2022 Shared Task Dataset - English

Data Type	Train	Val	Test	Total
Report text	162	50	50	262
Gold summaries	324	100	100	524

Table 2: FNS 2022 Shared Task Dataset - Spanish

[1] FNS 2022 – FNP 2022 (lancs.ac.uk)

Data Type	Train	Val	Test	Total
Report text	162	50	50	262
Gold summaries	324	100	100	524

Table 3: FNS 2022 Shared Task Dataset – Greek

We used training set of each language to fine-tune the model and used the validation set to determine the best performing model configurations.
In English training set, we had 3000 annual reports and 9873 gold summaries. On an average 3 golden summary available for each report. The average golden summary is 1084 words long and average annual report length is 46167 words. Table 1 has the details of the English dataset.
In Spanish training set (Table 2), we had 162 annual reports and 324 gold summaries, such that there are exactly 2 golden summaries for each annual report. The average golden summary is 878 words long and average annual report length is 39980 words.
In Greek training set (Table 3), we had 162 annual reports and 324 gold summaries, such that there are exactly 2 golden summaries for each annual report. The average annual report length is 28360 words and average golden summary is 7353 words long while the median length is 1514 words. It was noted that Greek summary length had a very skewed distribution due to outliers.

3. Systems

The final submission was composed of 3 systems. These systems were combination of 2 English and Greek solutions each and 1 Spanish Solution that we developed.

3.1 English Solutions

Only 0.01% of records were such where given summaries were not contiguous subsets of reports. We discarded these records from data. We divided each report into smaller text segments of 250 words. We experimented with segment of various lengths and empirically decided 250 as optimal cutoff.
We then compared these generated segments with the given summary text. Comparison was done at unigram token level. Any report segment with an overlap of more than 75-word tokens with summary text was considered to have potential towards summary creation and marked as positive. Segments with no overlap were marked as negative. Segments that had overlapping words between 0 to 74 were kept away from the modelling.

3.1.1 Summary Identification/Extraction Module

Above stated approach was used to generate train and validation dataset. We fine-tuned base version of the RoBERTa (Liu et al., 2017) model for classifying the report segment to be candidate summary segment or not. The best model achieved F1-score of 0.76 on the validation set.
During the inference, the report is first broken into segments of 250 words each except last segment. Each of these segments are scored using finetuned RoBERTa model.
Since the organizers have put a limit of max 1000-words for the system generated summaries, we select 4 candidate summary segments to make the final complete summary. We came up with 2 methods for final 4 segment selection.
In first solution, we select 4 continuous segments sequence such that the mean confidence score of prediction is maximized. This was done to mimic the process that was used for summary preparation by organizers.
In solution 2, we introduced the bi-gram variability score associated with each segment. We used this to reduce repetition of information across different segments for final summary. Bi-gram variability score for summary segment "S_i" was calculated based on count of bigrams in given candidate summary segment "C_i" and all other candidate summary segments "C_k" in given report:

$$S_i = \frac{Ci}{\sum_{k=1}^{y} Ck}$$

All the segments with score of more than 0.75 from RoBERTa model are considered as candidate segments. Top 4 candidates based on bi-gram variability score are selected as final summary of the report from all the candidate segments.

3.2 Spanish and Greek Solutions

The solutions for Spanish and Greek report summarization have 2 main submodules, summary identification and abstractive summarization. Both Greek and Spanish solutions are almost identical, with only difference being the base-model used for finetuning abstractive summarization task.
We divided each report into smaller segments delimited by the new line characters. We dropped lines with less than 5 words. Similarly, each summary was segmented into multiple lines and filtered.
Embeddings for each segmented line of report and summary was generated using the sentence transformer (Reimers & Gurevych, 2019) framework. We used multilingual-*mpnet-base-v2 model* (Song et al., 2020) *within this framework*. Using these embeddings, we calculated the cosine similarity of each report line against each summary line. The report lines with similarity score above 0.65 against any summary line, were marked as positive for candidate summary classification model dataset. All the remaining lines from reports were marked as negative.

3.2.1 Summary Identification/Extraction Module

Above stated approach was used to generate train and validation datasets. We finetuned a multilingual T5 model to classify between the positive and negative candidate report segments. The classifier achieved an f1 score of 0.29 on Spanish validation set and 0.65 on Greek validation set. We trained a single multilingual model for Spanish and Greek combined to classify report lines for being candidate input to summary extraction.

3.2.2 Abstractive Summarization Module

We scored the candidate segments using the previous module to generate the training data for this module. Since T5 (Raffel et al., 2020) is seq-to-seq model (Sutskever et al., 2014) we took all the lines where label 1 was generated output as candidates. We selected only such candidate report lines that had a cosine similarity score higher than 0.65 with any of the summary lines. Again, we used the same sentence transformer model for embedding generation. We generated the dataset for abstractive summarization model using each summary line as target sequence and top-4 similar candidate report lines as the input sequence. This approach was applied for generating both training and validation dataset.

We finetuned Google's mt5-small model for Greek and a Spanish-t5 model from flax community in Huggingface[2].

During inference, the report is broken into lines and scored using first submodule (classifier). Sentence embeddings are generated for all lines/segments from report which were classified as candidate input for summarization model.

We needed to group the candidate input lines into clusters so that a sizable text can be provided as input to the abstractive summarization model. We implemented two methods for Greek and one for Spanish after experimenting with few ideas. For Greek Solution-1 (first method), the classified summary segments of test set were grouped into 5 clusters. These 5 clusters were input to the abstractive summarization model and the output was the system generated summary segments.

Implementation of Spanish and 2nd Greek method (Solution-2) were same. We clustered the candidate report lines into 16 clusters and calculated centroid for each of these clusters. These 16 cluster centroids were used to select top-5 similar report lines to each cluster centroid. This resulted in 16 clusters of 5 similar lines each. These 16 clusters were input to the abstractive summarization model and the output was the system generated summary segments.

4. Experiments

4.1 English Solutions

We experimented with different overlap word lengths and segment word lengths for English summary identification model training dataset. RoBERTa-base model (Liu et al., 2017) variant was able to generalize well with overlap length in the range of 60-90 words and segment length of 250-350 words. We found the most optimal overlap length of 75 words and segment length of 250 words length. Also dropping the boundary case data points with overlap between 0-75 words improved the f1 score to 0.76. It was also critical to use the bigram variability score in final segment selection, which helped in ensuring the selected segments with least repetition of information. Final model was trained for 5 epochs, with learning rate of 1e-6 and AdamW (Loshchilov & Hutter, 2019) optimizer. We chose a batch size of 32 for both train and validation sets.

4.2 Spanish and Greek Solutions

Fine-tuned mT5-small model (Xue et al., 2021) performed the best compared to few other models we tried for candidate classification for both Greek and Spanish. It did not fare well for Spanish, when we used it for abstractive summarization as well. It performed well for Greek in abstractive summarization application though. Using a Spanish language specific model proved to be better since it clearly outdid mT5 model when we compared validation set performance of both the models using Rogue-2 (Ganesan, 2006) scores.

It was also critical to use semantic similarity embeddings for artificially creating summarization training dataset and clustering the semantically related lines for input generation for summarization submodule.

We observed that certain clusters with fewer lines tend to perform relatively worse due to lack of enough context for summarization which led to the idea of clustering with repetition. For Greek Solution-2 and Spanish, we clustered based on top-n similar data points to a given cluster centroid which enabled the consistent length and context for summarization model input.

The mT5 model used for candidate classification of both Spanish and Greek was trained with input sequence length of 128. Model was trained for 4 epochs with batch size of 8, learning rate of 1e-4 and AdamW (Loshchilov & Hutter, 2019) optimizer.

Abstractive summarization for Spanish was done by a T5 models pretrained for Spanish corpora. We finetuned it for input and output sequence lengths of 700 and 180 respectively. Model was finetuned for 40 epochs with learning rate of 3e-4 and batch size of 1.

We used the mT5 model for Abstractive summarization for Greek. We finetuned it for input and output sequence lengths of 1024 and 256 respectively. Model was finetuned for 30 epochs with learning rate of 3e-5 and batch size of 1.

All the models were finetuned on NVIDIA RTX3090 system.

5. Results

Rouge-2 (Ganesan, 2006) F1 score was the official metric for evaluating system performance for each language. The final score was weighted 0.5, 0.25, and 0.25 for English, Spanish, and Greek respectively. We submitted 3 systems to the competition and achieved an overall team rank 4. Our best scoring system was composed of solution-2 of both English and Greek sole, Spanish submission that we made. The final weighted score of best performing system was 0.228. Below table has the results for all the solutions that we submitted.

[2] Hugging Face – The AI community building the future.

Language	Solution	Rogue-2 Recall	Rogue-2 Precision	Rogue-2 F1-Score
English	Solution1	0.305	0.363	0.317
	Solution2	0.346	0.323	0.322
Greek	Solution1	0.043	0.415	0.072
	Solution2	0.097	0.321	0.138
Spanish	Solution1	0.134	0.149	0.131

Table 4: Results

6. Conclusion

We built the final system by dividing the problem into two. This division was done after analyzing the nature of input and output data. English summaries were purely extractive in nature whereas Greek and Spanish were abstractive.

Using a more sophisticated approach for final segment selection in English system could marginally improve the scores. Instead of picking the top-n segments, any seq2seq model could be trained to predict the start and end of summary on a combined corpus of selected sections.

We could also experiment using larger mt5 models for Spanish and Greek summarization which requires higher GPU memory for fine-tuning. Also, few language-specific text generation models could be finetuned to compare the performance with existing multilingual model for Greek and Spanish individually.

7. Bibliographical References

Ganesan, K. (2006). ROUGE 2.0: Updated and Improved Measures for Evaluation of Summarization Tasks. Computational Linguistics, 1(1).

Liu, Y., Ott, M., Goyal, N., Du, J., Joshi, M., Chen, D., ... & Stoyanov, V. (2019). RoBERTa: A Robustly Optimized BERT Pretraining Approach.

Loshchilov, I., & Hutter, F. (2018, September). Decoupled Weight Decay Regularization. In International Conference on Learning Representations.

Mahmoud El-Haj, et al., editors. (2022). Proceedings of the 4th Financial Narrative Processing Workshop, Marseille, France, 24 June. The 13th Language Resources and Evaluation Conference, LREC 2022.

Raffel, C., Shazeer, N., Roberts, A., Lee, K., Narang, S., Matena, M., ... & Liu, P. J. (2020). Exploring the Limits of Transfer Learning with a Unified Text-to-Text Transformer. Journal of Machine Learning Research, 21, 1-67.

Reimers, N., Gurevych, I., Reimers, N., Gurevych, I., Thakur, N., Reimers, N., ... & Gurevych, I. (2019). Sentence-BERT: Sentence Embeddings using Siamese BERT-Networks. In Proceedings of the 2019 Conference on Empirical Methods in Natural Language Processing (pp. 671-688). Association for Computational Linguistics.

Song, K., Tan, X., Qin, T., Lu, J., & Liu, T. Y. (2020). Mpnet: Masked and permuted pre-training for language understanding. Advances in Neural Information Processing Systems, 33, 16857-16867.

Sutskever, I., Vinyals, O., & Le, Q. V. (2014). Sequence to sequence learning with neural networks. Advances in neural information processing systems, 27.

Vaswani, A., Shazeer, N., Parmar, N., Uszkoreit, J., Jones, L., Gomez, A. N., ... & Polosukhin, I. (2017). Attention is all you need. Advances in neural information processing systems, 30.

Xue, L., Constant, N., Roberts, A., Kale, M., Al-Rfou, R., Siddhant, A., ... & Raffel, C. (2021, June). mT5: A Massively Multilingual Pre-trained Text-to-Text Transformer. In Proceedings of the 2021 Conference of the North American Chapter of the Association for Computational Linguistics: Human Language Technologies (pp. 483-498).

Zmandar, N., El-Haj, M., Rayson, P., Abura'Ed, A., Litvak, M., Giannakopoulos, G., Pittaras, N., Carbajo-Coronado, B., and Moreno-Sandoval, A. (2022). The financial narrative summarisation shared task (fns 2022). In Proceedings of the 4th Financial Narrative Processing Workshop, Marseille, France, 24June. The 13th Language Resources and Evaluation Conference, LREC 2022.

Proceedings of the 4th Financial Narrative Processing Workshop @ LREC 2022, pages 116–120
Marseille, 24 June 2022

DCU-Lorcan at FinCausal 2022: Span-based Causality Extraction from Financial Documents using Pre-trained Language Models

Chenyang Lyu, Tianbo Ji, Quanwei Sun, Liting Zhou
School of Computing, Dublin City University
Dublin, Ireland
chenyang.lyu2@mail.dcu.ie, tianbo.ji2@mail.dcu.ie, quanwei.sun@insight-centre.org, liting.zhou@dcu.ie

Abstract

In this paper, we describe our DCU-Lorcan system for the FinCausal 2022 shared task: span-based cause and effect extraction from financial documents. We frame the FinCausal 2022 causality extraction task as a span extraction/sequence labeling task, our submitted systems are based on the contextualized word representations produced by pre-trained language models and linear layers predicting the label for each word, followed by post-processing heuristics. In experiments, we employ pre-trained language models including DistilBERT, BERT and SpanBERT. Our best performed system achieves F-1, Recall, Precision and Exact Match scores of 92.76, 92.77, 92.76 and 68.60 respectively. Additionally, we conduct experiments investigating the effect of data size to the performance of causality extraction model and an error analysis investigating the outputs in predictions.

Keywords: FinCausal 2022, span-based causality extraction, financial documents, pre-trained language models, sequence labeling

1. Introduction

The FinCausal 2022 shared task, as a part of the Financial Narrative Processing Workshop (El-Haj et al., 2020; El-Haj et al., 2021), aims to extract *cause* and *effect* from financial documents, where both *cause* and corresponding *effect* are spans in the original documents. Extracting causality spans from financial documents is not only important for causal understanding in financial texts but also helpful for improving natural language understanding in finance domain. FinCausal 2020 (Mariko et al., 2020) and FinCausal 2021 (Mariko et al., 2021) have established benchmarks for causality extraction task and significantly facilitated the development of methodology in this area.

In this work, we employ advanced pre-trained language models (PLMs) to facilitate the causality extraction task as PLMs have been proven to be effective in many NLP tasks including text classification, text generation especially on span extraction/sequence labeling task such as Named-entity Recognition and Question Answering (Devlin et al., 2019; Lewis et al., 2020; Qiu et al., 2020). Build on PLMs, we also propose a heuristically-induced *post-processing* strategy to refine the system predictions. Our best system (BERT-large + *post-process*) achieves F-1, Recall, Precision and Exact Match scores of 92.76, 92.77, 92.76 and 68.60 respectively. More importantly, we focus on investigating the effect of data size to the performance of causality extraction model in order to provide useful information for the development of methodology. We found that causality extraction models obtain fewer benefit from increasing data size when the training data contains more than 60% examples of the full training set. Additionally, we conduct analysis towards the errors occurred in the predictions of PLMs as well as in the annotations of the examples in the dataset.

2. Data

The data used in FinCausal 2022 task is created from Qwam [1] and Edgar database [2]. We show some examples in Table 1, moreover we show the data size and average length of *document*, *cause* and *effect* in each version of FinCausal in Table 2. From the average length in Table 2, we can see that FinCausal 2022 data has shorter *documents* and longer *cause* spans compared to early version of FinCausal. Therefore, that might pose new challenges for the FinCausal 2022 task. In FinCausal 2022, the employed data consists of data created in FinCausal 2020 and FinCausal 2021 as well as newly annotated data. The pre-processing steps in this work are listed as follows:

- For the training data used in this work, we combine the *practice* and *trial* data in early versions of FinCausal task and half of the newly annotated data provided in FinCausal 2022, we use the other half of the new data as dev set. After filtering, the resulting training data contains 4386 examples and the dev data has 265 examples.
- Its worth noting that one document can possibly contain more than one *cause-effect* pair, thus for the examples whose id ends with *'.1'* we prepend a *'First'* to their documents, and for the examples whose id ends with *'.2'* we prepend a *'Second'* to their documents, see the second and the thrid example in Table1.
- To tokenize the texts (*document, cause* and *effect*)in dataset, we employ the $word\_tokenize$ function in NLTK (Bird et al., 2009) [3].

[1] http://www.qwamci.com/
[2] https://www.sec.gov/edgar/search-and-access
[3] https://www.nltk.org

Document	Cause	Effect
Incumbent RBS boss Ross McEwan announced in April his intention to step down from his role at the head of the 62% state-owned banking giant, saying it was the right time to go having delivered on his strategy of stabilising the bank following its post-crisis bailout.	it was the right time to go having delivered on his strategy of stabilising the bank following its post-crisis bailout.	Incumbent RBS boss Ross McEwan announced in April his intention to step down from his role at the head of the 62% state-owned banking giant
First. Finally, ValuEngine cut shares of Gladstone Commercial from a buy rating to a hold rating in a research report on Monday, July 22nd. Three investment analysts have rated the stock with a hold rating and two have assigned a buy rating to the company's stock. The stock presently has an average rating of Hold and an average price target of $22.50.	Finally, ValuEngine cut shares of Gladstone Commercial from a buy rating to a hold rating in a research report on Monday, July 22nd.	The stock presently has an average rating of Hold and an average price target of $22.50.
Second. Finally, ValuEngine lowered shares of Travelers Companies from a buy rating to a hold rating in a research report on Thursday, August 1st. Two equities research analysts have rated the stock with a sell rating, ten have issued a hold rating and two have assigned a buy rating to the company's stock. The stock presently has a consensus rating of Hold and an average price target of $148.78.	Two equities research analysts have rated the stock with a sell rating, ten have issued a hold rating and two have assigned a buy rating to the company's stock.	The stock presently has a consensus rating of Hold and an average price target of $148.78.

Table 1: Examples of *document* and corresponding *cause* and *effect*, where the second and the third example have the sample input *document* but different *cause* and *effect* spans, thus we prepend a *First* to the second example and a *Second* to the third one in order tot enable the model to be able to distinguish them.

Dataset	Data Size	Document	Cause	Effect
FinCausal 2020	1750	50.11	20.57	20.57
FinCausal 2021	1752	49.79	20.64	20.27
FinCausal 2022	538	45.80	24.10	19.01
Overall Training	4386	49.87	20.70	20.26
Overall Dev	265	48.91	25.75	20.15

Table 2: The data size of examples and average length of *document*, *cause* and *effect* in FinCausal 2020, FinCausal 2021 and FinCausal 2022 and the training and dev set used in this work. For FinCausal 2020 and FinCausal 2021, the statistics are calculated based on the combination of the *practice* and *trial* data.

- For the label of each word, if a word is in *cause* span, then its label is *B-Cause* if it is the start of *cause* span otherwise its label is *I-Cause*, the same rule applies to the words in *effect* span. For the words outside of *cause* and *effect* span, we give them a *O* label.

3. Experiments

3.1. System

In this work, we employ advanced pre-trained language models including DistilBERT, BERT and SpanBERT. DistilBERT (Sanh et al., 2019) is the distilled version of BERT which is smaller and faster with a price of slightly lower performance, BERT (Devlin et al., 2019) is a powerful natural language understanding model which has been shown to be very effective on many NLP tasks and SpanBERT (Joshi et al., 2020) is an improved version of BERT, which adopts a specially-designed pre-training objective that predicts a continuous span in text, resulting in superior performance in span extraction tasks. On top of the the contextualized word representations produced by PLMs, we add extra linear layers to predict the probability that each word belongs to which label (*O, B-Cause, I-Cause, B-Effect, I-Effect*). During training process, the system is optimized using AdamW (Loshchilov and Hutter, 2019) with a *CrossEntropy* loss. In the inference time, we select the most probable (the label with the largest probability) label for each word and then decode the label sequence to corresponding *cause* and *effect* span. Based on the observations that our systems tend to predict spans that end with incomplete phrases or sentences, we proposed a simple post-processing strategy that heuristically removes the incomplete phrases and sentences in the tail.

3.2. Experiment Setup

We use the implementations of DistilBERT, BERT and SpanBERT from Huggingface (Wolf et al., 2020) [4]. The learning rate is set to 5e-5, weight decay rate is 0, we set the dropout rate to 0.1. We train our systems 30 epochs with a batch size of 16. All experiments are conducted on a NNIDIA GTX 3090 GPU.

3.3. Results

We show the main experimental results in Table 3, the systems we used include *DistilBERT*, *BERT-*

[4]https://huggingface.co/models

	Dev Set				Test Set			
	F-1	Recall	Precision	EM	F-1	Recall	Precision	EM
DistilBERT	87.31	85.69	89.79	0.015	89.21	89.21	89.22	17.26
+ post-procss	88.44	86.83	91.34	54.72	90.34	90.30	90.42	67.63
BERT-base	86.88	86.61	87.41	0.023	91.08	91.09	91.07	17.90
+ post-procss	88.10	87.78	88.75	56.23	92.23	92.20	92.28	68.70
BERT-large	91.40	91.40	91.42	0.015	91.60	91.65	91.64	18.11
+ post-procss	92.71	92.62	92.85	56.98	**92.76**	**92.77**	**92.76**	68.60
BERT-large-wwm	92.55	92.44	92.69	0.011	91.47	91.50	91.46	17.90
+ post-procss	93.87	93.67	94.25	58.11	92.61	92.60	92.62	**69.02**
SpanBERT-base	92.22	92.30	92.19	0.015	90.29	90.27	90.31	17.36
+ post-procss	93.59	93.57	93.62	59.25	91.44	91.38	91.55	67.95
SpanBERT-large	93.18	93.25	93.12	0.011	91.18	91.21	91.16	17.90
+ post-procss	**94.55**	**94.52**	**94.6**	**59.25**	92.35	92.34	92.36	68.70

Table 3: Experimental results of all systems on dev set and blind test set. Highest performance is in bold.

base, BERT-large, BERT-large-whole-word-masking[5], *SpanBERT-base, SpanBERT-large*, we also show the effect of our proposed *post-process* strategy in Table 3. Our best performed system on blind test set (BERT-large + *post-process*) achieves F-1, Recall, Precise and Exact Match of 92.71, 92.62, 92.85, 56.9 on dev set and 92.76, 92.77, 92.76, 68.60 on the blind test set. The experimental results in Table 3 suggest:

- DistilBERT achieves comparable performance (slightly lower F-1, Recall and EM, higher Precision) with BERT-base while with a much smaller model size (40%×Bert-base) and faster training and inference speed (50%×Bert-base) compared to BERT-base, which is a huge advantage especially when deploying PLMs in production environment.
- For the same PLM, *large* model constantly yields performance better than *base* model. Moreover, the performance of PLMs is inline with their performance on other NLP tasks. For example, generally in terms of performance on NLP tasks: BERT-large-wwm > BERT-large > BERT-base, which is also true for FinCausal causality extraction task.
- The extremely low Exact Match score for all vanilla PLMs show that they struggle to precisely predict the correct boundary for the *cause* and *effect* spans in texts, suggesting that a vanilla PLM is still not enough for causality task although it can perform well on F-1, Recall and Precision scores.
- Our proposed *post-process* strategy substantially improve model's performance especially on Exact Match score. The results in Table 3 show that *post-process* can consistently give approximately 1.5 point improvements on F-1, Recall and Precision scores while significantly improve the Exact Match score. The results prove the effectiveness of our proposed *post-process* strategy.

[5]Referred to as BERT-large-wwm for simplicity

4. Analysis and Discussion

4.1. Effect of Data Size

We additionally conduct experiments investigating the effect of data size to the performance of causality extraction model. In experiment, we use increasing data sizes starting from 5% to 100% with intervals of 5%, we train our systems using the partial training data sampled from the full training set and evaluate all systems on the full dev set. For example, 5% training data means that we sample 5% examples from the full training set and use them to train a causality system and evaluate it on the dev set. The purpose of this experiment is to gain insights into how data size affects model's performance, in other words how much data is enough to yield a good performance. We show the curves of metrics (F-1, Recall, Precision and Exact Match) for the PLMs shown in Table 3 in Figure 1. The results show that all PLMs benefit from increasing data size at the early stage, however when data size exceeds 60% of the full training set (approximately 2600 examples) the performance has little improvements with increasing data size.

4.2. Error Analysis

We further analyse the errors in the predictions of PLMs, we randomly sampled some incorrect predictions from the output of *SpanBERT-large+post-process* and make manual analysis. The error type summarised from our manual analysis include:

- *Extra Content* (the predicted span contains more content than the golden one)
- *Less Content* (the predicted span contains fewer content than the golden one)

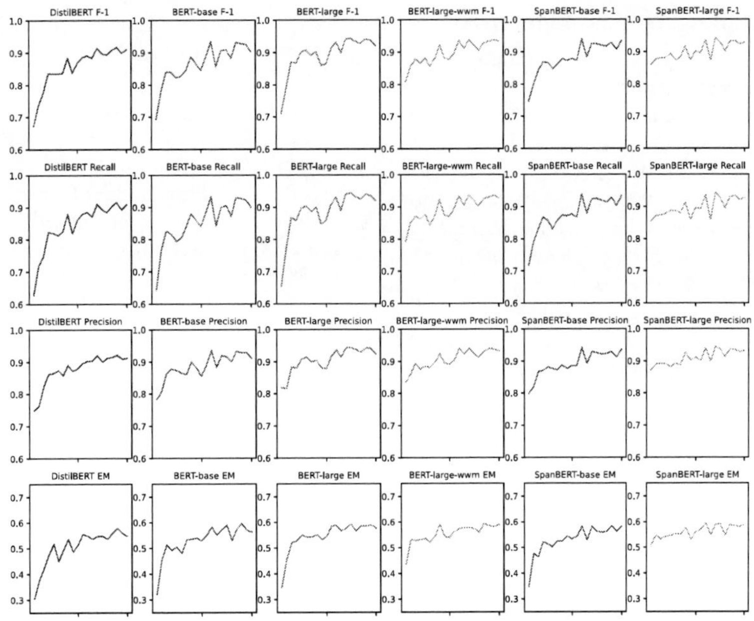

Figure 1: Visualization of metric curves of causality extraction models on different data sizes, where the y-axis is the metric score (F-1, Recall, Precision and Exact Match) and x-axis represents the data sizes starting from 5% to 100% with intervals of 5%.

Cause	Prediction	Error Type
the Company's Chief Executive Officer transition in 2011.	incremental costs associated with the Company's Chief Executive Officer transition in 2011.	*Extra Content*
Higher strategic SG&A costs in the technology businesses attributable to investments in strategic initiatives	Higher strategic SG&A costs in the technology businesses attributable to investments in strategic initiatives also	*Extra Content*
an after-tax charge of $305.1 million to settle certain patent litigation related to transcatheter mitral and tricuspid repair products.	settle certain patent litigation related to transcatheter mitral and tricuspid repair products.	*Less Content*
Working capital increased primarily due to the increase in accounts receivable and supplies inventory	Working capital increased	*Less Content*
lower incentive compensation costs in 2011 compared to 2010	lower incentive compensation costs in 2011 compared to 2010.	*Tail Punctuation*
Higher net charge-offs also contributed to the increase in the provision for credit losses and primarily reflect increases	as a result of the Merger.	*Completely Mismatch*

Table 4: Ground-truth *cause* span and corresponding prediction of *SpanBERT+post-process* associated with error type.

- *Tail Punctuation* (with an extra punctuation appended in the end of the predicted span)
- *Completely Mismatch* (completely different from the golden span)

We show some examples of incorrect predictions for *cause* spans in Table 4, these errors suggest that there is still room for improvements especially on Exact Match as both experiments results and error analysis show that PLMs have difficulty precisely predicting the boundary for *cause* and *effect* spans. Among all the errors, we think the *Tail Punctuation* is caused by the inconsitent annotation - if a ground-truth *cause* or *effect* span is a sentence or a clause including the end of a sentence or sub-sentence, it sometimes contains a punctuation (comma or full-stop) but sometimes it doesn't. That could cause confusion to the model in the training process, thus hindering the performance especially Exact Match score.

5. Bibliographical References

Bird, S., Klein, E., and Loper, E. (2009). *Natural language processing with Python: analyzing text with the natural language toolkit.* " O'Reilly Media, Inc.".

Devlin, J., Chang, M.-W., Lee, K., and Toutanova, K. (2019). BERT: Pre-training of deep bidirectional transformers for language understanding. In *Proceedings of the 2019 Conference of the North American Chapter of the Association for Computational Linguistics: Human Language Technologies, Volume 1 (Long and Short Papers)*, pages 4171–4186, Minneapolis, Minnesota, June. Association for Computational Linguistics.

Dr Mahmoud El-Haj, et al., editors. (2020). *Proceedings of the 1st Joint Workshop on Financial Narrative Processing and MultiLing Financial Summarisation*, Barcelona, Spain (Online), December. COLING.

Mahmoud El-Haj, et al., editors. (2021). *Proceedings of the 3rd Financial Narrative Processing Workshop*, Lancaster, United Kingdom, 15-16 September. Association for Computational Linguistics.

Joshi, M., Chen, D., Liu, Y., Weld, D. S., Zettlemoyer, L., and Levy, O. (2020). SpanBERT: Improving pre-training by representing and predicting spans. *Transactions of the Association for Computational Linguistics*, 8:64–77.

Lewis, M., Liu, Y., Goyal, N., Ghazvininejad, M., Mohamed, A., Levy, O., Stoyanov, V., and Zettlemoyer, L. (2020). BART: Denoising sequence-to-sequence pre-training for natural language generation, translation, and comprehension. In *Proceedings of the 58th Annual Meeting of the Association for Computational Linguistics*, pages 7871–7880, Online, July. Association for Computational Linguistics.

Loshchilov, I. and Hutter, F. (2019). Decoupled weight decay regularization. In *International Conference on Learning Representations.*

Mariko, D., Abi Akl, H., Labidurie, E., Durfort, S., De Mazancourt, H., and El-Haj, M. (2020). The financial document causality detection shared task (fincausal 2020). In *Proceedings of the 1st Joint Workshop on Financial Narrative Processing and MultiLing Financial Summarisation*, pages 23–32.

Mariko, D., Abi-Akl, H., Labidurie, E., Durfort, S., De Mazancourt, H., and El-Haj, M. (2021). The financial document causality detection shared task (fincausal 2021). In *Proceedings of the 3rd Financial Narrative Processing Workshop*, pages 58–60.

Qiu, X., Sun, T., Xu, Y., Shao, Y., Dai, N., and Huang, X. (2020). Pre-trained models for natural language processing: A survey. *Science China Technological Sciences*, pages 1–26.

Sanh, V., Debut, L., Chaumond, J., and Wolf, T. (2019). Distilbert, a distilled version of bert: smaller, faster, cheaper and lighter. *arXiv preprint arXiv:1910.01108.*

Wolf, T., Debut, L., Sanh, V., Chaumond, J., Delangue, C., Moi, A., Cistac, P., Rault, T., Louf, R., Funtowicz, M., Davison, J., Shleifer, S., von Platen, P., Ma, C., Jernite, Y., Plu, J., Xu, C., Le Scao, T., Gugger, S., Drame, M., Lhoest, Q., and Rush, A. (2020). Transformers: State-of-the-art natural language processing. In *Proceedings of the 2020 Conference on Empirical Methods in Natural Language Processing: System Demonstrations*, pages 38–45, Online, October. Association for Computational Linguistics.

Proceedings of the 4th Financial Narrative Processing Workshop @ LREC 2022, pages 121–123
Marseille, 24 June 2022

LIPI at FinCausal 2022: Mining Causes and Effects from Financial Texts

Sohom Ghosh[1,2], Sudip Kumar Naskar[2]
[1]Fidelity Investments, [2]Jadavpur University
[1]Bengaluru,India [2]Kolkata,India
{sohom1ghosh, sudip.naskar}@gmail.com

Abstract

While reading financial documents, investors need to know the causes and their effects. This empowers them to make data-driven decisions. Thus, there is a need to develop an automated system for extracting causes and their effects from financial texts using Natural Language Processing. In this paper, we present the approach our team LIPI followed while participating in the FinCausal 2022 shared task. This approach is based on the winning solution of the first edition of FinCausal held in the year 2020.

Keywords: Financial Texts, Causality Extraction, Natural Language Processing

1. Introduction

Recently, investors refer to financial content available online to educate themselves. Identifying causes and their effects help them in understanding financial markets better. For making investment-related decisions, they tend to strategize based on the causes and their effects. However, manually identifying causes and effects is extremely tedious and time-consuming. This paper proposes an approach for automating this. We pictorially represent such a scenario in Figure 1. This approaches consists of a BERT-base model fine-tuned for the task of token classification using BIO (Begin, Inside, Outside) tags. Subsequently, it uses Viterbi decoder (Forney, 1973) for finding out the best sentence.

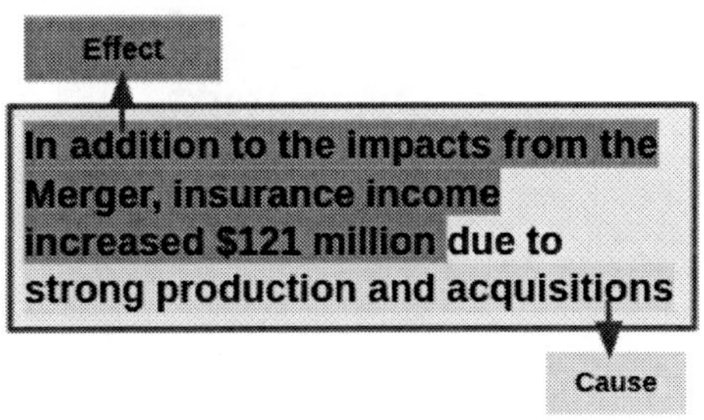

Figure 1: Extraction of a cause and it's effect.

2. Related Works

Relation extraction from documents has been one of the trending areas of research. Several SemEval (Hendrickx et al., 2010), (Gábor et al., 2018) shared task have been organized relating to this. FinCausal is a shared task that deals with extracting causes and effects specific to the financial domain. Its inaugural edition was held in the year 2020 (Mariko et al., 2020) and team NTUNLPL (Kao et al., 2020) secured the first position. They used BIO tagging and fine-tuned a BERT (Devlin et al., 2019) based pre-trained model for the task of token classification. The second edition of FinCausal (Mariko et al., 2021) was held in the following year. Team NUS-IDS (Tan and Ng, 2021) won the competition by leveraging Graph Neural Networks over the solution open-sourced by team NTUNLPL (Kao et al., 2020). We participated in the third edition of this shared task. We narrate our approach in the subsequent sections.

3. System Description

Our best performing system is the same as the one developed by team NTUNLPL (Kao et al., 2020) while participating in FinCausal-2020. It consists of three parts. They are:

1. Tagging each token of the input text using the BIO scheme. For causes (C) and effects (E) additional tags C and E are added.
2. Fine-tuning BERT-base model for the task of token classification
3. Using Viterbi decoder to select the best output sentence.

This is presented in Figure 2. The codebase has been open-sourced [1] We trained a BERT-base model on the full labelled dataset using the architecture proposed by team NTUNLPL (Kao et al., 2020). This dataset included the newly released labelled set for FinCausal 2022. Additionally, we scored the model released by team NTUNLPL (Kao et al., 2020) on the evaluation set of 2022. Finally, we ensembled the predictions by considering outputs from the former model when the one described latter was unable to generate predictions ('effects').

[1]`https://github.com/sohomghosh/FinCausal-2020_2022`.

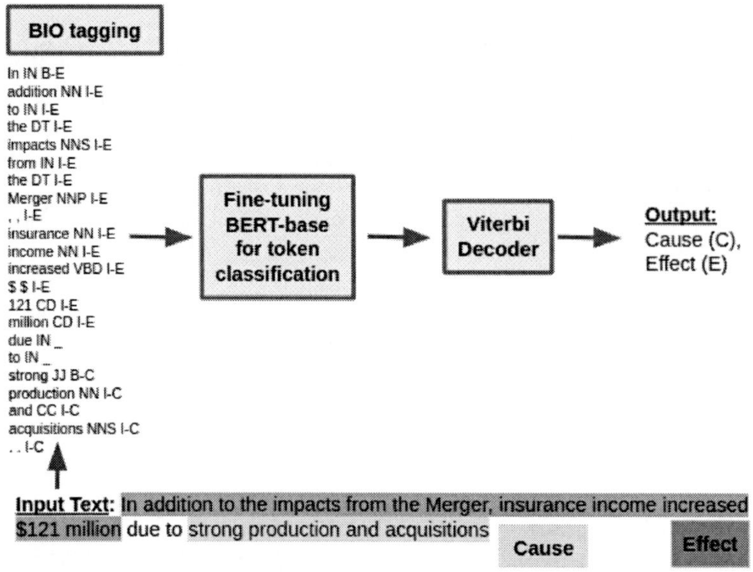

Figure 2: Cause and Effect extraction system

4. Experiments and Results

We present the results obtained from CodaLab[2] in Table 1.

We initiated our experiments by implementing two of the state of the art approaches (Nayak et al., 2022) and (Kao et al., 2020). Since the winning solution of FinCausal-2020 (Kao et al., 2020) is similar to that of FinCausal-2021 (Tan and Ng, 2021), we chose to move ahead with the former. We trained the CEPN (Nayak et al., 2022) architecture proposed by Nayak et al. separately on FinCausal-2020 and FinCausal-2021 datasets and evaluated them on the FinCausal-2022 data set. Subsequently, we combined the entire labelled dataset available till 2022 and re-trained the same architecture (Sl. No. 1). We experimented with both base and the large variant of BERT (Devlin et al., 2019). Furthermore, we replaced BERT embeddings with SEC-BERT-BASE (Loukas et al., 2022) embeddings which are specific to the financial domain (Sl. No. 2). For each of these cases, we maintained a train validation split of 80 to 20. For simplicity, we have modified the scoring logic slightly thereby generating only one set of cause and effect for each of the given texts. These codes are available in `https://github.com/sohomghosh/CEPN`.

After this, we started to experiment with the architecture presented by Kao et al. (team NTUNLPL) (Kao et al., 2020). Firstly, we scored their model on the evaluation set shared by organizers of FinCausal 2022 (Sl. No. 3). Subsequently, we re-trained it using the labelled dataset from all the three editions of FinCausal (Sl. No. 4). We also replaced the underlying BERT-base model with the one shared by Kao et al. (Kao et al., 2020) and fine-tuned it further for the task of token classification using the combined dataset mentioned above (Sl, No. 5).

Finally, combining ensembling results as discussed in the section 3 gave us the best results (Sl. No. 6).

Most of the systems were trained on Google Colab[3] using GPU as the hardware accelerator.

5. Future Works

In future, we would like to explore knowledge graphs for extracting chains of causes and their effects from financial documents. Moreover, we want to develop a tool for mining causes and effects in real-time.

6. Bibliographical References

Devlin, J., Chang, M.-W., Lee, K., and Toutanova, K. (2019). BERT: Pre-training of deep bidirectional transformers for language understanding. In *Proceedings of the 2019 Conference of the North American Chapter of the Association for Computational Linguistics: Human Language Technologies, Volume 1 (Long and Short Papers)*, pages 4171–4186, Minneapolis, Minnesota, June. Association for Computational Linguistics.

Forney, G. (1973). The viterbi algorithm. *Proceedings of the IEEE*, 61(3):268–278.

Gábor, K., Buscaldi, D., Schumann, A.-K., QasemiZadeh, B., Zargayouna, H., and Charnois, T.

[2] `https://codalab.lisn.upsaclay.fr/competitions/3802`

[3] `https://colab.research.google.com/`

Sl. No.	Base Model	Model Architecture	F1	Recall	Precision	Exact Match
1	BERT-large (re-train)	CEPN (simplified)	0.77	0.75	0.84	0.66
2	BERT-SEC (re-train)	CEPN (simplified)	0.74	0.72	0.81	0.58
3	BERT-NTUNLPL (scoring only)	NTUNLPL	**0.92**	**0.92**	0.92	0.78
4	BERT-base (re-train)	NTUNLPL	0.86	0.86	0.86	0.68
5	BERT-NTUNLPL (re-train)	NTUNLPL	0.30	0.38	0.25	0.00
6	Ensemble(3,4)	NTUNLPL	**0.92**	**0.92**	**0.93**	**0.79**

Table 1: Results after training on the labelled dataset available till 2022

(2018). SemEval-2018 task 7: Semantic relation extraction and classification in scientific papers. In *Proceedings of The 12th International Workshop on Semantic Evaluation*, pages 679–688, New Orleans, Louisiana, June. Association for Computational Linguistics.

Hendrickx, I., Kim, S. N., Kozareva, Z., Nakov, P., Ó Séaghdha, D., Padó, S., Pennacchiotti, M., Romano, L., and Szpakowicz, S. (2010). SemEval-2010 task 8: Multi-way classification of semantic relations between pairs of nominals. In *Proceedings of the 5th International Workshop on Semantic Evaluation*, pages 33–38, Uppsala, Sweden, July. Association for Computational Linguistics.

Kao, P.-W., Chen, C.-C., Huang, H.-H., and Chen, H.-H. (2020). NTUNLPL at FinCausal 2020, task 2:improving causality detection using Viterbi decoder. In *Proceedings of the 1st Joint Workshop on Financial Narrative Processing and MultiLing Financial Summarisation*, pages 69–73, Barcelona, Spain (Online), December. COLING.

Loukas, L., Fergadiotis, M., Chalkidis, I., Spyropoulou, E., Malakasiotis, P., Androutsopoulos, I., and George, P. (2022). Finer: Financial numeric entity recognition for xbrl tagging. In *Proceedings of the 60th Annual Meeting of the Association for Computational Linguistics (ACL 2022)*. Association for Computational Linguistics.

Mariko, D., Abi-Akl, H., Labidurie, E., Durfort, S., De Mazancourt, H., and El-Haj, M. (2020). The financial document causality detection shared task (FinCausal 2020). In *Proceedings of the 1st Joint Workshop on Financial Narrative Processing and MultiLing Financial Summarisation*, pages 23–32, Barcelona, Spain (Online), December. COLING.

Mariko, D., Akl, H. A., Labidurie, E., Durfort, S., de Mazancourt, H., and El-Haj, M. (2021). The financial document causality detection shared task (FinCausal 2021). In *Proceedings of the 3rd Financial Narrative Processing Workshop*, pages 58–60, Lancaster, United Kingdom, 15-16 September. Association for Computational Linguistics.

Nayak, T., Sharma, S., Butala, Y., Dasgupta, K., Goyal, P., and Ganguly, N. (2022). A generative approach for financial causality extraction. In *Companion Proceedings of the Web Conference 2022*, WWW '22, New York, NY, USA. Association for Computing Machinery.

Tan, F. A. and Ng, S.-K. (2021). NUS-IDS at FinCausal 2021: Dependency tree in graph neural network for better cause-effect span detection. In *Proceedings of the 3rd Financial Narrative Processing Workshop*, pages 37–43, Lancaster, United Kingdom, 15-16 September. Association for Computational Linguistics.

Proceedings of the 4th Financial Narrative Processing Workshop @ LREC 2022, pages 124–127
Marseille, 24 June 2022

iLab at FinCausal 2022: Enhancing Causality Detection with an External Cause-Effect Knowledge Graph

Ziwei Xu[1], Rungsiman Nararatwong[1], Natthawut Kertkeidkachorn[2], Ryutaro Ichise[3,1]
[1]National Institute of Advanced Science and Technology, Japan
[2]Japan Advanced Institute of Science and Technology, Japan
[3]Tokyo Institute of Technology, Japan
xuxiaowei23@hotmail.com, r.nararatwong@aist.go.jp, natt@jaist.ac.jp, ichise@iee.e.titech.ac.jp

Abstract

The application of span detection grows fast along with the increasing need of understanding the causes and effects of events, especially in the finance domain. However, once the syntactic clues are absent in the text, the model tends to reverse the cause and effect spans. To solve this problem, we introduce graph construction techniques to inject cause-effect graph knowledge for graph embedding. The graph features combining with BERT embedding, then are used to predict the cause effect spans. The results show our proposed graph builder method outperforms the other methods w/wo external knowledge.

Keywords: Graph builder, Cause effect graph, BERT

1. Introduction

Understanding cause and effect in financial documents help us to comprehend the movement of the financial market. Nevertheless, manual annotation is not feasible due to the massive volume of published financial papers. It is necessary to develop an automatic causality extraction method to facilitate financial analysis. Therefore, FinCausal (Mariko et al., 2020b) has been proposed to be the benchmark for causality extraction in the finance domain. The task description of FinCausal 2022 is a relation detection task where we need to identify a causal sentence or text block, the causal elements, and the consequential ones in a given sentence. For example, Given the sentence *"Zhao found himself 60 million yuan indebted after losing 9,000 BTC in a single day (February 10, 2014)"*, we could identify *"losing 9,000 BTC in a single day (February 10, 2014)"* as the cause while we annotate *"Zhao found himself 60 million yuan indebted)"* as the effect.

Recently, many methods have been proposed for FinCausal (Mariko et al., 2020a; Mariko et al., 2021). In FinCausal 2021, the system named DTGNN (Tan and Ng, 2021) achieved the best results in this task. DTGNN incorporates dependency relation features from a sentence through a graph neural network into BERT (Devlin et al., 2018) token classifier with Viterbi decoding (Kao et al., 2020). As a result, the system mainly focuses on adding syntactic features by the dependency features. However, the cause-effect relation of tokens is not explored yet. In this paper, we present our approach built on top of DTGNN and incorporate the cause-effect relation of tokens. We utilize external knowledge, particularly cause and effect graph in the financial domain (Li et al., 2021), to provide the cause-effect relation.

The rest of the paper is organized as follows. We presented our system in Section 2. In Section 3, we discussed our experiment and results. This paper is concluded in Section 4.

2. Proposed System

The competition task in FinCasual 2022 is to detect the cause span and effect span from a given textual span. The BIO scheme tags the **B**eginning tokens and **I**nner tokens in the objective spans and tags **O**thers in the rest of the string. The scheme defines this task as token classification, typically applied to Named Entity Recognition and Span Detection in the state-of-art methods.

2.1. Baseline

In previous competitions, we noticed the highlighted framework, DTGNN, proposed by the winner of Fincausal 2021 (Tan and Ng, 2021). This framework is composed of different functional modules attached to BERT architecture. We follow the major modules as shown in Figure 1: BERT encoder, graph builder, GNN+BiLSTM and Viterbi Decoder. Our contribution is mainly located in the graph builder module and GNN modules.

2.1.1. Graph Builder and GNN

In the baseline, the graph builder generates a subgraph for each textual span. The SAGEConv (Hamilton et al., 2017) operator embeds the subgraph into feature representations. In this way, the weights of edges in subgraph are neglected.

In our proposal, during the graph building process, we add the knowledge from Cause-Effect Graph [1] (CEG)(Li et al., 2020) in different manners. Then each subgraph would feed to the graph neural network (GNN), which contains two graph convolutional layers with GCNConv (Kipf and Welling, 2017) operator. In this way, not only do the connected nodes matter for

[1]`https://github.com/eecrazy/CausalBank.`

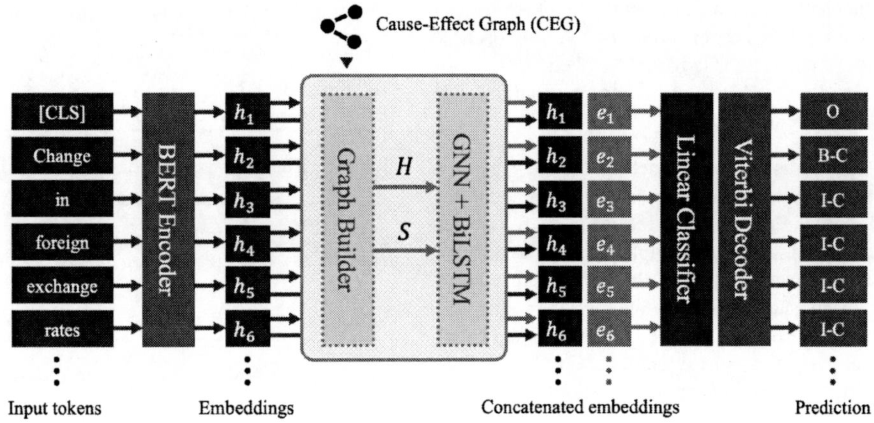

Figure 1: Our method consists of four main components: The BERT encoder, graph builder, GNN+BiLSTM, and Viterbi decoder. We proposed two approaches for the graph builder, which constructs a subgraph for GNN using the external cause-effect graph.

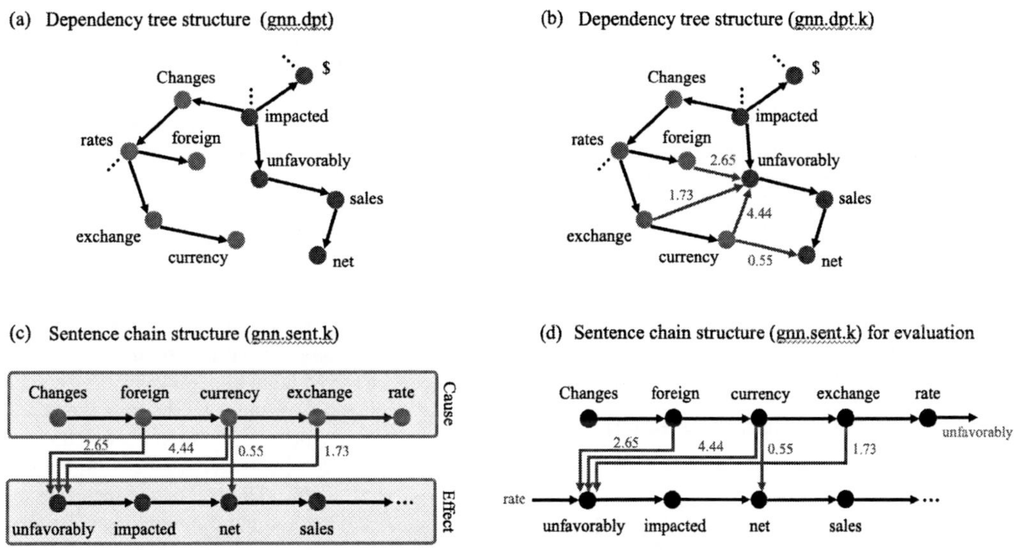

Figure 2: Our graph builder generates four types of sub-graph: (a) The original dependency tree-based subgraph in DTGNN, (b) the same subgraph with additional edges and weights (highlighted in red) for cause-effect relationships, (c) cause and effect chains with cause-effect edges for training, and (d) a single chain connecting the whole input sequence (except stopwords) for inference. All black edges in (b), (c), and (d) have the same small weight (0.1). The green nodes are tokens in the cause span, and the blue nodes are tokens in the effect span.

message passing, but the weight of connections is taken into account.

2.1.2. Viterbi Decoder

For token classification tasks, labels tend to be independent and discontinuous. Viterbi decoder (Kao et al., 2020) solves this problem by using the transition and emission matrices for those labels during the evaluation step, which correct predictions for continuous span labels. Thus we will applly this techniques as well in our framework.

2.2. Structure of knowledge injection

We expect this framework to use linguistic features to train the model. However, once the textual spans do not include the clear syntactic clues, e.g., *because* or *as*, the prediction of cause and effect spans can be reversed, resulting in the wrong prediction. We resort to injecting extra knowledge to distinguish cause spans and effect spans. Cause-Effect Graph (Li et al., 2020) stores the causality relations and weights between tokens pairs. In sentences, cause spans could potentially contain the tokens that have directed causality to the tokens inside effect spans. This section proposes two approaches to insert the target knowledge into embeddings using graph neural networks: sentence chain structure and dependency tree structure.

2.2.1. Dependency Tree Structure

For dependency tree structure, one sentence could be organized by the dependency tree relations, as shown in Figure 2(a). In this manner, tokens in the same sub-sentence tend to connect closer than those in the opposite. To insert causality knowledge, in Figure 2(b), we add the directed linkage between causality token pairs and assign weights for these relations. For the weights of dependency tree connections, we would equally assign them with the same low value (e.g., 0.1). Comparatively, the structure idea of the dependency tree has been implemented by previous work (Tan and Ng, 2021). In their work, the relation weights between tokens are not considered, which neglects much useful information.

2.2.2. Sentence Chain Structure

In sentence chain structure, cause span and effect span are separated into two chains. In each chain, tokens are linked to reserve their orders from beginning to end. In Figure 2(c), between two chains, the tokens holding causality relations are connected unidirectionally with the corresponding weights. As for the connection inside a chain, their weights are equally assigned with the same low value (e.g., 0.1). However, in the validation or test steps, we transform the textual span into an entire chain because of the lack of labels, the causality tokens pairs would be connected with the intra-chain links in Figure 2(d).

3. Experiments and Results

3.1. Data Preparation

We combined 2020, 2021, and 2022 versions of the FinCausal dataset for training, including both *practice* and *trial* sets. As we noticed several duplicate samples, we searched for and removed those with the exact input text and answers to ensure the reliability of our cross-validation data, resulting in 2,775 samples. We then split the reduced dataset into ten folds, nine of which were for training (2,497 samples) and one for validating (278 samples). While a sample may have multiple answer spans, the dataset format (csv) does not allow flexible multi-span labeling. As a result, a sample with multiple answers is split into multiple samples with the same input text. Therefore, we merged these samples and obtained the final 2,290 training samples and 255 samples for validation.

3.2. Replication Settings

Device and Time We used NVIDIA RTX 3090-24G, and it took 1h11min to simultaneously train three models, refer to the idea presented in sub-figure a,b,c of Figure 2. The best scores were achieved with random seed 123, 456, 123 for these models respectively.

	F1	Recall	Precision	EM
gnn.dpt	93.58	93.56	93.66	82.53
gnn.dpt.k	93.41	93.37	93.50	81.99
gnn.sent.k	93.90	93.89	93.95	82.64

Table 1: The best scores achieved on blind test set.

	F1	Recall	Precision	EM
gnn.dpt	89.70	89.66	89.77	73.38
gnn.dpt.k	88.38	88.36	88.42	73.02
gnn.sent.k	90.22	90.20	90.25	75.90

Table 2: The best scores achieved on our validation set.

Hyperparameter The pre-trained BERT model (bert-base-cased) is initialized by Huggingface [2]. All models were trained with ten epochs, learning rate 5e-5, and dropout 0.1. The maximum sequence length is set to 350, and the train batch size is 4. For GNN, the hidden and out graph dimension is 1024 and 512, respectively.

3.3. Results

Table 1 shows the best results in the test set. We notice that all models achieve similar high scores, but the sentence chain structure (*gnn.sent.k*) outperforms others by around 0.3% to 0.5% F1 score. As for knowledge injection variant *gnn.dpt.k*, it fails to improve the performance with the addition of extra knowledge compared to the original dependency tree structure (*gnn.dpt*). To sum up, the knowledge injection works well on our proposed sentence chain structure but not on the dependency tree structure. Ultimately, the inclusion of the Cause-Effect Graph in our proposed graph builder enhances the performance of span prediction tasks.

It is also worth mentioning that Table 2 shows the best scores achieved in the validation set. Surprisingly, we got lower values than the test set in general. We attribute this variance to the different evaluation metrics, in which the scikit-learn metrics that we applied in the validation set have stricter rules than used in competition.

Moreover, we experimented with 3-fold Cross-Validation (CV) and anticipated achieving higher performance. The precision on the train and validation set can be as high as 98% precision and 97% F1 score. However, on the test set, these models cannot reach the peak. They lay behind around 1% of those models without CV. Given these points, the application of CV introduces the over-fitting problem. It is not unsuitable for our models.

[2] `https://huggingface.co/`

4. Conclusion

We focus on generating better graph embedding with the proposed graph builders. Accordingly, the sentence chain structure with the injection of the Cause-Effect Graph outperforms the other structures w/wo knowledge, which helps distinguish between cause spans and effect spans. In the future, we will attempt to inject knowledge into different GNN variants to find the optimal way for knowledge embedding.

5. Bibliographical References

Devlin, J., Chang, M.-W., Lee, K., and Toutanova, K. (2018). Bert: Pre-training of deep bidirectional transformers for language understanding. *arXiv preprint arXiv:1810.04805.*

Hamilton, W. L., Ying, Z., and Leskovec, J. (2017). Inductive representation learning on large graphs. In *NIPS.*

Kao, P.-W., Chen, C.-C., Huang, H.-H., and Chen, H.-H. (2020). NTUNLPL at FinCausal 2020, task 2:improving causality detection using Viterbi decoder. In *Proceedings of the 1st Joint Workshop on Financial Narrative Processing and MultiLing Financial Summarisation*, pages 69–73, Barcelona, Spain (Online), December. COLING.

Kipf, T. and Welling, M. (2017). Semi-supervised classification with graph convolutional networks. *ArXiv*, abs/1609.02907.

Li, Z., Ding, X., Liu, T., Hu, J. E., and Van Durme, B. (2020). Guided generation of cause and effect. In Christian Bessiere, editor, *Proceedings of the Twenty-Ninth International Joint Conference on Artificial Intelligence, IJCAI-20*, pages 3629–3636. International Joint Conferences on Artificial Intelligence Organization, 7. Main track.

Li, Z., Ding, X., Liu, T., Hu, J. E., and Van Durme, B. (2021). Guided generation of cause and effect. *arXiv preprint arXiv:2107.09846.*

Mariko, D., Abi-Akl, H., Labidurie, E., Durfort, S., De Mazancourt, H., and El-Haj, M. (2020a). The financial document causality detection shared task (FinCausal 2020). In *Proceedings of the 1st Joint Workshop on Financial Narrative Processing and MultiLing Financial Summarisation*, pages 23–32, Barcelona, Spain (Online), December. COLING.

Mariko, D., Labidurie, E., Ozturk, Y., Akl, H. A., and de Mazancourt, H. (2020b). Data processing and annotation schemes for fincausal shared task. *arXiv preprint arXiv:2012.02498.*

Mariko, D., Akl, H. A., Labidurie, E., Durfort, S., de Mazancourt, H., and El-Haj, M. (2021). The financial document causality detection shared task (FinCausal 2021). In *Proceedings of the 3rd Financial Narrative Processing Workshop*, pages 58–60, Lancaster, United Kingdom, 15-16 September. Association for Computational Linguistics.

Tan, F. A. and Ng, S.-K. (2021). NUS-IDS at FinCausal 2021: Dependency tree in graph neural network for better cause-effect span detection. In *Proceedings of the 3rd Financial Narrative Processing Workshop*, pages 37–43, Lancaster, United Kingdom, 15-16 September. Association for Computational Linguistics.

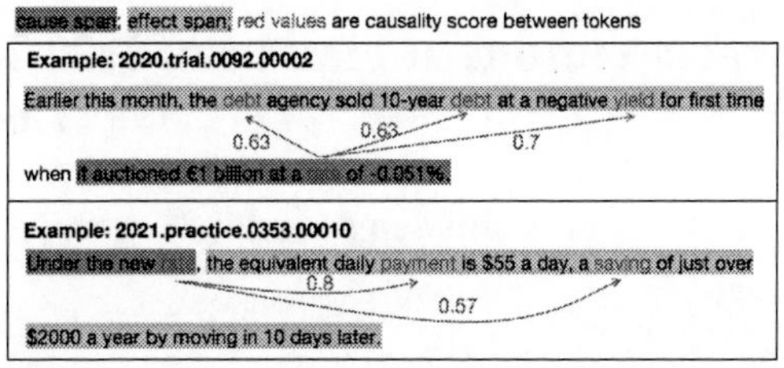

Figure 3: The example for which the model(*gnn.sent.k*) predict correctly.

6. Appendix

This section shows the typical examples when the models (*gnn.dpt* and *gnn.dpt.k*) mix up the cause span and effect span in Figure 3. In the opposite, with the addition of cause-effect knowledge, the model (*gnn.sent.k*) trained on sentence chain structure are able to predict the cause and effect span correctly.

Proceedings of the 4th Financial Narrative Processing Workshop @ LREC 2022, pages 128–130
Marseille, 24 June 2022

ExpertNeurons at FinCausal 2022 Task 2: Causality Extraction for Financial Documents

Joydeb Mondal, Nagaraj Bhat, Pramir Sarkar, Shahid Reza

Oracle AI Services
Bengaluru, India
{ joydeb.mondal, nagaraj.b.bhat, pramir.sarkar, shahid.reza }@ oracle.com

Abstract

This paper provides a novel approach based on transformer models and POS (part of speech) features with an ensemble approach for causality extraction of financial documents for FinCausal 2022 task 2. We provide a solution with intelligent pre-processing and post-processing to detect the number of cause and effect in a financial document and extract the same. Our given approach achieved 90% as F1 score(weighted-average) for the official blind evaluation dataset.

Keywords: financial information extraction, BERT, Causal Inference, Part Of Speech tagging.

1. Introduction

Causality extraction is the extraction of relationship between events in financial documents like finance reports/news etc. Generally the financial causality contains the set of cause and effect span. Extracting such relationship could help gather valuable insights from the documents. The dataset we considered here has both single as well as multiple cause effect relationships. Our approach is based on the sequence labelling of cause effect relationships with Part Of Speech feature support in a BIO scheme. The sequence labelling approach should help deal with extraction of causal text with variable length. We also explore the ensemble method with various transformer models. Our proposed solution outperforms the results on evaluation dataset provided in the task.

2. Dataset

The purpose of the task is to extract cause and effect. The trial & practice set are provided as a csv file with the headers of Index; Text; Cause; Effect. All are separate by semicolon (;). Below are the details of the header field:

- Index : Id of the sample
- Text : Sample text
- Cause: Sequence of text referring to as the cause of the event.
- Effect: Sequence of text referring to as the effect of the event.

Blind/evaluation dataset have only Index and Text.

We noticed that the dataset had samples with multiple cause effect relationships where in a single cause in the text can be mapped to multiple effects or vice versa.

Below table provides the details of Training and evaluation set. Along with the current task samples, we also used the samples from 2020 task.

Data Type	Sample Count
Train	1541
Dev	343
Test	343

Table 1: Data Stats

Index	Text	Cause	effect
1	The increase in net interest income was due primarily to a $152.9 billion increase in average outstanding loans, a $32.6 billion increase in average securities, partially offset by a 78 basis point decrease in earning asset yields.NIM was 3.22% for 2020, down 20 basis points compared to the prior year.	a $152.9 billion increase in average outstanding loans, a $32.6 billion increase in average securities, partially offset by a 78 basis point decrease in earning asset yields.	The increase in net interest income
2	Additional increases in noninterest income were primarily due to higher insurance income driven by improved production levels and acquisitions.	higher insurance income driven by improved production levels and acquisitions.	Additional increases in noninterest income

Table 2: Two Dataset Samples

3. Proposed Approach

3.1 Pre-processing

We have used Stanford CoreNLP Stanza (Manning et al., 2014; Qi et al., 2020) model to tokenize each sample text and created the POS tag and corresponding token.

For sample of multiple cause-effect events, we added an index as special number token and the part of speech tag as

'CD' before each sample to represent it separately with respect to inputs for the model. For extracting causal relations we have used BIO(Begin, Inside, and Outside) tagging scheme with 'C for cause and 'E' for Effect as labels to represent the positional information of the tokens and the semantic roles of the causal events.

Cause			Effect		
Token	**POS Tag**	**BIO Tag**	**Token**	**POS Tag**	**BIO Tag**
The	DT	B-E	It	PRP	B-C
Sunshine	NNP	I-E	is	VBZ	I-C
State	NNP	I-E	consistently	RB	I-C
drew	VBD	I-E	one	CD	I-C
in	IN	I-E	of	IN	I-C
. . .	. . .	. . .	. . .	. . .	. . .
17.7	CD	I-E	low	JJ	I-C
billion	CD	I-E	taxes	NNS	I-C

Table 3: Pre-processed Dataset Samples

3.2 Applied Method

We have used pretrained text encoder BERT which generally performs very well in many NLP tasks (Devlin et al., 2018). We use the BERT-base cased model as a pretrained model which consists of 12 transformer layers with hidden dimension of 768. We have used huggingface (Wolf et al., 2019). library which is the most commonly used for this kind of pretrained models. We also experimented with uncased versions and noticed that the cased version performed much better. Hence all of our base models adopted the cased version.

We started with a baseline structure, where we finetuned the BERT-base cased model into simple token classifier where we have added a linear layer given the tokens as inputs and corresponding sequence labels as target.

We have taken the max length as 350 (based on the max text size in the given sample set), batch size as 32, and initial learning rate is set to 5e-05, and we used cross entropy as the loss function. We use cross entropy loss along with Adam Optimizer.

We have extended the model architecture with POS embedding features. We have used POS tags as an embedding and concatenated it with the last hidden state output of BERT's embedding and pass it through the final linear layer. We have used Tesla V100-SXM2 with 16 core to train our system.

3.3 Post-Processing

The predictions from the models are in the form of BIO tags. After concatenating B & I tags we are infer the cause and effect. We also added a set of heuristics to find out the cause-affect pair.

- For prediction, we send the index value to detect multiple events
- If any event has a length less than 4, then we merge it.

We select the longest cause-effect pair if multiple causal chains are present in a given data instance.

4. Evaluation

We have trained multiple pretrained models with the typical loss functions on the train dataset and evaluated the results on the provided blind dataset as well as the test data. We extracted F1 score, Recall, and Precision from codalab evaluation and added our computed F1 score on model. Transformer models including RoBERTa (Robustly Optimized BERT Pre-training Approach) (Liu et al., 2019), BERT Base (Devlin et al., 2018), BERT Large-Cased Whole Word Masking (Devlin et al., 2018) (BWM) were experimented with different hyper-parameter settings. The mentioned results on Table3 indicates the effectiveness of our approach.

Models	F1	Recall	Precision	Exact Match	Test Data Eval Score
Bert base	0.90	0.90	0.90	0.70	0.87
Bert large	0.90	0.90	0.90	0.70	0.89
Roberta	0.90	0.90	0.90	0.70	0.88
Bert base+ Bert large+ Roberta	0.90	0.90	0.91	0.71	0.88

Table 4: Evaluated Model Result on test data

Error analysis show that the cases that were missed were mostly due to wrong linking of cause and effect in multiple cause/inference scenario (Cases that had one cause mapped to two/more effect and vice versa.).

5. Conclusion

In this paper, we explore the causal inference for Fincausal Task 2. Our approach involved experimenting with various transformer models viz, BERT, Roberta, Bert Large with part of speech feature support. We observed that the best results were achieved with an ensemble model of Bert base, Roberta and Bert large with max voting strategy. In future, we would like to explore the pretrained Finance BERT with cause effort link modeling. This should improve the errors due to multiple cause effect linking.

6. Bibliographical References

Jacob Devlin, Ming-Wei Chang, Kenton Lee, and Kristina Toutanova. 2018. BERT: pre-training of deep bidirectional transformers for language understanding. CoRR, abs/1810.04805.

Christopher D. Manning, Mihai Surdeanu, John Bauer, Jenny Finkel, Steven J. Bethard, and David McClosky. 2014. The Stanford CoreNLP natural language processing toolkit. In Association for Computational Linguistics (ACL) System Demonstrations, pages 55–60.

Yinhan Liu, Myle Ott, Naman Goyal, Jingfei Du, Mandar Joshi, Danqi Chen, Omer Levy, Mike Lewis, Luke Zettlemoyer, and Veselin Stoyanov. 2019. Roberta: A robustly optimized bert pretraining approach. arXiv preprint arXiv:1907.11692.

Thomas Wolf, Lysandre Debut, Victor Sanh, Julien Chaumond, Clement Delangue, Anthony Moi, Pierric Cistac, Tim Rault, Rémi Louf, Morgan Funtowicz, and Jamie Brew. 2019. Huggingface's transformers: State-of-the-art natural language processing. CoRR, abs/1910.03771.

Proceedings of the 4th Financial Narrative Processing Workshop @ LREC 2022, pages 131–134
Marseille, 24 June 2022

ATL at FinCausal 2022: Transformer based Architecture for Automatic Causal Sentence Detection and Cause-Effect Extraction

Abir Naskar, Tirthankar Dasgupta , Sudeshna Jana, Lipika Dey
TCS Research
{abir.naskar, dasgupta.tirthankar, sudeshna.jana,lipika.dey}@tcs.com

Abstract

Automatic extraction of cause-effect relationships from natural language texts is a challenging open problem in Artificial Intelligence. Most of the early attempts at its solution used manually constructed linguistic and syntactic rules on restricted domain data sets. With the advent of big data, and the recent popularization of deep learning, the paradigm to tackle this problem has slowly shifted. In this work we proposed a transformer based architecture to automatically detect causal sentences from textual mentions and then identify the corresponding cause-effect relations. We describe our submission to the FinCausal 2022 shared task based on this method. Our model achieves a F1-score of 0.99 for the Task-1 and F1-score of 0.60 for Task-2 on the shared task data set on financial documents.

Keywords: Causality extraction, Explicit causality , Implicit causality, Inter-sentential causality, BERT Transformer

1. Introduction

The proliferation of advance Natural language Processing and Machine Learning techniques (Bui et al., 2010) has tremendously helped develop intelligent agents that can extract meaningful information from various sources like, web pages, blogs, news articles, tweets and social media posts. Assimilation of such information with proper reasoning strategies can help these agents in the quest for new knowledge. One of the key abilities of such an agent is to perceive an event and reason about its cause and the potential impacts through causal reasoning.

The concept of causality can be informally introduced as a relationship between two events e_1 and e_2 such that occurrence of e_1 results in the occurrence of e_2 (Girju and Moldovan, 2002; Chan et al., 2002). For example, in the sentence "*Aston Martin is recalling 7,256 vehicles because the seat heaters are getting too hot*", the event "*seat heaters are getting too hot*" is causing the event "*Aston Martin is recalling 7,256 vehicles.*". The extraction of causal relations from textual mentions is an important step for the improvement of many Natural Language Processing applications such as question answering (Sorgente et al., 2013; Blanco et al., 2008), information extraction, knowledge graphs and document summarization. In particular, it enables the possibility to reason about the detected events (Girju, 2003) beside creation of new insights and for the support of the predictive analysis. Natural language texts contain an abundance of such relations appearing in different forms. Even a single sentence expressing causal relations can be arbitrarily complex and varied in structure that makes the extraction task challenging. Indeed, there are few explicit lexico-syntactic patterns that are in exact correspondence with a causal relation while there is a huge number of cases that can evoke a causal relation not in a uniquely way.

Most of the traditional approaches of causality detection are are either based on pattern or rule engineering techniques or use statistical machine learning (ML) models (Khoo et al., 1998; Khoo et al., 2001). Rule based approaches are restricted to particular domains, and thus, cannot be generalized in a real-world scenario. On the other hand, ML models uses sparse features such as bag-of-words, part-of-speech tags and dependency relations, which can suffer from the drawbacks of time-consuming feature engineering problem. There is a recent surge of interest in deep neural network-based models that are based on continuous-space representation (Yih et al., 2015) of the input and non-linear functions. Thus, such models are capable of modeling complex patterns in data and since they do not depend on manual engineering of features, they can be applied to solve problems in an end-to-end fashion.

In this paper we present two independent transformer based deep neural network architectures for the causal sentence classification and cause-effect relation extraction task. We have used the fine-tuned Bidirectional Encoder Representations from Transformers (BERT) language model cascaded with a sequence-labeling architecture (Zhou and Xu, 2015). The proposed models solves the two tasks comprised of - (i). classifying sentences into two categories - causal and non-causal (ii). Labeling appropriate sub-sequences in a causal sentence as cause, effect and connective. The labeling of connectives is a unique proposition of the work, which along with its companion cause and effect pair, helps in detection of causal relations from complex sentences more effectively.

2. The Task Definition and Data sets

As part of the Financial Narrative workshop, the FinCausal-2022 [1] focused on detecting if an object, an event or a chain of events is considered a cause for a

[1] https://wp.lancs.ac.uk/cfie/shared-tasks/

	Task-1	Task-2
Avg. no. of sentences	1.3	1.6
Avg. no. of words	34.7	48.2
Max no. of word in document	298	176
Max no. of sentence in document	5	5
number of positive label	1281	N.A
number of negative label	12228	N.A

Table 1: Data statistics for task-1 and task-2.

prior event. This shared task focuses on determining causality associated with a quantified fact. Accordingly the shared task is composed of the following two subtasks:

- **Task 1:** is a binary classification task. The data set consists of a sample of text sections labeled with 1 if the text section is considered containing a causal relation, 0 otherwise. The data set is by nature unbalanced, as to reflect the proportion of causal sentences extracted from the original news and SEC corpus, with provisional distribution approximately 5% 1 and 95% 0.
- **Task-2:** is a relation extraction task. The text sections will correspond to the ones labeled as 1 in the Task 1 data set, though for the purpose of results evaluation, they will not be exactly the same in the blind test set. The purpose of this task is to extract, in a causal text section, the sub-string identifying the causal elements and the sub-string describing the effects.

The data are extracted from a corpus of 2019 financial news provided by QWAM. The original raw corpus is an ensemble of HTML pages corresponding to daily information retrieval from financial news feed. These news mostly inform on the 2019 financial landscape, but can also contain information related to politics, micro economics or other topic considered relevant for finance information. There are 13516 documents for task1. For task2, there are 2014 unique documents. For each document cause and effect parts are marked. For some documents there may be multiple cause and effect pair. Total 2290 pair are annotated for all documents. The details about the data statistics for both Task-1 and Task-2 [2]. is depicted in Table 1.

3. Overview of proposed causal entity extraction and classification framework

BERT (Bidirectional Encoder Representations from Transformers) (Vaswani et al., 2017) is widely used now a days in several NLP tasks and it actually works well in most of the cases. We implemented a sequence-to-sequence model for cause and effect term extraction and a binary classifier for classification of the causal documents. Initially several rule based systems (Mirza and Tonelli, 2016; Sorgente et al., 2013) are used to extract cause ans effect from sentences or to classify causal sentences. Then several deep learning models (Dasgupta et al., 2018) were came into fashion. We use transformer based architecture with pre-trained BERT to train our both models.

3.1. Architecture for causal document classification model

A BERT based classification model in figure:1 is used to classify a document is a causal sentence or not.

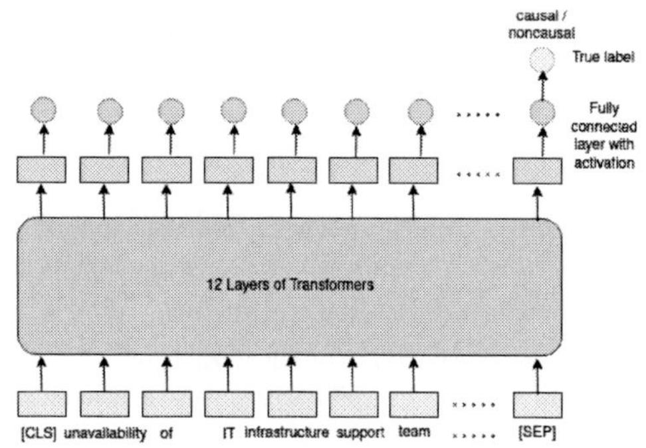

Figure 1: Proposed architecture for Causal sentence classification (Task-1).

In our proposed model we pass the document $D = \{w_1, w_2, \ldots, w_n\}$ which consists of n words and the goal of this sub task is to predict the binary label y of the document D, where $y \in \{0, 1\}$ where the label 0 stands for non causal document and 1 is for causal document. For example, take the document below,

D= *"If the energy sector in Canada continues down this steep decline that's been caused by legislation over the last three or four years, it will get so much worse for Canadians in terms of jobs and also in terms of revenue across all three levels of government which provide the social services and the public programs that Canadians deserve and expect."*

This example document is a causal document. And for another document,

D= *"While the Speaker's office disclaimed the leaked version, saying it is out of date, the draft reveals several noteworthy Democratic policy options likely being discussed including Medicare negotiation, capping drug prices at an International Price Index, capping out-of-pocket costs for Part D beneficiaries, and establishing an inflation rebate for drugs whose prices rise too fast."*

This is not a causal document.

For the purpose of many to one set up, we take the BERT output and send them into a fully connected layer for multiclass classification. Then the output of the fully connected layer is matched with the original label. To deal with over-fitting a Dropout mechanism in the fully connected layer is used.

[2] https://github.com/yseop/YseopLab

3.2. Architecture for cause effect term extraction model

An almost similar BERT based classification model in figure: 2 is used to identify the portion of the document as cause or effect or none of that. Here we pass

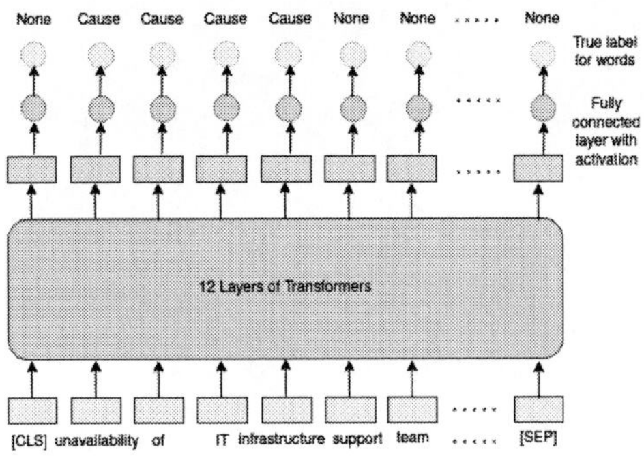

Figure 2: Proposed architecture for Cause-effect extraction (Task-2).

the full document $D = \{w_1, w_2, \ldots, w_n\}$ which consist n word tokens into the BERT based transformer module and the goal of this sub task is to predict the target t, where $t = \{t_1, t_2, \ldots t_n\}$ where $t_i \in \{cause, effect, none\}$. For example, for the document,

D= *"NPAs increased $703 million year over year, primarily due to PCI loans that would have been classified as nonperforming at December 31, 2019 and loans exiting certain accommodation programs related to the CARES Act.Noninterest income increased $3.6 billion for the year with nearly all categories of noninterest income being impacted by the Merger."*

In this example document, The cause portion is *"PCI loans that would have been classified as nonperforming at December 31, 2019 and loans exiting certain accommodation programs related to the CARES Act."*. And the effect part is *"NPAs increased $703 million year over year"*.

For that purpose we send the BERT output sequence into a fully connected sequence to sequence module for predicting the sequence tag $S = \{s_1, s_2, \ldots, s_n\}$. This is then matched with the original sequence label, $Y = \{y_1, y_2, \ldots, y_n\}$. The Dropout technique is used in the fully connected layer to cope up with the overfitting issue. The Cross Entropy Loss is used for back propagation.

4. Experiments and Results

4.1. Experimental settings

We use bert-base-uncased (Devlin et al., 2018) as default backbone network. This use 12 layers, 768-dimensional embeddings. Total 110 million parameters for 12 heads per layer. For both task we keep the hyper-parameters same. We use Adam optimizer with learning rate 2×10^{-5}. The dropout rate is used was 0.1. We took batch size of 4 and run that for 10 epoch. We mostly set the same setup for both of our model. The entire data was broken three parts randomly. the 60% data is taken for training purpose, 20% is for evaluation and 20% for test purpose. We run the entire system and test our model in CPU only. It took around 50 minutes to complete 1 epoch.

4.2. Results

We had achieved F-measure 94.3 for Task1. For Task2 we have got exact match for 21.3% and when we proceed with token accuracy excluding the [CLS] and [SEP] tokens we have got the F-measure value as 63.6. Initially we had trained our system for 5 epochs, when we train it for 10 epochs we saw slight improve over accuracy. the precision, recall, F-measure calculated are given below.

	Task1	Task2
Precision	93.2	62.2
Recell	95.6	65.1
F-measure	94.3	63.6
Exact match	N.A	21.3

5. Conclusion

The key idea of the task and build the model is to automatically detecting the causal documents and extracting the cause and effect information. Initially several rules (Guo et al., 2020) and statistical models (Khoo et al., 1998; Khoo et al., 2001) were used for that purpose. in our end-to-end system the document is passed through our proposed model as input and output will be the extracted entities and the class where the document belongs to. Our proposed model focuses all the causes and effects in a document. But it fails to understand the relation between the cause and effect where multiple causal instances and their effect present in the document. For example if for one cause multiple effect happened, or may be there are multiple cause and effects present in the document, we are failing to identify which cause inspires which effect. In some cases the cause portion and the effect portion is so far away from one another that to identify their dependencies will be very difficult. And for our BERT based transformers model there is always a constraint about the number of tokens as input. And we need large corpus of annotated data for that. So we intended to work on those aspects to facilitate research.

6. Bibliographical References

Blanco, E., Castell, N., and Moldovan, D. (2008). Causal relation extraction. In *Lrec*.

Bui, Q.-C., Nualláin, B. Ó., Boucher, C. A., and Sloot, P. M. (2010). Extracting causal relations on hiv drug resistance from literature. *BMC bioinformatics*, 11(1).

Chan, K., Low, B.-T., Lam, W., and Lam, K.-P. (2002). Extracting causation knowledge from natural language texts. In *Pacific-Asia Conference on Knowledge Discovery and Data Mining*, pages 555–560. Springer.

Dasgupta, T., Saha, R., Dey, L., and Naskar, A. (2018). Automatic extraction of causal relations from text using linguistically informed deep neural networks. In *Proceedings of the 19th Annual SIGdial Meeting on Discourse and Dialogue*, pages 306–316.

Devlin, J., Chang, M., Lee, K., and Toutanova, K. (2018). BERT: pre-training of deep bidirectional transformers for language understanding. *CoRR*, abs/1810.04805.

Girju, R. and Moldovan, D. (2002). Mining answers for causation questions. In *AAAI symposium on mining answers from texts and knowledge bases*.

Girju, R. (2003). Automatic detection of causal relations for question answering. In *Proceedings of the ACL 2003 workshop on Multilingual summarization and question answering-Volume 12*. Association for Computational Linguistics.

Guo, S., Jin, L., Yang, J., Jiang, M., Han, L., and An, N. (2020). Causal extraction from the literature of pressure injury and risk factors. In *2020 IEEE International Conference on Knowledge Graph (ICKG)*, pages 581–585. IEEE.

Khoo, C. S., Kornfilt, J., Oddy, R. N., and Myaeng, S. H. (1998). Automatic extraction of cause-effect information from newspaper text without knowledge-based inferencing. *Literary and Linguistic Computing*, 13(4):177–186.

Khoo, C. S., Myaeng, S. H., and Oddy, R. N. (2001). Using cause-effect relations in text to improve information retrieval precision. *Information processing & management*, 37(1):119–145.

Mirza, P. and Tonelli, S. (2016). Catena: Causal and temporal relation extraction from natural language texts. In *The 26th international conference on computational linguistics*, pages 64–75. ACL.

Sorgente, A., Vettigli, G., and Mele, F. (2013). Automatic extraction of cause-effect relations in natural language text. *DART@ AI* IA*, 2013:37–48.

Vaswani, A., Shazeer, N., Parmar, N., Uszkoreit, J., Jones, L., Gomez, A. N., Kaiser, Ł., and Polosukhin, I. (2017). Attention is all you need. In *Advances in neural information processing systems*, pages 5998–6008.

Yih, W.-t., He, X., and Gao, J. (2015). Deep learning and continuous representations for natural language processing. In *Proceedings of the 2015 Conference of the North American Chapter of the Association for Computational Linguistics: Tutorial Abstracts*, pages 6–8.

Zhou, J. and Xu, W. (2015). End-to-end learning of semantic role labeling using recurrent neural networks. In *Proceedings of the 53rd Annual Meeting of the Association for Computational Linguistics and the 7th International Joint Conference on Natural Language Processing (Volume 1: Long Papers)*, pages 1127–1137.

Proceedings of the 4th Financial Narrative Processing Workshop @ LREC 2022, pages 135–138
Marseille, 24 June 2022

MNLP at FinCausal2022: Nested NER with a Generative Model

Jooyeon Lee **Luan Huy Pham** **Özlem Uzuner**
George Mason University
Fairfax, Virginia, USA
{jlee252,lpham6,ouzuner}@gmu.edu

Abstract

This paper describes work performed for the FinCasual 2022 Shared Task "Financial Document Causality Detection" (FinCausal 2022). As the name implies, the task involves extraction of casual and consequential elements from financial text. Our approach focuses employing Nested NER using the Text-to-Text Transformer (T5) (Raffel et al., 2020) generative transformer models while applying different combinations of datasets and tagging methods. Our system reports accuracy of 79% in Exact Match comparison and F-measure score of 92% token level measurement.

Keywords: Nest NER, Transformer Model, Generative Model, T5, NER

1. Introduction

In the field of financial analysis, the ability to swiftly and accurately comprehend the root causes and effects of events imparts valuable advantages in real-time decision making. The core obstacle to such a feat is the sheer volume and volatility of financial information which is being produced constantly. Our effort in this work is our contribution to this ongoing effort and research to address these challenges. The structure of the paper is simply: i) Methodology and Data, ii) Results and Discussion.

2. Methodology and Data

Our methodology generally leverages traditional generative systems. In a sequential manner, we started with text pre-processing, followed by fine-tuning the T5 model. Then, we employed post-processing to extract the correct span and entity. During the post-processing step, the system leverages specialized logic to select results among the output of multiple models to balance the strengths and weaknesses of each model in different scenarios.

2.1. Dataset Formulation

In addition to the official Fincausal dataset, we leveraged the Penn Discourse Treebank (PTDB) Version 3.0 Dataset (Miltsakaki et al., 2004). The third release of the PDTB, produced in 2020, contains data extracted from 2,499 stories from the Wall Street Journal over a three-year period, containing 53,676 tokens of annotated relations. It claims to be the largest such corpus of annotated relations available (Webber et al., 2019). We trained our model with different batches: 1) FNP only, 2) FNP and PDTB, 3) FNP and PDTB numeric values only, 4) FNP and PDTB Cause relations only 5) FNP and PDTB Result relations only 6) FNP and PDTB Implicit relations only 7) FNP and PDTB Explicit relations only.

2.1.1. FNP Dataset

The official Fincausal 2020 and 2022 dataset (FNP) of 2789 entries was extracted from a corpus of 2019 financial news as crawled and provided by Qwam. The official dataset, released and utilized since 2020, only includes entries with a 3-sentence distance between the cause and effect.

2.1.2. PDTB

The PDTB-style annotation uses a special pipeline-delimited format to identify spans of text and associated relationships. These relationships specified various forms of causal relations, identified as a subset of "Contingency Relations", where the "situation described by one argument provides the reason, explanation, or justification" (Webber et al., 2019) for the other. We extracted only the examples within the PDTB which resembled the cause-effect pattern, resulting in 7986 entries. For each cause-effect pair, we extracted the associated span of text which includes both members of the pair, as opposed to the entire full-length annotated article, thus maintaining consistency with the length of the official FNP dataset.

2.2. Pre-processing

To leverage the Generative Model, we created corresponding pairs of input and output and investigated the performance of different tagging methods. Examples of the raw dataset are shown in Table 1 and the tagged output in Table 2. We explored four methods. **Method 1** tags only the output, with the output including only the cause tags and effect entities, discarding all tokens which do reside in the entities. The effect span begins with a tag <e0> or <e1> and ends with a corresponding tag </e0> or </e1>. The cause span begins with a tag <c0> or <c1> and ends with the a corresponding tag </c0> or </c1>. **Method 2** is similar to Method 1, but retains the tokens outside of the cause and effect entities. **Method 3** involves tags on both input and output. Output is tagged using the same method as **Method 1**. For the input, we inserted a <causality> tag in front of the tokens indicating the causality, such as 'Due to', 'because', 'therefore', 'since', 'thus', 'if', 'as', 'when', 'after', 'as a result', 'subsequently', 'then', 'enhance', 'degrade', 'lead'. **Method 4** tags the output only, separating cause and effect with the tag <causality>, where a phrase before the tag is Cause, a phrase after the tag is Effect. This is the simplest method, though it does not consider nested cases. In this method, if two separate cause and effect pairs exist in one input, it is considered as two different inputs: one cause and effect pair is considered one input and second cause and effect are a separate, second input.

2.3. T5

One of the most challenging Natural Language Processing tasks is correctly recognizing named entities and their span, as they can partially overlap across different entities or also can be nested inside other entities altogether (Finkel and Manning, 2009). To address the issue of Nested NER, we use a generative model, T5 Transformer (Raffel et al., 2020), to generate the cause and effect from an input. In this paper, we compare the performance between models fine-tuned on a different dataset. We optimized hyper-parameters for each architecture using grid searches. This optimization includes varying learning rate (0.001, 0.002, 0.003, 0.0001, 0.0004 and 0.0005), batch size (8 and 16) and training epochs (2, 4, 6, 8, 10, 12, 14, 16, 18, 20, 22, 24, 26, 28 and 30). We report results for each model using the hyper-parameters that yielded the highest accuracy. For all models, we set the max input length and output length to 200. For the generation step, beam size was set to 2 and repetition penalty was fixed to 2.5. All the experiments were conducted on the Google Colab Pro platform. The T5-base model available on Huggingface [1] [2] was used to fine-tune to our dataset.

2.4. Post-processing

We employed three sequential steps during the post-processing step. The first step is to correct common errors found during the validation testing. The second step is to extract the actual cause and effect using the cause tag (<c0>, <c1>, </c0>, </c1>) and effect tag (<e0>, <e1>, </e0>, </e1>). Finally, we select the best output from the different models.

- Step 1: Output Cleaning We have applied a cleaning process based on the validation output analysis that is described in the Section 3.2. The primary rule of cleaning are as follows: if there is any tag that is closed but not opened, then add the opening tag at the front of the entire output text.
- Step 2: Cause and Effect Extraction We simply extract cause by finding a phrase between open and close tag of cause, and effect by finding a phrase located between open and close tag of effect.
- Step 3: Model Selection We use ensemble learning techniques which shows higher accuracies in variety of tasks (Husain et al., 2020; Lee et al., 2021; Dang et al., 2020). Based on the validation accuracies, we selected the top 3 models: 1) Model trained with FNP only dataset with epoch 20 with learning rate 0.0001. 2) Model trained with FNP only dataset with epoch 28 with learning rate 0.0001 3) Model trained with FNP dataset and PDTB that contains numeric values with epoch 24 with learning rate of 0.0005.

3. Results and Discussion

3.1. Results

Accuracy is measured using an exact match of the gold standard string and generated strings for the validation. The validation sets are a randomly selected 20% portion of FNP data. The validation accuracy for data combinations are shown in Table 3a. The validation accuracy for different tagging methods are shown in Table 3b. The accuracy data shown in Table 3a are experiment results using tagging Method 1. The Table 3b has experiment results with dataset 1). The submitted output for the competition is a result of a model trained with both the training set and validation set we have.

3.2. Discussion

In this section, we show in depth error analysis to provide system implications for future development considerations. We focus on two different types of errors: tagging errors and span errors.

3.2.1. Common Tagging Errors

Case 1. Unclosed & unopened tags This is the case where a tag is opened, but never closed with the corresponding tag (i.e. <c0> exists, but </c0> not found).

- <c1> They set a sector perform rating and a $21.00 price target for the company. **</c0>** **<c0>** Seven equities research analysts have rated the stock with a hold rating and six have issued a buy rating to the stock. </c1> <e0> <e1> The company has an average rating of Hold and an average target price of $20.79. </e1> </e0>

Case 2. Cause and Effect Switched When cause is tagged as effect or effect is tagged as cause, it belongs to this case.

- Input: Consumer Banking and Wealth average total deposits increased $119.5 billion, or 120.4%, compared to 2019 driven primarily by the Merger and COVID-19 stimulus impacts.
- Gold Standard: <e0> Corporate and Commercial Banking average loans and leases held for investment increased $81.6 billion, or 95.9%, compared to 2019 </e0> <c0> the Merger and growth in corporate loans. </c0>
- Machine Output: <c0> Corporate and Commercial Banking average loans and leases held for investment increased $81.6 billion, or 95.9%, compared to 2019 </c0> <e0> the Merger and growth in corporate loans. <e0>

[1] https://huggingface.co/docs/transformers/model_doc/t5

[2] Our code is publicly available at https://github.com/jlee24282/FNP2022_MNLP

Index	Text	Cause	Effect
0009.00052.1	Things got worse when the Wall came down. GDP fell 20% between 1988 and 1993. There were suddenly hundreds of thousands of unemployed in a country that, under Communism, had had full employment.	Things got worse when the Wall came down.	GDP fell 20% between 1988 and 1993.
0009.00052.2	Things got worse when the Wall came down. GDP fell 20% between 1988 and 1993. There were suddenly hundreds of thousands of unemployed in a country that, under Communism, had had full employment. and PDTB	Things got worse when the Wall came down.	There were suddenly hundreds of thousands of unemployed in a country that, under Communism, had had full employment.
23.00006	In case where SGST refund is not applicable, the state is offering a 15% capital subsidy on investments made in Tamil Nadu till end of 2025	In case where SGST refund is not applicable	the state is offering a 15% capital subsidy on investments made in Tamil Nadu till end of 2025

Table 1: Three examples from FinCausal 2021 Corpus - Practice Dataset

	Input	Output
Method 1 (Single Relation)	Average short-term borrowings decreased as a percentage of funding sources due to strong deposit growth.	<e0> Average short-term borrowings decreased as a percentage of funding sources </e0> <c0> strong deposit growth. </c0>
Method 1 (Multiple Relations)	Things got worse when the Wall came down. GDP fell 20% between 1988 and 1993. There were suddenly hundreds of thousands of unemployed in a country that, under Communism, had had full employment.	**<c0>** <c1> Things got worse when the Wall came down.**</c1>** </c0> **<e0>** GDP fell 20% between 1988 and 1993. **</e0>** **<e1>** There were suddenly hundreds of thousands of unemployed in a country that, under Communism, had had full employment. <e1>
Method 2 (Single Relation)	Average short-term borrowings decreased as a percentage of funding sources due to strong deposit growth.	**<e0>** Average short-term borrowings decreased as a percentage of funding sources **</e0>** due to **<c0>** strong deposit growth. **</c0>**
Method 2 (Multiple Relations)	Things got worse when the Wall came down. GDP fell 20% between 1988 and 1993. There were suddenly hundreds of thousands of unemployed in a country that, under Communism, had had full employment.	**<c0>** **<c1>** Things got worse when the Wall came down.**</c1>** **</c0>** **<e0>** GDP fell 20% between 1988 and 1993. **</e0>** **<e1>** There were suddenly hundreds of thousands of unemployed in a country that, under Communism, had had full employment. <**e1**>
Method 3	**<causality>** In case where SGST refund is not applicable, the state is offering a 15% capital subsidy on investments made in Tamil Nadu till end of 2025	**<c0>** In case where SGST refund is not applicable **</c0>** **<e0>** the state is offering a 15% capital subsidy on investments made in Tamil Nadu till end of 2025 **</e0>**
Method 4	In case where SGST refund is not applicable, the state is offering a 15% capital subsidy on investments made in Tamil Nadu till end of 2025	In case where SGST refund is not applicable **<causality>** the state is offering a 15% capital subsidy on investments made in Tamil Nadu till end of 2025

Table 2: Examples of Nested NER format tagging from FinCausal 2021 Corpus Pre-processed.

Case 3. Incorrect Link between Cause and Effect We consider <c0> is a cause of <e0>, and <c1> is a cause of <e1>, while there should not be any link between (<c0> and <e0>) and (<c1> and <e1>). The following example shows a case where <e0> exists but not <c1>, <c1> exists not but not <e1>.

- Input: Consumer Banking and Wealth average total deposits increased $119.5 billion, or 120.4%, compared to 2019 driven primarily by the Merger and COVID-19 stimulus impacts.
- Gold Standard: <e0> Corporate and Commercial Banking average loans and leases held for investment increased $81.6 billion, or 95.9%, compared to 2019 </e0> <c0> the Merger and growth in corporate loans. </c0>
- Machine Output: <e0> Corporate and Commercial Banking average loans and leases held for investment increased $81.6 billion, or 95.9%, compared to 2019 </e0> <c1> the Merger and growth in corporate loans. </c1>

Case 4. Repetition When the tag meaninglessly repeats and causes an incorrect tag extraction, it belongs to this case.

- <c1> They set a sector perform rating and a $21.00 price target for the company.</c0> **<c0>** **<e0>** **<e0>** **<c0>** **<c0>** Seven equities research analysts have rated the stock with a hold rating and six have issued a buy rating to the stock. </c1> **<e0>** **<e0>**

	Dataset	Cause	Effect
1)	FNP	72.28	83.47
2)	FNP and PDTB	58.10	58.33
3)	FNP and PDTB numeric values only	68.60	69.53
4)	FNP and PDTB Cause relations only	67.9	67.33
5)	FNP and PDTB Result relations only	56.25	56.94
6)	FNP and PDTB Implicit relations only	53.01	49.5
7)	FNP and PDTB Explicit relations only	71.63	72.09

(a) Performance comparison between different dataset.

	Cause	Effect
Method 1	72.28	83.47
Method 2	69.60	74.53
Method 3	52.02	62.43
Method 4	66.89	65.21

(b) Performance comparison between different tagging method.

<**e0**> <e1> The company has an average rating of Hold and an average target price of $20.79. </e1> </e0>

3.2.2. Span Error

With the test output, we see that average exact match accuracy of the participants of Fincausal 2022 is 77.83%, while the F-measure score (measured at the token level) of 93.67%. This may be an indication that span errors are common among participants, given that considering relaxed match vs exact match increases accuracy by 14.8%. Our model shows the same tendency. Example of span error is as below.

- Input: Consumer Banking and Wealth average total deposits increased $119.5 billion, or 120.4%, compared to 2019 driven primarily by the Merger and COVID-19 stimulus impacts.
- Gold Standard: <e0> Consumer Banking and Wealth average total deposits increased $119.5 billion, or 120.4%, compared to 2019 </e0> <c0> the Merger and COVID-19 stimulus impacts.</c0>
- Machine Output: <e0> Consumer Banking and Wealth average total deposits increased 119.5 billion, or 120.4 <e0>, compared to <c0> 2019 driven primarily by the Merger and COVID-19 stimulus impacts.</c0>.

4. Conclusion

This paper shows a model submitted to FinCausal 2022 shared task as team MNLP. We studied different tagging methods and showed clear performance differences on the T5 generative model for the Nested NER task. We also explored the possibility of data amplification on the domain of financial cause and effect detection. The end result of our efforts culminated in a 79% Exact Match comparison score and a 92% F-measure score. With our experiments, we show the potential future directions with generative models for the Nest NER.

5. Bibliographical References

Dang, H., Lee, K., Henry, S., and Uzuner, Ö. (2020). Ensemble BERT for classifying medication-mentioning tweets. In *Proceedings of the Fifth Social Media Mining for Health Applications Workshop & Shared Task*, pages 37–41, Barcelona, Spain (Online), December. Association for Computational Linguistics.

Finkel, J. R. and Manning, C. D. (2009). Nested named entity recognition. In *Proceedings of the 2009 Conference on Empirical Methods in Natural Language Processing*, pages 141–150, Singapore, August. Association for Computational Linguistics.

Husain, F., Lee, J., Henry, S., and Uzuner, O. (2020). SalamNET at SemEval-2020 task 12: Deep learning approach for Arabic offensive language detection. In *Proceedings of the Fourteenth Workshop on Semantic Evaluation*, pages 2133–2139, Barcelona (online), December. International Committee for Computational Linguistics.

Lee, J., Dang, H., Uzuner, O., and Henry, S. (2021). MNLP at MEDIQA 2021: Fine-tuning PEGASUS for consumer health question summarization. In *Proceedings of the 20th Workshop on Biomedical Language Processing*, pages 320–327, Online, June. Association for Computational Linguistics.

Miltsakaki, E., Prasad, R., Joshi, A. K., and Webber, B. L. (2004). The penn discourse treebank. In *LREC*. Citeseer.

Raffel, C., Shazeer, N., Roberts, A., Lee, K., Narang, S., Matena, M., Zhou, Y., Li, W., and Liu, P. J. (2020). Exploring the limits of transfer learning with a unified text-to-text transformer. *Journal of Machine Learning Research*, 21(140):1–67.

Webber, B., Prasad, R., Lee, A., and Joshi, A. (2019). The penn discourse treebank 3.0 annotation manual. *Philadelphia, University of Pennsylvania.*

Author Index

Aberer, Karl, 53
Abi-Akl, Hanna, 105
AbuRa'ed, Ahmed, 43
Ait Azzi, Abderrahim, 83

Barbero Jiménez, Álvaro, 59
Beheshti, Amin, 73
Bellato, Sandra, 83
Belyaeva, Oksana Vladimirovna, 89
Betancur, David, 59
Bhat, Nagaraj, 128
Bogatenkova, Anastasiia, 89

Carbajo Coronado, Blanca, 83
Carbajo-Coronado, Blanca, 43
Cassotti, Pierluigi, 95
Chersoni, Emmanuele, 10
Chopra, Ankush, 112

Dasgupta, Tirthankar, 131
DeGemmis, Marco, 95
Dey, Lipika, 131

El-Haj, Mahmoud, 43, 79, 83, 105
El Maarouf, Ismail, 83

Foroutan, Negar, 53

Gan, Mei, 83
Ghodratnama, Samira, 73
Ghosh, Sohom, 1, 121
Giannakopoulos, George, 43
Giguet, Emmanuel, 100
Gisbert, Ana, 83
Gittens, Alex, 108

Hassanzadeh, Oktie, 108
Hsu, Yu-Yin, 10
Huang, Chu-Ren, 10

Ichise, Ryutaro, 124

Jana, Sudeshna, 131
Ji, Tianbo, 116

Kang, Juyeon, 83

Katikeri, Raghu, 65
Keeriyadath, Sangeeth, 65
Kertkeidkachorn, Natthawut, 124
Khanna, Urvashi, 73
Kosmopoulos, Aris, 43
Kozlov, Ilya Sergeevich, 89

Lebret, Rémi, 53
Lee, Jooyeon, 135
Lekkas, Georgios, 95
Liew, Jasy Suet Yan, 36
Litvak, Marina, 43
Lončarski, Igor, 17
Lucas, Nadine, 100
Lyu, Chenyang, 116

Mariko, Dominique, 105
Massonnet, Stéphane, 53
Mohamad Zamani, Nur Azmina, 36
Moll´a, Diego, 73
Mondal, Joydeb, 128
Moreno Sandoval, Antonio, 83
Moreno-Sandoval, Antonio, 43
Musto, Cataldo, 95

Nararatwong, Rungsiman, 124
Naskar, Abir, 131
Naskar, Sudip, 1, 121
Ni, Jian, 108

Ogden, Andrew, 79

Pant, Manish, 112
Pelicon, Andraž, 17
Peng, Bo, 10
Perminov, Andrew Igorevich, 89
Pham, Luan Huy, 135
Pittaras, Nikiforos, 43
Pollak, Senja, 17

Raja, Msp, 65
Rayson, Paul, 43
Reza, Shahid, 128
Romanou, Angelika, 53

Saha, Anik, 108

Sarkar, Pramir, 128
Segurado, Alba, 59
Semeraro, Giovanni, 95
Sengupta, Shovon, 1
Shukla, Neelesh, 65
Singh, Sunny Kumar, 1
Škrlj, Blaž, 17
Srinivas, Kavitha, 108
Stepišnik-Perdih, Timen, 17
Sun, Quanwei, 116

Trottier, Kim, 105
Tsutsumi, Gakuto, 27

Utsuro, Takehito, 27
Uzuner, Özlem, 135

Vaca, Alejandro, 59
Vaid, Amit, 65

Xu, Ziwei, 124

Yener, Bulent, 108
Yusof, Ahmad Muhyiddin, 36

Zhou, Liting, 116
ZMANDAR, Nadhem, 43
Žnidaršič, Martin, 17

Association for Computational Linguistics
209 N. Eighth Street
Stroudsburg, Pennsylvania 18360

CURRAN ASSOCIATES INC. proceedings.com

ISBN 978-1-7138-6120-1

9 781713 861201